This

. . . is an authorized facsimile made from the master copy of the original book. Further unauthorized copying is prohibited.

Books on Demand is a publishing service of UMI. The program offers xerographic reprints of more than 130,000 books that are no longer in print.

The primary focus of Books on Demand is academic and professional resource materials originally published by university presses, academic societies, and trade book publishers worldwide.

BLACK WRITERS IN LATIN AMERICA

Black Writers
in Latin America

Richard L. Jackson

UNIVERSITY OF NEW MEXICO PRESS

Albuquerque

Library of Congress Cataloging in Publication Data

Jackson, Richard L.   1937–
    Black writers in Latin America

    Bibliography: p. 213
    Includes index.
    1. Spanish American-literature—Black authors—
History and criticism.   I. Title.
PQ7081.J264   860'.9   78-21431
ISBN 0-8263-0501-6

6003770129

© 1979 by the University of New Mexico Press. All rights reserved.
Manufactured in the United States of America.
Library of Congress Catalog Card Number 78–21431
International Standard Book Number 0–8263–0501–6

For Lillian

Art with no message or human content
has, to me, the same value as a
blank sheet of paper.

Nicolás Guillén

Contents

Part Three: CONTEMPORARY AUTHORS (1950-)

Preface

The study of Afro-Latin American literature and culture is experiencing its own kind of boom in the seventies. The recent activities involve conferences, publications, and new courses—such as the Panel on the Black Writer in Latin America (Sixth National Convention of the Popular Culture Association in Chicago, 24–26 April 1976); the Medgar Evers College, CUNY, Symposia on Afro-Hispanic Literature (the first one in the series was held at the Center for Inter-American Relations in New York, 18 June 1976); the planning for an American Society for Afro-Hispanic Literature; the appearance in Caracas, Venezuela, of *Cuadernos afro-americanos*, a new journal of Afro-American studies; two other proposed journals one based in New York, *Studies in Afro-Hispanic Literature*, and the other *Revista de Estudios Negrigenistas*, promised by Alberto M. Pamies; the Congreso de Literatura Afro-Americana held in Miami at the Florida International University in November 1976; the 1977 SECOLAS program at Tuskegee on Race and Class in Latin America, 21–23 April 1977; the Primer Congreso de la Cultura Negra de las Américas that took place in Cali, Colombia, in August 1977; the numerous panels and sessions on the black in Latin America at the Latin American Studies Association–African Studies Association joint meeting held in Houston, Texas, in November 1977; the First New World Festival of the African Diaspora held in Brazil in August 1978; the increasing number of new courses on Afro-Latin American literature and culture, especially at Howard University in Washington, D.C.; the Colección Ebano y Canela, a new series of publications (Ediciones Universal in Miami) under the direction of Alberto M. Pamies and other new publications, many of them reviewed in the bibliographic guide I include at the end of this study. Interest in Afro-Hispanic letters is higher now than it was in the fifties and sixties, higher even than it was in the celebrated high period of *poesía negra* during the thirties and forties.

The big difference now is that more black scholars than ever before are focusing attention on the black experience in Latin

America. Further, I believe there is more interest in authentic black literature, that is, in literature by blacks in Latin America rather than in Latin American literature simply on black themes. In fact, until recently, one associated black literature in Latin America for the most part with Brazil and the Caribbean; now, however, we are becoming more aware that other Latin American countries, even such "white" ones as Costa Rica and Uruguay, had traditions of black consciousness, some dating back to the nineteenth century and before, that produced black folklore, black newspapers, black journals, black political parties, and black writers. It is precisely the literary products of this black consciousness that prompt this present volume, as it is the black writer in Latin America who is of central concern in this new upsurge of interest.

By focusing on the black writer and on the problems of literary blackness in Latin America, I hope to provide a better understanding of the ethnicity factor, that is, of the level of black consciousness in countries in that part of the world where black communities continue to exist (persist). And I particularly have tried to clarify whether black writers in such countries as Costa Rica, Cuba, Colombia, Ecuador, Panama, Peru, Uruguay, and Venezuela have seen themselves as part of a Unified Black (or First) World, where black liberation, black identity, black solidarity and equality of rights and opportunity have high priority, or whether they have allowed these concerns—and ethnic memory—to be erased or overruled by socialist revolutionary consciousness, *mestizaje* (miscegenation), and cultural assimilation. Whether, in effect, there is a pull in Latin America toward ethnic consciousness, or ethnogenesis, and a First World Black Aesthetic or toward a Proletarian World or a Third World consciousness not limited by race. By taking into consideration the effect of the ethnicity factor, and the parameters of literary blackness that control it, on the artistic and social sensibilities of the black writer in Latin America who wrote in Spanish from the colonial period to the present day, I pick up where my *The Black Image in Latin American Literature*—which dealt primarily with nonblack Latin American writers—left off.

In that volume I focused largely on the black as subject and on the literary manifestations of the Hispanic heritage of white racial consciousness. The present study, on the other hand, is on the development of black self-awareness or the black as author from the controlled expression of the black writer of slavery times to the more assertive and aggressive black literature of our day. A chronological overview was necessary because there is a continuum in the literary history of the black experience in Latin America; black consciousness can be seen, if we look closely enough, even in the controlled literature of early black writers. The present volume calls attention, as well, to the black experience in Latin America reflected in oral literature, whose tradition of protest under the cloak of anonymity is picked up and continued later in the written literature.

To illustrate that this definable awareness of being black in white (or, at best, miscegenetic) societies has resulted in more than just public service protest statements, however, I have drawn on such terms in recent use as *black sensibility, black perspective, new black aesthetic, true black experience, black diaspora, forced* or *counter poetics, ethnopoetics, ethnic memory, ethnogenesis, false consciousness, dynamic Africanity, Third Worldism, First Worldism, creative dialogue, mestizaje positivo* and *mestizaje negativo*, as they help us understand how many of the works discussed here, which are, in essence, philosophical, spiritual and ideological journeys toward blackness, reveal not only an outward but an inward *toma de conciencia* as well, one that is, of necessity, preliminary to black protest literature, to public stance, and to broader visions, both political and humanistic. It is this awakening or commitment to blackness, whether worked out within the system or in the streets against it, that has been a major thematic constant in the literary aesthetics of black Latin American writers represented in this study. Although I deal here more with the thematics than with the poetics of literary blackness, I do highlight certain stylistic, lyric, structural, and narrative devices when they facilitate our understanding of the black writer and of the problems of literary blackness in Latin America. But while the overriding concern throughout this chronological overview is to illustrate Afro-Latin American commitment to literary blackness, the critical orientation of each chapter is not always the same, as dominant features of works that best illustrate this commitment rather than a rigid outside "model" determine the emphasis.

The periodization of this chronological overview is divided into three parts. Part 1, "Early Literature" (1821–1921), covers oral literature and what can be called the first hundred years of Afro-Latin American writings in Spanish, and chapters 2 to 6 discuss black literature from 1821 (the date of Juan Francisco Manzano's *Cantos a Lesbia*, the first book of poetry published by a black in Spanish America) to 1921. Part 2, "Major Period" (1922–49), leads off with a chapter on Nicolás Guillén (whose first book of poetry dates from 1922) and the impact of his *Motivos de son*, which he published in 1930. I consider the publication of that volume to be the real starting date for what became a major period of authentic black literary expression in Spanish America, a period that coincides with the high period of negristic poetry written largely by white writers in Spanish America, with the negritude movement in the French Caribbean, and with the development of black literary consciousness in Brazil. This period could also properly be said to begin with 1929, the date Nicolás Guillén published "Pequeña oda a un negro boxeador cubano," which he has called his first *black* poem. Part 3, "Contemporary Authors" (1950–), includes discussion of younger writers and others like Nicolás Guillén who, in the fifties, sixties, and seventies continue to focus a large portion of their literary attention on their increasing awareness of the United States, on international black consciousness, and on Third Worldism. The sixteen chapters in these three parts are bounded by an Introduction where I explore some of the theoretical problems of literary blackness in Latin America and by a speculative Conclusion.

Many of the writers discussed here have been overlooked even in Latin American literary histories and anthologies and most have not appeared anywhere in English. For these reasons I have translated liberally from many of their works for, to paraphrase Don Lee (Haki R. Madhubuti), black writers do not die of overexposure in Latin America. Perhaps through more exposure the following words from an Afro-Uruguayan poem, "La hora de la tierra en que tú duermes," by Virginia Brindis de Salas (one of the few black female authors in Latin America), will prove prophetic:

> La hora de la tierra en que tú duermes
> La hora ciega a los otros
> que viven del otro lado.
> Amigo, quítate la venda
> quítate la venda
> que a ti te ciega en este,
> quítate la venda
>
> . . . .
> Quítate la venda, quítate;
> quítate la venda de tus ojos.
>   (*Pregón de Marimorena*, pp. 21–22)

Asleep on Earth at a Propitious Time
Time has blinded those
who live on the other side.
Amigo, remove the blindfold
that keeps you from seeing us,
remove the blindfold
. . . .
Remove the blindfold, remove it;
remove the blindfold from your eyes.

I would like to express my appreciation to the Canada Council for a research grant that helped make this volume and the previous one possible, to Carleton University for research assistance and for the sabbatical leave that gave me the free time to write, to students at Carleton, and to audiences and colleagues in New York City, New York, Ithaca, New York, San José, California, Chicago, Illinois, Tuskegee, Alabama, Jackson, Mississippi, Atlanta, Georgia, Houston, Texas, Waterloo, Ontario, Washington, D.C., and Providence, Rhode Island, where much of this material was first discussed in lectures, papers, seminars, and panels.

I would like to mention here also the cooperation I received from staff members at the Carleton University Library who had to find material difficult to acquire, from Lic. Nuria F. de González, Director of the Library, University of Panama, and from María E. Prieto de Frade, Reference Librarian of the National Library of Uruguay in Montevideo, who made available to me photocopied material essential to this study.

Thanks also to Marisa Bortolussi who made first drafts of many of the translations, to Carl Mora for his guidance, to David V. Holtby for his aid in editing the manuscript, to Carlos Guillermo Wilson, Nelson Estupiñán Bass, and Lemuel Johnson for their helpful suggestions, to Mrs. Nicolette Bravo who always does a first-rate job of anything that has to be done, especially if it involves expert typing, and to my wife, Lillian, who is always my first and last reader.

Introduction:
The Problems of Literary Blackness in Latin America

> Literature is what happens in a man certainly. What can happen "in" him, however, will be partly conditioned by what has happened "to" him. . . .
>
> John F. Danby

In approaching the subject of literary blackness in Latin America, numerous questions arise. How does one approach such a topic in an area such as Latin America where racial mixing and myths of racial harmony would seem to render redundant, at first glance, even the posing of any question associated with specific racial origin and distinct pride in color? Any attempt to answer that question must take into account other complex issues. What are the problems of literary blackness in an area some would have us believe is "without races"? Is there a black experience in Latin America distinct from an African, a Latin, and an Anglo-American experience? Does this experience have an impact on the black writer's expression of his New World vision? Does this expression culminate in a form of literary blackness, the artistic manifestation of a *black* way of viewing, sensing, and expressing the Afro-Latin American experience? And, regardless of adherence to European forms, does this literary blackness operate as an overriding organizing principle in Afro-Latin American literature? In short, is there an ethnicity factor in Latin American literature and, if so, what are the prospects for an authentic literature of the Black Aesthetic in that part of the world?

I would like to start off by affirming that there is a very real black experience in Latin America and that this experience is reflected in the literature of the area. I would also like to indicate from the outset that black literature in Latin America, though very much a literature of black awareness and of the black experience, is not—at least not yet—a literature of the Black Aesthetic in the strict United States Black Nationalist sense.

I can best illustrate this point by referring to an article by Sandra Govan, of Luther College, entitled "The Poetry of Black Experience as Counterpoint to the Poetry of the Black Aesthetic."[1] Her short, excellent essay should receive wide exposure in the Afro-Latin American field because I believe her comments, though limited to the United States scene, can, at the same time, be used to illustrate better than any other analysis the essential difference between Afro-Latin American literature and contemporary black literature in the United States. Black literature in America recently has been designated a literature in revolution that, by mixing rebellion, protest, and the avant-garde, is "giving rise to a new black consciousness of ideological, political, and literary possibilities"[2] not yet as noticeable and perhaps not as possible in Latin America.

In distinguishing between the poetry of Black Experience and the poetry of the Black Aesthetic in the strict United States Black Nationalist sense, Sandra Govan's first premise is "that the poetry of Black Aesthetic is more 'structured' or 'directed' to the *responsibilities* of the artist, both artistically and politically; he must reflect a Black experience and he or she must do it in such a fashion that the art 'teaches and instructs' the Black community" (p. 288). On the other hand, "the poetry of the Black Experience," she writes, "simply reflects a Black experience or any other experience that has in some fashion touched the artist and that he considers worthy of artistic treatment or comment, without imposing any particular responsibilities" (p. 288).

Govan points out that many writers of the Black Experience use racial incidents, the black heritage, and themes from black history as reference points, but unlike poets of the Black Aesthetic they do not restrict themselves to these thematic concerns. In fact I would add that the black experience in Latin America generally is cast into a broadened "democracy for all" context as the commitment of black authors there often extends beyond the black community. Central to the literature of the Black Experience, too, is a reliance on European or Western poetic thought and practice rather than on African and Afro-American techniques. Elaborating on this last point, Govan thinks a very definite case can be made for distinctions in form between the poetry of the Black Aesthetic and the poetry of Black Experience. "The poets of Black Experience," she writes, "are not only familiar with Western/European techniques and modes, they use these modes in their poetry. They may borrow from a variety of poetic schools for various stanza forms—the ode, sonnet, lyric or structured free verse. They may use such devices as rhyming couplets or a particular European metre. Generally, the diction is Western. . . . " (p. 290). Black poets in Latin America, both in Brazil and in Spanish America, are masters of Western poetic technique even though some, as we illustrate later on, do incorporate folk forms from the black oral tradition into their formal literature.

Govan makes what I consider the crucial point in her characterization of poetry of the Black Experience (and this same point can be useful when making a distinction between poetry of the Black Experience and poetry on black themes by nonblack authors) when she writes that "perhaps what makes the poetry that uses the Black Experience truly 'Black' is the personal feeling and insight that Black writers, people close in kinship to the experience, invest in their poetry" (p. 291). This "secret sympathy" or subjective vision from within is the one thing, or one of the things, together with theme and attention to roots and shared history, that Govan sees as intrinsic to both the poetry of the Black Aesthetic and to poetry of the Black Experience, a point well worth keeping in mind when we discuss the ethnicity factor in literary aesthetics.

For the moment we should reemphasize that unlike the poetry of the Black Experience, the poetry of the Black Aesthetic in the United States "in its most radical sense does not," Govan writes, "tolerate white (Western or European or American) critical standards" (p. 289). Sometimes the poetry of the Black Aesthetic does not even tolerate poetry itself: "Maybe i shouldn't write / at all . . . perhaps these are not poetic times at all," writes Nikki Giovanni in her "Poem for Sandra." Some poems provide an excellent guide to the new black poetics in the United States when they come to stand, for example, for the collective consciousness of black America. "Let the world be a black poem . . . " Amiri Baraka has said. From the new black poetry in the United States we could compile a guide to the new black poetics simply by listing such poems as Baraka's "Black Art" ("Poems are bullshit unless they are / teeth or trees piled on a step"); Nikki Giovanni's "Poem for Sandra" (i wanted to write / a poem / that rhymes / but revolution doesn't lend itself to be-bopping"); Ethridge Knight's "For Black Poets Who Think of Suicide" ("Black poets should live—not leap from steel bridges, like the white boys do"); and especially Val Benson's "Poetry to the People" ("We need poems / We need poems Now."). We have nothing like this in Latin America. No such poetic guidelines exist.

While we do not have in Latin America a poetry of the Black Aesthetic in the strict United States Black Nationalist sense, what we do have there, as Doris J. Turner and Antonio Olliz Boyd (whose work on Machado de Assis, Nicolás Guillén, and Adalberto Ortiz is the most extensive study yet done on the subject) have shown,[3] is an ethnicity factor that influences the aesthetics of black writers. There is no question that ethnic blackness is an influential and motivating factor in the aesthetics of Afro-Latin American writers; even a cursory glance at the literature of the area would reveal that "black authors in Latin America treat ethnically oriented material from a basis of conscious experience. . . ."[4] For in Latin America, too, "it is rather ludicrous to think that a Black writer—if he is honest—can project his art without showing some of the scars that racism has inflicted upon him."[5] In Latin America, as elsewhere, it is inevitable that racism and the white aesthetic have had some bearing on the black man and his relationship to his color. In fact, as Boyd has said, "The biggest single unalterable circumstance in the life of any black writer is his consanguineal affiliation to an oppressed group. Whether he admits or denies this fundamental, his psychology will in some way be governed by this relationship."[6] The "in-group" sensitivity Boyd sees operating in Latin America, which is indicative of a black consciousness, could very well form the core of a Black Aesthetic should systematic and radical literary theories based on ethnic affiliation develop.

A black aesthetic in the strictest sense is not yet operable in Latin America, but this does not negate Boyd's basic "victim" and "victimizer" hypothesis, namely, that blacks do not perceive their literary world in the same manner as whites; that blacks reflect racial attachments from a "living in a society" perspective rather than through an outsider, exotic approach; that personal identification with blackness and personal experience with the black experience have a great deal to do with a black writer's choice of words, symbols, and images; that race and color, in short, do make a difference. These are the same distinctions that Doris J. Turner illustrates brilliantly in her recent analysis of contrasting symbols, words, and images in two Afro-Brazilian works, *Jubiabá* (1935), by the white Brazilian Jorge Amado, and *Sortilégio* (1951), by Abdias de Nascimento, a black Brazilian.

This view is hardly one shared by Jahnheinz Jahn, the noted German scholar, who in the sixties took one of the most controversial positions ever taken in the field of black, or to use his term, Neo-African literature, when he asserted that the color of an author's skin contributed little toward determining what literary family he belongs to.[7] His theory means that white authors whose works show "africanisms," or African stylistic features and patterns of expression can be included in Neo-African literature. Further, his theory also suggests that black writers whose work shows no such africanisms can be excluded. This approach is risky in that it reduces an author's work to so much stylistic posturing. When we read Jahn's assessment of the achievement of Nicolás Guillén, for example, we are left with the impression that Guillén's main contributions lie in his incorporation of African cheerfulness, sensuality, and stylistic patterns into a European language.[8] There is, needless to say, much more to Nicolás Guillén than that.

The advent of the ethnicity factor during the decade of the seventies has given the relationship between skin color and literary aesthetics more recognition and respectability. Martha K. Cobb, for example, has shown that the aesthetic effectiveness of black poets (her examples are Jacques Roumain, Langston Hughes, and Nicolás Guillén) relates to the perceptions and values drawn from the black experience in the Americas.[9] Emphasizing the strengths and validity of a black aesthetic in relation to the heritage of western literature, Cobb takes into account the importance of point of view. More specifically, she writes that "images of plantation life," to take one example, "conceived out of the feelings and memories of a black writer would bear little resemblance to images created from a white point of view."[10] Boyd, in showing that race and color do make a difference, has explored what he calls the "deep structures" of literary expression to illustrate just how an author's telling choice of words, images, and symbols reflects that difference. Speech patterns and descriptive words are the telling choices, according to Turner, that weaken Amado's symbolic but negative black stereotype in *Jubiabá*.

The ethnic signals and clues to ethnic identification Boyd sees in covert linguistic signs, while not the overt thematic indicators that form the basis of Cobb's approach, nevertheless are present even in the works of those writers, mainly nineteenth century ones, whose overt racial empathy is suspect and who of necessity write "white" but rarely feel comfortable doing it. The literature of these writers, though devoid of "black language" and "black themes," is still "colored," if you will, with indicators of ethnic affiliation, for the writers never seem to be at one or at home racially with the larger societies whose racist pressures and white standards reward whiteness and restrict "africanity" in literature.

Following the lead set by Boyd who sees the white symbols of Cruz e Sousa, for example, not as the reverse of negritude, or negritude in reverse as Preto-Rodas[11] thought, but rather as black awareness, it is clear that black awareness still informs the aesthetics of black writers in Latin America even when those aesthetics are diverted into an exaggerated cult of whiteness. In other words, even if a black writer shows no inclination toward race conscious social protest literature and even if his content, stylistic features, and patterns of literary expression are clearly Western (as with Juan Francisco Manzano, the slave poet in Cuba) or decidedly Modernist (as with Gaspar Octavio Hernández in Panama), there can still be something there that can label that author "black" even when, or especially when, that black author is trying to write "white" for a white audience. What I am saying here certainly does not constitute hard-core literary theory, but knowing an author's ethnic affiliation at times does open up to us one more avenue for exploratory interpretation of the literary work, especially in the case of black writers who write "white" in racist or slave societies, since racism and slavery, it must be borne in mind, can be primary causes for the suppression of overt black awareness in the first place.

In short, even black writers who write "white" often call attention indirectly to the racist pressures they encounter in the societies in which they live. Recognizing the relationship between these pressures and the literary aesthetics of these writers is just as important as recognizing africanisms, linguistic signs, and thematic indicators of literary blackness in others, if we are to understand what black authors who suppress their blackness have to tell us. I have always thought that black writers who choose to say little or nothing overtly about the black experience in Latin America are, at the same time, telling us much about it. That is why our studies on the aesthetic tendencies of the black psyche cannot be limited only to cases where the black origin of an author is under suspicion (Machado de Assis) or where the black identity of the author is not only obvious but clearly affirmed (Nicolás Guillén or Adalberto Ortiz). We must consider as well the impact of ethnicity in the "white" aesthetics of black authors whose black ethnic origin is obvious physically but whose literary orientation, on the surface, seems to have been diverted into directions other than race.

These considerations—ethnicity and literary orientation—are related to the question, "What is black poetry?" raised by Stephen Henderson in his landmark book *Understanding the New Black Poetry*, which contains some guidelines applicable to Latin America. Henderson refines the question, "What is black poetry?" by outlining five logical possibilities, and I give them in full below:

1. Any poetry by any person or group of persons of known Black African ancestry, whether the poetry is designated Black or not.
2. Poetry which is somehow *structurally* Black, irrespective of authorship.
3. Poetry by any person or group of known Black African ancestry, which is *also identifiably* Black, in terms of structure, theme, or other characteristics.
4. Poetry by any identifiably Black person who can be classed as a "poet" by Black people. Judgment may or may not coincide with judgments of whites.
5. Poetry by any identifiably Black person whose ideological stance vis-à-vis the history and the aspirations of his people since slavery is adjudged by them to be "correct." [12]

These possibilities in turn are related to the problem of racial identity in Latin America where the process of *mestizaje* has complicated the question, "Who or what is Black?". Angela Gilliam in a recent attempt to answer that question chose the following definition: *Anyone who claims Black heritage is an African.* [13] This definition, understood to include blacks who are recognizably so and others who accept this ethnic identity, makes sense, especially in view of the fact that there are signs of an increasing polarization or hardening of racial identities into black and white in Latin America, despite a history of amalgamation and cultural assimilation.

It would be nice to accept that in the final analysis the human spirit has no color, that the necessity for races to "harden" into black

or white, or for values to have to be specified as white or black
ideally should never exist. It must be understood, however, as Sylvia
Washington Ba understands it, that "in view of the division produced by history it is rather naive to expect the black man to vindi-
cate his humanity without first vindicating that aspect of it
[pigmentation] that has been so discredited."[14] Small wonder, therefore, that black writers in Latin America inevitably and understandably allow a black perspective to influence their literature.

This black perspective in Afro-Latin American literature has less
to do with African retentions or survivals and "cultural tenacity,"
the Neo-Africanisms popularized by Jahnheinz Jahn, than with "dynamic Africanity," which Anani Dzidzienyo defined as "the socio-
political expressions of these survivals and, above all, how they are
viewed in relation to postslavery continental and diasporic Africa."[15]
A black perspective, then, not limited to "Afrolotry" in J. Mbelolo
Ya Mpiku's term,[16] or to *africanización perpétua*, expressed by Gastón Baquero[17]—since it is by now a foregone conclusion that the African heritage is ever present in the New World—but one that has
been shaped by the "true black experience";[18] namely, the devastating
historical experience of slavery, imperialism, racism, and color conscious colonialism (all of these are what Malcolm X, I believe, called
negative or "vulturistic isms"), in the New World, on the "continent
of the Black man's suffering."[19]

One other problem of Neo-African literature as conceived by
Jahnheinz Jahn—in addition to leaving open the inclusion of white
authors and to ruling out color as a factor in literary expression—is
the total stress his concept puts on African retentions while rejecting
race conscious social protest literature growing out of the black experience in America. Even Leopold Sédar Senghor, the main pro-
ponent of a "Negritude des sources," recognizes the significance of
the social history of the New World black in confrontation with the
white world outside Africa where blacks, he writes, "whether they
be from the United States, from Brazil, or from the West Indies,
insist on the specificity of their condition because of their original
experience: on the social inheritance more than the biological inheritance."[20] While the African heritage through "soul-force," that
"quality of life that has enabled Black people to survive the horrors
of their 'diaspora'"[21] is important, it is the héroic survival of the
Neo-African himself during his four centuries here rather than
African survivals, though they certainly played a role in that sur-

vival, that should also be kept in perspective and in memory. It should be kept in mind, then, that negritude is largely a concept of the New World. There blacks, as many chapters in this book illustrate, are confronted with those negative or "vulturistic isms" and with such other realities as *mestizaje*, assimilation, and alienation not experienced in Africa, for these are the realities that represent the true black experience in the New World.

The expression of these realities in Afro-Latin American literature, in turn, is often conditioned by New World concepts or parameters of literary blackness. These parameters, the keys to recognizing an authentic black perspective in a work of literature, help us over the obstacle presented by the second possibility posed by Stephen Henderson in answer to the question, "What is black poetry?"; that is, poetry which is somehow *structurally black* irrespective of authorship. In raising the question, "Can nonblacks write authentic black poetry?" Henderson recognizes that there would be real problems if a nonblack writer elected to write on a black theme using a black persona and successfully absorbing black expressive patterns.

In evaluating "black" literature irrespective of authorship, we should first test for authenticity or credibility by looking to such parameters or indicators of a black perspective as those recently developed by Martha K. Cobb.[22] Cobb conceptualizes the black experience into the following minimum thematic schema, which though allowing for individual variations on the black experience can be and should be used, certainly as a starting point, for the comparative exploration of black literature in any part of the New World: (1) *confrontation* with an alien and usually hostile society; (2) *dualism*, or a sense of division between one's own self and that of the dominant culture; (3) *identity*, a search that embraces the question who am I?; and (4) *liberation*, both spiritual and political.

Such concepts as these, when infused or "saturated"—to use another by now well-known term—with the personal feelings and insight of black writers, help reveal the peculiarly black perspective, that closeness and understanding conditioned by racial memory and by ethnic kinship to the shared history of the black as victim. Perspective, to use Richard Wright's definition, is "that fixed point in intellectual space where a writer stands to view the struggles, hopes and sufferings of *his* [italics mine] people. . . . At its best, perspective is a preconscious assumption, something which a writer takes for granted, something which he wins through his living."[23] Such closeness and understanding, which derive from the black writer's subjective vision from within we spoke of earlier or from that "something" won by his living, cannot be matched in credibility and therefore in authenticity by the objective vision from without of nonblack writers who, regardless of good intentions and black structural features relied on, do not share this closeness, understanding and lived history and therefore the "sensibility," to use George Kent's word, that inform black writing. This sensibility, "the writer's means of sensing, apprehending, his characteristic emotional, psychic, and intellectual response to existence,"[24] is not "something that can be so easily borrowed by others,"[25] or by the Other, to be more specific. When Julian Mayfield wrote, "soul gut music alone does not a black man make,"[26] he was talking about blacks and also about Tom Jones and Janis Joplin and about whites who wore afros and dashikis, and who sang black songs and who talked black talk. We can apply the phrase broadly to Latin America and to Spain where nonblacks for centuries have been simulating blackness, trying to talk "black" talk, particularly as we all know, during the negristic poetry craze popularized by white poets mainly in the Caribbean between the two world wars. Real or authentic black poetry, though, goes beyond the facile imitation of the African sound in Spanish, a point I elaborate on in chapter seven.

The real challenge, then, is charting blackness, especially in early Afro-Latin American literature where accommodationist—to use Fanon's term—or assimilationist verse shows black writers to be highly imitative and conventional and corresponding "point by point" with white writers, for being authors of their ages, we cannot fail to recognize that blacks have written in the prevailing styles of their periods; that is, in the "white (or European) style of the time," and perhaps more so than whites, to prove they could do it as well as, if not better than, whites themselves. It is easy to see Plácido, for example, as Cuba's romantic poet, or to fit black writers into standard literary molds. It is easy to see Martín Morúa Delgado as perhaps Cuba's first naturalist writer, or to cast the Afro-Colombian Arnoldo Palacios in this same mold. There is no question that Gaspar Octavio Hernández was more Modernist than most in Panama, or that Nicolás Guillén throughout his career has been the classic Spanish poet. Yet, just as we have to look beyond the formalistic exterior for credibility in literature on blacks by nonblack writers, so too do we have to look within the standard literary categories or generations for the ethnicity or motivating factor that shapes the *idea*, as Don Lee has popularized the notion, which, in turn, gives black writing in Latin America and elsewhere ethnic perspective as well as aesthetic form.

That is why when looking at black literature in Latin America we should turn to new concepts and definitions and re-examine old ones more closely to fully understand the problems of literary blackness in that part of the world. The concept of *mulatez*, for example, which is a form of *mestizaje*, is central to an understanding of the black experience in Latin America in that it is the one parameter of literary blackness that seems, in one form or another, to relate to all the above mentioned concepts as well as to Senghor's theory of a civilization of the universal, and I might add, to Sartre's famous theory of negritude elaborated in "Black Orpheus," [27] where he makes among other controversial judgments what is now widely seen to have been a mistake, when he saw the ultimate objective of negritude to be a society without races rather than a society simply without racism. If, however, we recognize the *mestizaje* factor at work in Latin America and if we accept Senghor's concept of *métissage culturel*, which lies at the core of his negritude theory of a civilization of the universal, taking them to mean a symbiotic mixture of cultures and races, then Sartre's mistake would seem to warrant more than a passing reference in a discussion of literary blackness in Latin America where cultural and biological mixing has gone on at an unprecedented rate throughout the history of the black experience on this continent.

Further, in recognizing *mestizaje* to be an indisputable fact of the black experience in Latin America, I wrote not long ago that "*mestizaje* has done much to validate the prediction of Sartre who, realizing that some black poets transcended race, had stated that the black struggle and negritude as the exaltation of blackness would give way to the proletarian struggle, suggesting, in effect, that the black song of black poets was destined to be one without color." [28] It is important to realize, however, that even though the synthesis or realization of the human in a society "without races" in the sense of without ethnic privilege is nowhere desired more than among blacks in Latin America, one can desire—though Sartre doubted it—the abolition of all kinds of ethnic privilege through a show of solidarity with the oppressed of every color without, of course, giving up the "ethnic notion of negritude." One can identify with class, with the worldwide proletariat, without deserting race. This is essentially what Ascensión Lastre, star black man in Adalberto Ortiz's prizewinning Ecuadorian novel *Juyungo*, does. As we shall see in a later chapter, Lastre mixes the "notion of race" with the "notion of class" throughout the novel and, though ambivalent at times, does seem to confound Sartre's view in the end.

In Latin America the synthesis or realization of the human being in a raceless society is not inconsistent with the hopes whites have pinned on *mestizaje* or the whitening process there or with the class leaning of blacks. The black, however, much like Ascensión Lastre who often puts class before race and who has much pride as a man, does not "strip his pride" as a black for other men. Ascensión Lastre, an excellent case in point, as we shall see, retains his black pride more than "for a moment"; indeed, it persists right up until he goes down fighting, we are to believe, for his country. The strength he summoned for his final heroic deeds derives from his blackness, not from unguided patriotism, class action, or even from instant madness, as was recently suggested.[29] Ascensión Lastre does not "through supreme generosity" abandon his black pride. Nor even does Nicolás Guillén, perhaps the leading Third World writer.

The concept of *mulatez*, then, is one parameter of literary blackness with a very high profile in Latin America related as it is to a larger concept of liberty and human solidarity (confrontation, identity, and dualism resolved) in the ideal sense of black and white together in a world of universal brotherhood without races (ethnic privilege) and without racism. From José Martí to Sartre the humanistic vision that Wilfred Cartey defines as the "shared participation in the common good"[30] seems to point toward the Hegelian synthesis, toward Teilhard de Chardin's theory of cultural pluralism, and in a less racist sense toward Gobineau's concept of *métissage culturel*, all popularized by Senghor in his theory of a civilization of the universal, a humanistic universalism much like the kingdoms of culture envisaged by Dubois years ago that will be as much a part of the twenty-first century as racism and the color line are a part of this century and slavery the nineteenth century. In a speech not too long ago in North America,[31] Senghor saw the Americas significantly as a prototype of this civilization of the future.

With those considerations in mind, it becomes clear that ethnicity as a factor retains its importance even in a civilization of the universal. Any exploration of the problems of literary blackness in Latin America must confront the "colorless nudity" theory that Sartre uses to characterize negritude, and emphasize that the black man in Latin America even when he writes a "black song without color" is not abandoning his blackness to love his neighbor, since it is not the black man who must go beyond race and color, but the white man who must renounce his traditional universal (white) values and pride in race and color to let the black man in, a point that becomes especially important when we discuss Nicolás Guillén in a later chapter. The black man does not have to "lose himself in the Other" to live comfortably in the future civilization of the universal nor does he have to return to Africa. That is why the "black song" of black writers in Latin America, though often reflecting a *mestizo* reality that recognizes the "very wide process of acculturation"[32] in Brazil and elsewhere in Latin America, is a universal song that is, at the same time, fully black in that it lays great emphasis on the racial, cultural, and historical realities of the black experience in the New World.

This black experience, which has been defined as the most intense experience in the modern world,[33] is at the same time one of the most universal experiences the world has ever known "because it includes all the pain, sorrow, hardships, frustrations that are fundamental to man."[34] The concept of *mulatez*, too, in a sense opens on to the universal through a human oneness that emphasizes a universal brotherhood into which all (black and white) races "meld" biologically and culturally. There is a further universality, too, one "that encompasses and encourages tolerant forms of individual, national, and ethnic consciousness."[35] It is partly on this concept of universality that *ethnic blackness* in Latin America and *ethnopoetics*,[36] an avant-garde term, come together as neither underestimates the importance of the ethnicity factor in literary aesthetics. Both terms recognize the need to set to order a new system that can incorporate a people's need for self-awareness, self-realization, and self-definition, whether expressed through oral or written literature.

Whatever the form universality takes in relation to literary blackness in Latin America, then, it must be remembered that in the final analysis, universality resides in a decision "to recognize and accept the reciprocal relativism of different cultures."[37] Or, as Abraham Chapman, echoing this sentiment, put it, "it is the duty of literary scholars to examine fully the racist influences on western concepts of the universal and to correct racist distortions with the understanding that the universal means being receptive to, and consciously welcoming, the diverse aesthetic creations of Black people of the world for the cultural enrichment of humanity." [38] Even in *mestizo* societies the "legitimate universalism" of which George Kent spoke can derive from a black perspective projected when a writer discovers his true origins and his transcendant values, rather than by flying over, reducing, or avoiding, as Kent says, "the tensions inherent in the black experience by reaching for some preexisting Western universal." [39]

In other words, even in *mestizo* societies black writing can be fully black and universal too, but we have to recognize the distinction between what has been called *mestizaje positivo* and *mestizaje negativo* since, as we shall see, black writers in Latin America insist on this distinction. Quite simply, the first means a blending of cultures in which there is equal respect for both. The second means that a minority culture is absorbed as an inferior culture. [40]

Black ethnicity, then, has its place even in the "miscegenetic utopia" [41] of Latin America where the "minimum basis for personal dignity" [42] can be found in perhaps the most important necessity of all, namely, the "compelling necessity of accepting—and insisting on—one's origins" [43] even when, or especially when, government policy and the historical process of acculturation prevent a realistic and all-out return to some of those origins. The acceptance of one's origins—and accommodating that acceptance to a New World reality that often denies it validity—is an overriding principle that guides the aesthetics of much of the black literature discussed in the following chapters.

Part One

EARLY LITERATURE, 1821–1921

In the Beginning:
Oral Literature and the "True Black Experience"

> No study of Latin American literature, even in the
> twentieth century, is balanced unless oral performance
> is taken into account and unless there is some notion
> of the dialectics of oral and written literatures.
>
> Jean Franco

The very first literary manifestation of the "true black experience" in Latin America is found in the folk literature that blacks cultivated orally before learning to write European languages. Whatever the "strata"[1] of the folklore of black America, whether pure African, Negro (or Creole), or white folklore but absorbed by blacks, and regardless of origin, whether uniquely black American or from Africa, Europe, or even Aesop's fables, folklore used by blacks in the New World tells us much about black survival reflecting as it does their unique New World experience. Origin of black folklore is often extraneous, since source is not as significant as meaning when one looks for *how* versions are applied to and are illustrative of the true black experience and *what* they mean in terms of black survival.

This distinction between origin and content is discussed by Langston Hughes: "Let it be said quickly that Negro folklore, like almost any other kind, can be traced in its origin to a dim past when it drew on a common cultural heritage, which most of the folk of the world appear to have shared. In any case the telling of tales is a time honored custom in Africa. By what steps the Fables of Aesop (Ethiop) became the animal stories of West Africa, of the West Indies, and of the slave states of the U.S.A. is a lively question but not to the point here."[2] What does interest me in this study is the use to which this folklore has been put in Latin America since the protest element and the humor of the oppressed, common to the folklore of all races, are also present in the black oral tradition in Latin America, a fact that cannot be overemphasized.

Interest in Afro-Latin American folk literature has focused largely on the folktale, but rarely on it as a reflection of the true black experience in Latin America; that is, on the folktale as socio-racial statement, perhaps because, as in the United States, it has been the "white hand" that has been most responsible for what has come down to us in written form. The surge of current interest in Latin American black folk expression, particularly in Cuba, indicated by the same kind of "diligence and popularity of collections, anthologists, musicologists, and interpreters"[3] Sterling Brown saw in the fifties in the United States, makes one wonder, as Brown did, whether such commercializing "will affect the genuineness of the stuff."[4] This concern is valid and partly explains why, since from the days of Joel Chandler Harris and his Uncle Remus tales to the present, "collectors being of different race or class or both, have been viewed by the folk with natural distrust."[5]

This natural distrust is understandable not only because it is difficult to see black folktales reworked by upper class whites as authentic black folktales "by the folk for the folk,"[6] but also because the far ranging control the artistic presence of the paternalistic white hand has can make them suspect, as art sometimes has a tendency to get in the way of insight and credible image. This danger is a real one particularly as black folktales in their written forms are transposed and largely designed to give pleasure, amuse, and entertain whites, much like the early oral versions did for white masters and slave owners and their children.

This kind of "collaboration between black folklore and its white mediator"[7] is perhaps best illustrated in the Afro-Cuban folktales collected and authored by Lidia Cabrera. Her collections are, by far, the most readily available today as they, like most of her other work in the Afro-Cuban field, are regularly published or reissued by Librería Universal, a thriving publisher and distributor in Miami of Cuban and Latin American books. Her works recently have been dealt with by Hilda Perera, Josefina Inclán, and Rosa M. Valdés-Cruz in book-length studies[8] that show that Cabrera, like Joel Chandler Harris in his Uncle Remus tales, uses such devices as invention and imagination common to all good short story writers.

Their studies show specifically that Cabrera's stories combine African elements with "narrative development and technique *derived from* [italics mine] the creative imagination of Lidia Cabrera." [9]

While one might be able to see "the core of negritude," [10] as Perera claims, in these "reworkings," [11] to use Valdés-Cruz's term, one can also see without having to look too closely that they have the very problems of credibility mentioned above particularly in tales where black features are the focus ("Las Nariguetas de los negros están hechas de Fayanca"); in tales where such stereotypes as the happy-go-lucky or lazy black are perpetuated ("Taita Hicotea y Taita Tigre", "Susudamba no se muestra de día", "La vida suave", "La loma de Mambiala"); and in tales where antiblack or rationalizations of racism and racial hierarchy are proffered ("Hay hombres blancos, pardos y negros").

Without a doubt Cabrera's monumental work with the Afro-Cuban folktale has retained much that is African flavored: the *jitanjá-foras*, for example, so typical of *negrista* poetry, are there in such *estribillos* as "Grín grín grín, / Grín grín grín, / Grín grín grín, / Bongo Monasengo, Si Kengó! / Bongo Monasengo, Si Kengó." [12] and "¡Yé yé yé, Lukénde, yéyé / yéyé, lukénde, yéyé! " [13] There is no question, however, that she has overlaid these *cuentos* with her own narrative and creative skill complete with "stylistic affinities with Lorca's generation." [14] But what is worse, her strong "love for the Cuba of the nineteenth century, a vague nostalgia for the colonial period" [15] preempts identification with "the social or sexual problematic of the black within a society governed by whites," [16] a problem further compounded by "the absence of the themes of slavery, of the slave's fight for liberty, and of his rebelliousness." [17]

Despite this onesidedness, perhaps understandable in one who here in the late seventies can still refer to "*my* [italics mine] Cuban blacks" [18] and who sees Africans more to blame for slavery than whites, [19] there are New World settings for some of Cabrera's tales where references to and reflections of the true black experience are inevitable. The preponderance of animal tales in particular where the weak traditionally wins out or outsmarts the bigger and stronger suggests the attraction this kind of symbolic tale had for the underdog slave. These stories, often dogmatic, were more than humorous entertainment to the slave. Like the *jicotea*, the most popular animal "hero" of the folktale in Cuba, the black slaves "felt obligated to turn to cunning, false humility, hypocrisy and even magic in order to defeat those with the upper hand." [20] One of the most important qualities of the *jicotea* was his ability to survive: "The turtle suffers punishment and blows; when it seems as though all is lost it comes back stronger like the black spirit which does not buckle under either to slave labor or ill treatment."[21]

Significantly, one of the best reflections of the true black experience in the New World comes not from Cabrera's reworked tales but from her *El monte*, a book that unlike her "transposiciones," was taken down "as is," that is, as narrated to her by her black informants. "I have limited myself rigorously," she writes of this book, "to stating with absolute objectivity and without prejudice that which I have heard and that which I have seen."[22] Her intention in the story was simply to show the significance to the Afro-Cuban of the "sacred" *ceiba* tree, but what emerges is a moving account about a defiant black slave who refused to allow a white "superior" to sleep with his wife and who, anticipating revenge for taking care of his own, had to take flight, escaping death through superhuman efforts afforded him by strength derived from the *ceiba* tree.[23]

The runaway slave hunted down by dogs figures as well in black proverbs—also reproduced faithfully—that Lidia Cabrera collected and published in her *Refranes de negros viejos* (Miami: Editorial C.R., 1970): "When a dog attacks us, our cries do not defend us." "With the club we have in our hands, with that we kill the dog." Such proverbs as these and others that show the true black experience in the New World, like "A slave has a father and a mother," and "If the ox is not born, the black pulls the cart," indicate a black awareness not inconsistent with that seen, for example, in "Cuento del jigüe,"[24] a tale collected by Ramón Guirao and included in his *Cuentos y leyendas de Cuba* (La Habana: Ediciones Mirador, 1942). This tale, which really deals with black pride, is typical of this collection, more noted for its reflection of the true black experience in the New World than for the imposition of a strong white hand. In this sense Guirao is closer to Rómulo Lachatañeré who in his ¡Oh, mío Yemayá! (Mansanillo: Editorial "El Arte," 1938) tries to be "faithful to the tale of his simple informers even in the language."[25] This judgment is not too unlike Nicolás Guillén's assessment of Lachatañeré's *Manual de Santería* (La Habana: Editorial Caribe, 1942):

The *Manual de Santería* is different. In it Lachatañeré proposed to examine the phenomena of religious syncretism in

Cuba from various new angles, in opposition to the academic methods. It is a valuable book both for that which it affirms and that which it denies; a book written from the bottom up, that is to say, according to the author's experiences living among the *santeros*, who he approaches free from intellectual or professional prejudice. This way he allows them to speak, and not their "learned" interpreters who often end up betraying them.[26]

Several black folktales in which the white hand is minimal collected elsewhere in Latin America represent black attempts, for example, to offset an inferiority complex. One example,[27] which is really about the survival of black dignity in the face of the white aesthetic, is a black version of the biblical story of Noah, told to Max Radiguet in Peru, a version that, by making Noah a black, shows blacks trying to gain the upper hand while pointing up in historical perspective how whites are and how they got to be that way. Another tale, given below, by creating an unflattering origin of the white race, shows the same intent. It is reproduced from Colombia by Paulo de Carvalho-Neto:

> God created a man and a woman. Both were black. As time went by, the couple had two sons named Cain and Abel. Cain was wicked and perverse, for ever since he was a child, he devoted himself to drink, women and gambling. Abel, on the other hand, was good. He went to mass, respected his parents and his fellow man; and he fulfilled his promises. Cain, envious of his brother, killed him one afternoon upon returning from his work. But as there is no crime that remains hidden, God appeared to him, reproached him for his faults and cursed him. So great was Cain's wickedness that he began to grow pale until he was all white, a color he maintained until his death.
>
> Cain was the father of the white nation on this earth.[28]

Even the folklore of Pai João, the legendary Brazilian Uncle Remus, who was popular among whites because of his resignation, managed to reflect the true black experience in the New World by subtly expressing in his tales "the spirit of revolt against the slave condition."[29] Pai João's folktales in Brazil spoke not only "of African traditions but also of the long and hateful history of slavery, of oppression and martyrdom: the punishment of slaves, the master's persecutions, the nostalgia for free lands. . . . " [30] It is this symbolic or protest aspect of black folklore that gave it a dimension that went far beyond mere entertainment for whites, since what was important was "how these tales affected the slave's attitudes toward himself, not whether his thinking or behavior would impress a society which considered black people little better than animals." [31] Black folklore as social statement, then, had a significance as a source of survival for black listeners and readers when it spoke to their needs and sentiments, a significance that was important not only to black survival but to the survival of black folklore itself.

In a recent study on mechanisms or strategies of survival Richard K. Barksdale wrote that the black American ever since he was brought to the New World "has had to resort to many strategies of offense and defense in order to cope with the manipulative devices and subtle depredations of a powerful white majority." [32] Among the several strategies he reviews are the strategy of angry physical confrontation and revolt; the strategy of accommodation; the strategy of nonviolence; and the "subtle but effective offensive strategy" [33] known as comic ridicule.

It is this last strategy—comic ridicule or therapeutic laughter—that is "as old as the Black man's presence in America," [34] that interests us here. The hidden black laughter in songs and ballads and stories in which the white slaveholder was subtly ridiculed is also heard in Latin America, where, as we mentioned earlier, the theme of weakness overcoming strength, particularly in the animal tales, had obvious appeal—both amusing and instructive—to the black slave who saw, for example, in the stories of *jicotea* (who certainly knew how to protect itself) the same paradigms for human survival seen in the Anansi stories in the West Indies. In short, without understanding what humor meant to slaves themselves, namely, "a means of survival," [35] one is not likely to rise above "the superficiality of a Stephen Foster or a Joel Chandler Harris." [36]

Blacks have also put their humor to good use in verbal battles with white opponents. In these literary contests, the black improviser could protest his state and ridicule whites, and sometimes do both things at the same time, since the black, "who had excellent reasons for wanting to release his pent-up fury against the white man, could now do so with impunity, since the whole thing was just a game." [37] Indeed, some of the strongest battles on race seem to have been fought with words in the direct confrontations of these *desa-*

fíos or *contrapunteos* and in circulating *coplas* where racist and racial feelings of the people are perpetuated in song and sayings.

Much black humor is seen, too, in early folk poetry of the anonymous *copla*, which is also the source of some of the most rampant and blatant antiblack consciousness ever recorded in Latin America. Paulo de Carvalho-Neto has recently published a book on this subject with numerous examples of what he calls "racist folklore,"[38] that is, a folklore devised by whites designed to perpetuate negative and sterotyped images of blacks.

Arthur Ramos earlier in this century had already recognized oral literature to be a valid indicator of the true black experience in America when he saw, for example, in the folk *copla* "the true story of the social and domestic life of the black Brazilian."[39] Carvalho-Neto added to our knowledge on this subject through his own field work in Ecuador, for example, where he found the black is a frequent protagonist in folktales as well as in folk poetry. But regardless of location or forum, and whether *contrapunteo, copla*, or *cuento*, pejorative feelings against blacks are recorded. Small wonder, therefore, that blacks have developed as a mechanism or strategy of survival a "black folklore of protest,"[40] that can also be called a *forced poetics* or a *counter-poetics*,[41] in which they attempt to "get even" in equally anonymous folk literature.

Carvalho-Neto cites some of these examples of racial antipathy:

Cantor blanco	White singer
Hay mucho negro insolente	There are many insolent blacks
Con ellos no quiero ilusionarme;	I don't want to fool myself about them;
Observe que no somos	Notice that we are not
Tela del mismo tejido.	Cloth of the same texture.
Cantor negro	Black singer
Soy negro pero huelo bien	I am black but I smell good
Tú eres un blanco rubio,	You are a blond white man
Si quieres cantar conmigo;	If you wish to sing with me
Primero vayas a bañarte;[42]	First go and take a bath;

There is much black pride in this defensive oral literature:

Dices que soy Negro	You say I am a black
Negro soy, en verdad;	Indeed, black I am
Pero soy un Negro de bien,	But I'm an honest black
Y tú, un blanco sinvergüenza.[43]	And you, a shameless white.

José Juan Arróm[44] in his well-known study has shown that the black is a widespread theme in folkloric poetry, particularly in the *copla*, the most popular form, and his findings support what I have been saying, namely, that the black motif in popular literature ranges from antiblack prejudice to affirmation of black pride, and that folk poetry like oral stories tells us as much about the true black experience as erudite literature. In fact, such anonymous verse as

El ser negro no es ofrenta	Being black is nothing shameful
Ni color que quite fama	Nor is the color defaming
Porque el zapatito negro	Because little black shoes
Lo calza la mejor dama.[45]	Are worn by the finest ladies.

that reflects a "certain diversion of some popular singer," [46] precedes, and in intent is like, later written literature of black protest. Under the cloak of anonymity the black folk singer or storyteller could be more defiant in his protest than blacks in early authored literature; for that reason oral literature is a valid source for insight into the true black experience in the new world. Jean Franco has gone so far as to say that "in order to understand the colonial period at all, it is necessary to study oral literature and poetry not simply as folklore (a nineteenth-century invention [she calls it]) but as an integral part of a living culture which as in medieval Europe provided an outlet for the unofficial activities and responses of the people." [47] Citing Walter Benjamin, she writes that "experience which is passed from mouth to mouth is the source from which all storytellers have drawn. . . . The storyteller takes what he tells from experience—his own or that reported by others. And he, in turn, makes it the experience of those who are listening to his tale." [48] And she adds that it is this "direct contact between the oral performer and the community experience which makes the persistent survival of oral narrative and poetry in Latin America a matter of more than antiquarian interest." [49]

Jean Franco is, of course, right, then, to conclude that oral literature can teach us much, particularly oral literature which under the cloak of anonymity escaped the censorship and control early written literature had to endure. It is not difficult, therefore, to trace in later print literature themes of freedom, injustice, humor, and pride in blackness back to early oral improvisations popular among blacks.

José Vasconcelos, the famous "El Negrito Poeta" of eighteenth-century Mexico, escaped anonymity because his improvised *coplas* were written down by admirers of his talent as composer of humorous verse. His caustic response to affronts include the following defense of his blackness:

No tengo la culpa yo.   I am not to blame.
una mano oculta y sabia   A hidden and wise hand
esta piel negra me dió   Gave to me this black skin
cual si naciera en Arabia.[50]   As though I had been born in Arabia.

And again:

Ser negro no es culpa mía,   Being black is no fault of mine,
a todos doy alegría   Everyone I make happy
y con esto me reintegro.[51]   And with that I am recompensed.

In the *contrapunteo* tradition, "El Negrito Poeta" carried on "controversies in verse" with other improvisers, criticizing, for example, the white aesthetic of one who looks down on blacks:

Calla la boca, embustero,   Be quiet, you liar
y no te jactes de blanco,   and don't boast that you are white
saliste del mismo banco,   You came out of the same mold
y tiene el mismo cuero.[52]   And you have the same hide.

Other forms of oral literature in Latin America portray the true black experience, including the more subterranean and internal ritual songs and liturgical songs that are famous more for their onomatopoeic effects than for racial confrontation with whites. Whatever form or forerunner of later literature examined, though, one will find that thematically in Latin America, as in the United States, "the reflected experience"[53] is the same, an experience perhaps best summed up in the following oral, "remembered" history:

Fuimos ayer esclavos   Yesterday we were slaves
Hoy no lo somos ya.   Today we are not.
¡Qué crueles penas   What cruel suffering!
que balbalilá![54]   What nonsense it all was!

Slave Poetry and Slave Narrative:
Juan Francisco Manzano and Black Autobiography

Writing in that age was, for the slave, a form of heroism.
Ildefonso Pereda Valdés

Slavery, whether a remembered history or an actual experience, was living hell for blacks. Times were hard especially for the slave man of letters if he dared deal overtly with his plight. Even white writers who lived under the system were not free to write whatever they wanted about it. In Cuba slavery lasted until 1886, and an antislavery consciousness in literature emerged amidst the controls and censorship supporting slavery. Indeed, this control and censorship sometimes came, as we shall see, from within the abolitionist circle itself. The influential Cuban group, which was led by Domingo del Monte, dictated, for example, the *manso* "portrait of the slave,"[1] that is, they gave the slave a meek image, the only one deemed acceptable and able to escape censorship during the first half of the nineteenth century.

Considering the obstacles to receiving an education free blacks encountered in the nineteenth century, one can imagine the difficulties slaves faced in becoming literate. Slaves were not even supposed to learn to read and write, let alone publish. But some blacks did all of these activities, and predictably these early black writers tried to write "white." What better way to show an intellect equal to whites? And how else would a slave have any chance at all of getting it said? But even in this literature under control, where overt blackness is conspicuous by its absence, the impact of slave status left its mark. This is true in poetry of the time, for example, where slavery, ironically and unrealistically, though understandably, is never mentioned.

We will never have a definitive literary history of slave writing in Latin America. Much of what survived down through the years is difficult to come by, but more tragically much of what was written by slaves especially in Cuba had no chance at all for survival. Many blacks destroyed their own work in the wake of the purge of blacks— slave and free—that followed the infamous "Conspiración de la Escalera" in 1844, one of the attempts in Cuban history to suppress or to stamp out blackness, particularly its political expression. Carlos Trelles, in his "Bibliografía de autores de la raza de color de Cuba," which he published in *Cuba Contemporánea* (pp. 33-78) in Havana in 1927, admits that even then many of the items he mentions he knew only by hearsay, not actually having been able to locate them.

Francisco Calcagno, writing his *Poetas de color* in 1867, was fortunate to have been able to examine some slave poetry, making his book a remarkable document of enormous importance because it was the first to deal exclusively with black writers in a Latin American country. It still remains among the very few books or anthologies of its kind. Recognizing slave testimonies to be invaluable examples of their "tenacious fight against the impossible,"[2] Calcagno discusses slave and free black poets, among them José del Carmen Díaz, Ambrosio Echemendía, Antonio Medina, Agustín Baldomero Rodríguez, and, of course, the two most important figures—Gabriel de la Concepción Valdés, known as "Plácido," and Juan Francisco Manzano.

Juan Francisco Manzano (1797?–1854) was the only slave poet who matched the fame of Plácido, his free counterpart. Older than Plácido, Manzano was also the first black to publish a book of poetry in Cuba, *Poesías líricas* (*Cantos a Lesbia*) in 1821. This work was a considerable achievement, whatever its literary value, when we realize that the author had begun to teach himself to read and write just three years before, in 1818. His second book of poetry, *Flores pasajeras*, of which there are no extant copies, was published in 1830. These two books, some poems such as his much anthologized "Mis treinta años," his letters, his *Autobiografía* (published first in English in 1840), and his *Zafira* (1842), a play, represent the corpus of Manzano's work that has come down to us.

Although Manzano continued to write after gaining his freedom in 1836, the devastating purge of blacks in 1844 surely made writing even more difficult than it had been. It is not surprising, therefore, that we have nothing from Manzano during the last ten years of his life. The year 1836 was perhaps Manzano's best: he gained his freedom as well as garnered a wider forum for his literature. In that year he was allowed to appear before the prestigious Del Monte literary *tertulia* (group) to read his poem "Mis treinta años," which continues to enjoy success even today. This sonnet, which speaks of his "thirty unhappy years,"[3] does not mention slavery directly nor does it need to as oblique references leave little doubt what his thirty years spent as a slave have been like.

These oblique references in Manzano's poetry tell us as much about the slave poet's integrity as dissimulation does about Plácido's, especially in the latter's "revolutionary" verse. Both poets are noted for what could be termed escapist literature but what is in reality poetry of evasion, an evasion not of reality itself but of the authorities. We marvel at Manzano's restraint in suppressing direct reference to external circumstances of which he, a black and a slave writing in a slave society, had to be acutely aware.

In demonstrating, moreover, his ability to write a verse as conventional as that produced by white poets of the time, Manzano moves beyond convention. His subtle mastery of blending conventions into fresh expressions is seen, for example, in his "Ilusiones"—the title itself being highly suggestive—which begins "Oh why does this burning flame in my chest / that I try so hard to put out / return with such passion?"; or his "Oda a la luna," where he contemplates "another happy world"; or his "El reloj adelantado":

En vano, reloj mío,
te aceleras y afanas,
marcando silencio
las horas que no pasan[4]
. . . .

In vain, my watch,
you accelerate and toil,
marking silently
the hours that do not pass
. . . .

or "La música," with its references to the poet's "unhappy star." Behind the stylizing conventions of his work is the expression of the sensitive soul of one in bondage who, deeply touched by love and music, sees time, the moon, and music, for example, as extensions of a repressed self, of a "dead being," in the words Manzano uses to describe to Del Monte, his benefactor, what a slave is "to his master."[5]

This Del Monte is the same "liberal" responsible for Manzano's freedom and for his *Autobiografía*, which he "commissioned" Manzano to write. This *Autobiografía*, which has just received new life

in a very fine modernized edition by Ivan Schulman,[6] is perhaps
Manzano's greatest claim to fame: it is the only slave autobiography
that we know of that was written during that long period in Cuban
history, and perhaps it is Latin America's first and only slave
narrative.

In the United States and Africa black autobiographies, some of
them classics, abound. The slave narrative itself was a prominent
literary genre in the United States, and black autobiographies and
autobiographical books continued to pour forth following the Civil
War. To date an estimated four hundred of these books have been
published in the United States.[7] In Latin America, however, the black
autobiography is not a primary form, although autobiographical
books by Afro-Latin Americans do exist, including Candelario
Obeso's *La lucha de la vida* (1882), Manuel Zapata Olivella's *Pasión vagabunda* (1949) and his *He visto la noche* (1959) in Colombia, Martín Morúa Delgado's *La familia Unzúazu* (1901), and
Biografía de un cimarrón (1966) in Cuba.[8]

Were it not for Del Monte's insistence, we would not have Manzano's *Autobiografía*. The circumstances of its creation, therefore,
are illuminating and warrant some attention if we are to appreciate
this slave narrative and the unique view from below it affords us, a
view partly shaped by Del Monte's view from above. Del Monte,
who has been called "the first great patriarch of Cuban belles-
lettres,"[9] was, in a sense, the Carl Van Vechten of his time. Del
Monte's relation to black Cubans like Manzano was similar to the
position Carl Van Vechten, who published his own *Nigger Heaven*
in 1926, had in relation to black Americans like Langston Hughes,
and indeed, to the Harlem Renaissance in early twentieth-century
America. Both men were wealthy white critic-patrons who spon-
sored black art. It must be remembered that in Manzano's time, as
in the early days of Langston Hughes, blacks, and some whites too
when dealing with black themes, wrote what influential whites
wanted and expected them to write, a fact of great significance in
the history of antislavery literature in Cuba.

Both Manzano's *Autobiografía* and *Francisco* by Anselmo Suárez
y Romero, the Cuban antislavery novel that has the distinction of
preceding *Uncle Tom's Cabin* by several years, were written at the
request of Del Monte, who had them produced largely for foreign
readers. Both works were in fact first published out of the country:
Francisco in New York in 1880 and Manzano's *Autobiografía* in

English in London in 1840. Both works, however, did circulate in Cuba in manuscript form, although Manzano's was not published in the original Spanish until 1937. Foreign exposure for these two works was to be gained through Richard Madden, the Englishman author and friend of Del Monte who was entrusted with an antislavery portfolio containing them. Madden chose Manzano's *Autobiografía* rather than Suárez y Romero's *Francisco* to translate into English in London.

These two works were partly designed to reveal to the world outside Cuba the progressive and humanitarian positions of the concerned citizens within the country or at least those represented by Del Monte's group. The major limitation, though, was that neither book was allowed to go "beyond what are the 'official' criteria of the group."[10] The standard imposed by the Del Monte group, which was more reformist than abolitionist, called for "moderation and restraint"[11] in the depiction of the black slave. For this reason Manzano's own *Autobiografía*, controlled from above by Del Monte, and like other antislavery works written around the same time, had to play down the threatening image of the rebellious slave while playing up the image of the docile and submissive slave "in order to call forth a sympathetic reaction to slavery's abuses from the more enlightened members of the community, who would probably have been offended by a rebellious protagonist."[12]

Del Monte achieved something of a literary coup by having Manzano, an authentic black slave and an "admirable example of meekness and resignation,"[13] conform to these guidelines. Conforming was the only way Manzano could hope for continued support and protection. Since Del Monte knew he had a showpiece black with a good image and intellectual capacity, why not display him. His talent made him one of the *excellent exceptions:* a slave who was not *vile, stupid,* and *immoral,* defects Del Monte felt people born and raised as slaves inevitably had.[14] Further, and perhaps even more important, this display would prove that such exceptions could be produced under slavery providing, of course, they had good masters.

The phrase "being a slave owner is no crime, but abusing that privilege is,"[15] (which Francisco Calcagno introduced) is of enormous importance both in understanding the meaning of Manzano's *Autobiografía* and in clarifying Del Monte's reasons for supporting it. Manzano recounts numerous cruelties and punishments suffered for much of his life at the hands of the Marquesa de Prado Ameno, a sadistic, warped owner. Now, if Manzano represented one of the excellent exceptions to the mass of undesirable slaves, so too, it is inferred, was the Marquesa an exception to other *amitos*, some of whom Manzano served under, who were paragons of kindness and goodness.

Manzano readers take note of his mistreatment at the hands of that cruel lady, and Calcagno asks the telling question in his *Poetas de color*, "Why could not the fate that made Manzano a slave at least have made him always a slave of Cárdenas? He would not have suffered the horrible treatment of which he often lamented with such humility and good reason; perhaps we would not today be reading this autobiography of his written with such bitterness . . . " [16] It was during the period Manzano served with this *amito*, who was "correct, benevolent and magnanimous," [17] that he taught himself to read and write, patterning his behavior on the good example set by his master. But the implications of the question Calcagno raises are clear, namely, that slavery, when not poisoned by bad masters or mistresses who abuse the system, is not really evil. This was a message even the censors would take kindly to, especially if the system could produce a man like Manzano.

Del Monte's reasons for wanting the book written along with Manzano's concern about his personal safety, meant the work essentially misrepresented slavery. Were it not written under control its publication would have been "the biggest anathema of all" [18] against slavery. But as it turned out Manzano had very little to fear since his *Autobiografía* is not really an indictment of slavery but only of abuses by some misguided owners. Further, perhaps Manzano had Del Monte's assurances that no harm would come to him in any event as his book was destined largely for a foreign audience. We should remember that when Manzano dared publish his first book of poems approximately twenty years earlier, it was done "under guarantee," Calcagno tells us, "since slaves were not allowed to publish anything." [19]

Manzano's insistence on assurances or guarantees could perhaps account for his reluctance to get on with the writing of his *Autobiografía*. We knew that he made four false starts before getting it under way. We know too, from his letter to Del Monte dated 4 June 1835, that once Manzano reconciled himself to the undertaking he practiced the selective censorship required to bring his story in line with his benefactor's guidelines. In that letter he writes, "I have prepared myself to account to Your Grace for a *part* of the story of my life, *reserving its most interesting events* for some day when, seated in some corner of my homeland, tranquil, *certain of my destiny* and my means of livelihood, I could write a truly Cuban novel" [20] [italics added].

This letter, I believe, tells us more about Manzano than his entire *Autobiografía*, which, by the way, he labeled Part 1. Part 2, as we shall discuss shortly, was mysteriously "lost." This letter suggests more than just intention to comply with the acceptable image, for the italicized parts are the keys to a fuller reading of Manzano's intentions. He is well aware that he is putting down only "a part" of his life story, that he is "reserving its most interesting events" for another time when "certain of my destiny" he could write what he calls a "truly Cuban Novel." Manzano knew very well, in short, that it would take more assurances than those Del Monte guaranteed to get him to reveal more of his life story. But two questions linger: Did he dare elaborate in Part 2, and is that why that volume was so quickly "lost"?

The fate of Part Two of Manzano's *Autobiografía* is problematic, and its disappearance "shortly after having been written and copied" [21] has not been satisfactorily explained. Madden suspects foul play. Writing in the prologue to his translation of the first part he says: "The work was written in two parts; the second one fell in the hands of persons connected with the former master, and I fear it is not likely to be restored to the person to whom I am indebted for the first portion of this manuscript [Del Monte]." [22] Del Monte reports that the second part "was lost in the care of [Ramón de] Palma and was never seen again." [23]

When we recall that Manzano at the end of Part 1 of his *Autobiografía* was finally beginning to come out from under the lamblike image he had so carefully constructed in that volume, we can assume that Part 2 could well have been more frank than Part 1. Perhaps Manzano in Part 2 forgot the original guidelines and expressed some views that for all concerned, including Manzano, were better left unsaid. Perhaps Manzano had tired of being circumspect and wanted to go faster and farther than his liberal, white friends were prepared to go. This certainly was the case with Plácido, as we shall see in Chapter 3. At any rate, it is unfortunate that Part 2 was lost, or destroyed, particularly as it could well have come as close as he ever got to writing the book he tells us he was saving up for. Certainly the purge in 1844 seems to have silenced him—and many other blacks.

As it turns out, we are left only with Part 1, which because it is written by a black slave who could tell us much, is, perhaps, the most tragically controlled piece of literature coming out of that period of Cuban and Latin American literary history, certainly more so than Anselmo Suárez y Romero's *Francisco*, even though Suárez y Romero's novel did have the *subversivo* excised from it by the Del Monte group[24] to make it conform to their requirement of presenting blacks as submissive.

It is precisely this unacceptable conformity that has moved Cuban filmmakers to produce a corrective view of the black slave in the recent film "The Other Francisco" (1975). Sergio Giral, the director, is on the right track by questioning the authenticity of the meek, humble nature of Francisco as he is depicted by Anselmo Suárez y Romero in his novel *Francisco*, which the movie version, by contrast, takes as its point of departure. The movie version is also provocative in its suggestion that the meekness superimposed on the character Francisco in the novel is in fact a reflection of the submissive, controlled character of mid-nineteenth century liberal reformers like Suárez y Romero who were reluctant to push openly for the abolition of slavery. There is also historical veracity in the movie's ending that strongly implies a connection between slave insurrection and the wars of liberation and independence from Spain that followed.

But since the movie draws on a fictitious character to give this corrective view in retrospect, I could not help wondering how much more effective the revision could have been had the movie examined the life of Manzano, a real person. A more forceful film, for example, could have come from a hypothetical reconstruction of that part of his *Autobiografía* that was lost. A revisionist Part 2 brought to the screen could be set against the background of slave suffering and insurrection found in "The Other Francisco," but it would have the added advantage of using a real black slave who wrote as a point of departure. Equally fascinating would have been this same background but as backdrop to cinematographic speculation regarding the controversial role of Plácido, another real historical figure, who, as we shall see in the next chapter, was charged with involvement in some of the same slave insurrections mentioned in the movie.

At any rate, even tragically controlled, the first part of Manzano's *Autobiografía* does stand as an early example of black writing in Latin America, and as such it does bequeath something to following generations in terms of its faithfulness to themes and traditions relevant to black history in the New World. The theme of liberty, for example, that runs throughout the history of Afro-Latin American literature does exist in a very basic form in the *Autobiografía*. Manzano's search for identity (the development of which was interrupted by the division of his work into two parts) within the confines of his New World environment is also evident. With Part 2 missing we can only guess whether his motivation in that second part derived from some radical change in his life that might have led to an "internal transformation of the individual." [25] We can only wonder, in other words, whether Manzano "describes not only what has happened to him at a different time in his life, but above all how he became—out of what he was—what he presently is." [26] Self formulation or the discovery of the present self that was just beginning to take over at the end of Part 1 could well have formed the organizing principle for Part 2 of Manzano's *Autobiografía*. "Black autobiographies, including the slave narratives, are unique statements about identity," [27] and Manzano's, even though he concealed a lot, is no exception.

This is so even though Manzano presents himself in Part 1 not as an *engaged* activist but as a *disengaged* pacifist, a harmless victim of the system and no danger to it. These two categories, black autobiographies of the *engaged* and of the *disengaged*, which have been defined by Saundra Towns,[28] help us understand and categorize Part 1 of Manzano's *Autobiografía*. In Towns' first group are authors who make a personal commitment to black liberation. But the single-minded pursuit by these men—political activists, social reformers, and public men—of their goals is absent in the other category, the autobiography of the disengaged, whose authors show little interest in their ancestry or at best are reluctant to acknowledge it.

Arriving at what I consider a key phrase in her characterization of the second group, Towns writes that black writers in this group find it far better to forget the past, and to subsume one's blackness under one's Americanness. I find this phrase crucial because I believe that is precisely what Manzano did. If we substitute "Cubanness" for "Americanness" we have what is a fairly accurate assessment of Manzano's integrationist concept of the future he desired in his *patria*. Manzano, being the artist that he was with a sensitivity to match his inclination, could not help but hope for some quiet moments to develop his art and his identity. These quiet moments for Manzano could come only with his emancipation from slavery. But, again we must remember, that the purge in 1844 epitomized the hostile white enviornment of his time and put a quick end to whatever quiet moments he was able to have.

Manzano, then, not only wanted to be free but also to be left to quietly blend into the Cuban landscape, for he felt as Cuban as anyone else. This is the same desire for integration that will be picked up later by Martín Morúa Delgado with a political zeal matched only by his political clout. But Morúa, writing in the late nineteenth century, when slavery and colonialism were on the wane, was in a much better position to bring to fruition his ideas of belonging for himself and for his people in Cuba. Part 1 of Manzano's *Autobiografía* largely covers his period as a child slave and rightly belongs to the category of the black autobiography of the disengaged. We cannot help but wonder whether Part 2, which probably reflected more consciousness of being a man, would have belonged to the category of the engaged.

We do not know how Manzano took the loss or the destruction of Part 2 of his *Autobiografía*. We do know that he published very little after 1840. But among the little he did publish we have *Zafira* (1842). This play, his only attempt at dramatic form, is set in sixteenth-century Northern Africa and comes complete with such *exótica* as an Arabian Princess and Turkish warriors. It is clear that in this play Manzano also has mastered an art for which Plácido is famous, namely, the art of dissimulation and veiled protest of current times in his homeland by dealing with injustice in far-off places and in bygone times.

The faults of the work as a dramatic piece aside, *Zafira* can be read as an allegory on Cuba, and the dissimulated feelings expressed are similar to those we see in many of the "revolutionary" poems of Plácido set in foreign lands. In this play Manzano speaks of heroism and tyrants. Shouts of "Kill the tyrant!" are heard. He speaks of vassals, human grief, victims, justice, liberty, and human dignity. There are such lines as:

> Yo detesto el furor de la violencia
> Que impone la opresión al desgraciado[29]

> I detest the fury of violence
> Which oppression imposes on the unfortunate

and

> Por vivir en el lujo y la opulencia
> Deben cobardes ser, o por lo menos
> Degradados amantes del reposo[30]

> To live in luxury and opulence
> Cowards they must be, or at least
> Degenerate lovers of repose

and

> . . . al fin soy hombre
> Y a los sensibles seres peternezco

> . . . at least I am a man
> and to sensitive beings I belong.

In these early days in the history of black writing in Latin America, dissimulation, often under the cloak of *exótica* was, like the cloak of anonymity, one of the few ways (call them strategies as well) blacks could speak to the tragedies of mankind. How else could it be when blackness was so thoroughly ingrained as a negative attribute. Even this historical brainwashing can be seen in Manzano's *Zafira* where the author makes repeated references, for example, to *black* signs, *black* origin, *black* toil, *black* hurricanes, *black* tempest, *black* cloak, the *blackest* treason, and *black* slander.

With his freedom Manzano joined the other colored segment of colonial society, the free black. Ironically, Manzano's plight worsened after gaining his freedom, and he even served a prison term. Life for free blacks, especially writers who were under constant supervision in slave societies, was difficult as they faced obstacles and persecutions even worse than those facing slaves, as we shall see in the example, a fatal one, of Plácido, Manzano's Cuban compatriot, and in the frustrations of José Manuel Valdés, the first black writer in Peru.

Slave Societies and the Free Black Writer:
José Manuel Valdés and "Plácido"

*It is not the heights to which I have risen that matter, but
the depths from which I have come.*

Booker T. Washington

One of the recent trends in historical research is reassessing the role of the free people of color in slave societies in the New World.[1] These early second class citizens, who "outnumbered their slave counterparts in Spanish America well before the struggles for political independence,"[2] were not slaves, but they too had their problems and obstacles to overcome. Occupying "an ambiguous intermediate position between the fully free and the enslaved"[3] the free black, since he, in a sense, was more of a threat than the slave, was, as a result, more feared and treated worse in some cases. We repeatedly read such statements as the following: "For the Government, the free black, who was more intelligent, was more dangerous than the slave,"[4] and "the dangers of Cuba come not so much from the slaves as from the multitude of free blacks and mulattoes."[5]

The free black writers especially were caught in this ambiguous (precarious) position, and often they had to bring their literature under control by writing "white" as Manzano, their slave counterpart, had done. The result in the case of José Manuel Valdés, the first black writer to publish in Peru, was a mystical verse in which the poet internalized his anguish over the injustices he had to suffer because of his color. Plácido (Gabriel de la Concepción Valdés), who started to publish in 1838, almost twenty years after Manzano, turned, on the other hand, to open but veiled protest against these injustices.

José Manuel Valdés (1767–1844), whose published medical articles date from 1791, was more than a writer of religious verse. This accomplished physician, who was a university professor well known in Europe for his medical theories was, nevertheless, not allowed to enter the priesthood, because "Spanish American whites firmly intended to preserve the income and perquisites of the church for themselves." [6] The same exclusionist attitudes prevailed in higher education. Valdés did, however, earn medical certificates from practical training and went on to be a noted physician. Ironically, only after establishing this fine reputation was he allowed to enter the University of Lima and obtain degrees, including a doctorate in medicine.

Despite such obstacles as having universities and the priesthood closed to them, many ambitious free blacks achieved much, but few were as important as Valdés. His struggles, though, led him to religion and religious verse for solace. When he writes,

> El señor vivifica y da la muerte,
> . . . .
> al pobre y miserable que yacía
> Sobre el estiércol, su poder levanta;
> Y en el excelso tronco le coloca,
> Donde los reyes a los pueblos mandan [7]

> The Lord gives life and he takes it away,
> . . . .
> His power raises the poor and miserable up
> from the dung heap;
> To sit on a higher rung
> where kings rule

we see the spiritual liberation that provides him that solace. Just as ethnicity will influence later black writers, so too does this same factor shape even the religious verse of this early black poet. In the following verses from his *Peruvian Psalter* (1833),

> El poderoso Dios viene a Salvarme,
> Y viene como padre el más benigno.
> Para que no le tema como esclavo
> Sino que le ame con respeto de hijo [8]

> All powerful God comes to save me,
> And he comes as the most benign father
> So that I may not fear him as a slave
> But love him respectfully as a son.

where the word "slave" is hardly rhetorical, it is suggested that only before God does Valdés feel at ease, respecting, and truly respected in kind.

Valdés celebrated those he admired, and he wrote a biography of Fray Martín de Porres, another black Peruvian like himself who rose above his preordained status in life, and left odes to San Martín and Bolívar, generals who preached and helped achieve some measure of racial equality for blacks in Latin America. It is unfortunate that a black who achieved so much in his own right during those difficult times was not able to feel comfortable in his color despite his success. We are told, for example, that Valdés did not want his picture made because he thought blacks came out badly in them.[9] This is the same white aesthetic in force in twentieth-century Panama, for example, where Gaspar Octavio Hernández, despite his accomplishments, deeply regretted his blackness and lamented not having European features, as we shall see in chapter 6.

It is unfortunate, too, that Valdés had to look to the other world of religion through his own kind of evasion, an "enforced evasion,"[10] for justice, for a "supreme justice."[11] Plácido, on the other hand, first tried for it in this world. Valdés, then, despite being a learned man was, like Plácido, not free from or immune to the racist pressures and practices of his time. Valdés reacted to his trials and tribulations by internalizing his anguish and by writing and translating a mystical private poetry. This reaction is quite different from that of Plácido who, as we shall see, wrote a more public, "revolutionary" poetry, in which he mastered the art of a dissimulation of another kind.

Plácido (1804–44), a very public man, was forced by human decency into that stance. Nowhere is the following quote more true than in his case: "Consciously and unconsciously, free blacks and free mulattoes offered the seeds of revolt or threatened revolt to the unfree blacks. The free colored were usually among the first to raise the issues of personal liberty and class discrimination in the societies."[12] Free blacks, particularly in Cuba, had no choice but to react since "by the nineteenth century, racism was a prominent feature of Cuba's white society, and its most hostile manifestation was toward the free colored community."[13] This society, paranoid from suspicion and "blinded by fear and racial prejudice,"[14] came down hardest on the free black in 1844 and after, when the purge of that year practically decimated the free black community for its involvement in political and racial plotting designed to free the slaves and give independence to Cuba. Plácido was executed on 28 June in that year after having been charged with acting as "president of the principal junta, recruiting officer, instigator, and one of the first conspiracy agents."[15]

Plácido's role in that 1844 conspiracy, known as the "Conspiración de la Escalera," has been scrutinized by Frederick Stimson in *Cuba's Romantic Poet: The Story of Plácido* (Chapel Hill: The University of North Carolina Press, 1964), the only book in English on this poet. Stimson's book is a thorough discussion of Plácido's life and works. He marshalls his evidence impressively, but his conclusions, that is, his interpretations of this evidence, often leave much to be desired. For example, regarding Plácido's involvement in the conspiracy, Stimson writes:

> For many reasons Plácido was called to trial. General reasons include his prominence in colored society; prominent Negroes were the first to be arrested, for it was thought that they were sufficiently influential to have helped to organize revolts. Of course many of Plácido's poems seemed to contain thinly disguised expressions of sedition; Calcagno observed that all Cubans were familiar with, for instance, the "Juramento," "¡Habaneros, libertad!" and others, such as "A un cometa." The fact that the almost white poet married a Negress might have indicated that he sympathized with the Negroes or considered himself as belonging to their race. Though it has never been proved conclusively that he and Turnbull were close friends, Cuban authorities considered them so. And last but not least among these bits of circumstantial evidence were the mysterious trips inland and the arrests, especially the arrest in Villa Clara. (p. 79)

Then, after reviewing even more specific charges amassed against the poet and after admitting that new material coming to light further indicates "fairly conclusively" that Plácido "was indeed one of the leaders," Stimson strangely concludes: "But in view of what is known about his character and personality, it is hard to conceive of him as the power behind this or any other conspiracy. Apparently mercurial and temperamental, a 'true poet' concerned with love and art, he would seem to lack the drive, stability, and cunning to direct a revolt" (p. 88). Further, Stimson somehow believes "one might make of Plácido a critical psychopathic case" (p. 140), a maladjusted, emotional cripple with an Oedipus complex.

One of Plácido's last requests (made in his will) was that a certain ode of the Spaniard Manuel José Quintana be copied in gold letters and sent to Spain, his executioner. For this request Stimson wonders whether the poet has lost his reason (p. 85). But this request does not seem extravagant. It is perhaps flamboyant but not insane, for we must take into consideration that Quintana, one who had sung of freedom and liberty for Spain, was Plácido's poet-hero, another singer of freedom and liberty. What we have in this request is a bit of irony: what better way to remind Spain of her intolerance and of the foolishness of her actions than by sending there this ode of Quintana who, "for the Spaniards of his time was a great poet and fighter of liberty, a victim of intolerance and tyranny." [16]

Central to much of Stimson's assessment of Plácido is the role of the poet's mother, Concepción, and he sets out to correct the biographers on the question of Plácido's emotional ties to her. Stimson concludes that Plácido "apparently" loved her more than most critics have realized. Yet, even though Stimson realizes that Concepción "had nothing to do with raising the child" (p. 49), that she did not support him publicly, and that the poet referred to her not as "mother" but as *señora*, he does not explore the equally plausible theory advanced by Martha K. Cobb that Plácido's references to his "mother," especially in his famous "Despedida a mi madre," written during his last imprisonment and just before execution, refer to the black grandmother who raised him. It is possible, as Cobb points out, that the Cuban poet, "like many black young people in the United States called the grandmother who raised him Mama or Mother." [17] (I even called my great grandmother Mama. We called our grandmother "Muddie," our way of saying Mother.)

There is also a tendency in Stimson's book to belittle or to be bothered by the fact that his poetry was overshadowed by a stronger interest in the sensational aspects of Plácido's life and death in the United States in the nineteenth century. The brutality surrounding the poet's death and the racial conflict implicit in the story of Plácido, Stimson thinks, took precedence in the United States' public eye over his "aesthetic values," "his artistry," his "artistic genius." But Stimson makes the mistake, I believe, of regretting—and this is his final conclusion—"that Plácido's fame has not resulted from his less pretentious and more delicate poems dealing with Cuba's customs and scenery' (p. 145). Granted Plácido's sensational and untimely death, to be sure, did not hurt his reputation. But we must remember that he was already quite famous, a legend in his own time, even before his execution. He had even been the protagonist, "a unique case in our literary history," [18] of a novel by Cirilo Villaverde, *La peineta calada* (1843), a year before his death. We should remember, too, that Plácido's reputation as a poet and dissident with revolutionary potential had also been established long before the "Conspiración de la Escalera". He had been arrested several times prior to 1844, often for such poems as "¡Habaneros! ¡libertad!," where he adds "Are we free or are we not free?" [19] and the equally famous "El juramento," where he swears "to be an eternal enemy of the tyrant." [20] His revolutionary verse was taken seriously, especially by the authorities. Some of his so-called subversive poetry even turned up at the trial, and poems like "El cometa" were used as "conviction pieces." [21] Plácido in a real sense was feared "for his verses," [22] and he was executed partly because of them, but hardly because of his "blossom" and siboney poems, except only indirectly, in that they did help establish his popularity.

Part of Plácido's legacy to the generations that follow him was his love of liberty, and this passion comes through time and time again in his poetry. As Stimson points out, his "sedition-tinged poetry" had made him a marked man not only in the fatal year 1844 but also the year before, in 1843, when he suffered a long imprisonment after being "arrested on suspicion of being involved with abolitionists plotting to overthrow slaveholders" (p. 75). Though dissimulation was his trademark, he was not too discreet in such poems as "Muerte de César," "La muerte de Gesseler," "A la Grecia," "A Polonia," and in "Despedida al General Mejicano (hijo de Cuba), Don Andrés de la Flor," where he writes

> Cansado de vivir cual siervo esclavo,
> ....
> Que hay en tu patria hermosa y desgraciada,
> Millares de hombres fuertes e instruidos,
> En la inacción y esclavitud sumidos,
> Que con valor y espada,
> Héroes pudieran ser, y no son nada. [23]

> Tired of living as any poor devil of a slave,
> ....
> That there are in your beautiful and unfortunate country
> Millions of strong and educated men,

> Subjected to inactivity and slavery
> Who with valour and arms
> Could be heroes, but are nothing.

Unrelenting in his attacks on tyranny and tyrants, Plácido is as heroic and defiant in some of his poems as he is "romantic" and flippant in others. For this reason, of all the many statements that have been made over the years by Plácido critics, perhaps the one farthest off the mark was made by A. M. Eligio de la Puente in 1930, who sees in Plácido's poetry "On the whole, very little which could win for Plácido the honored title of revolutionary poet."[24] Just seven years after Plácido's death, the Paris journal *Revue des Deux Mondes* (15 December 1851) noted exactly the opposite: "The most essentially revolutionary poet of Cuba is Plácido, G. de la Concepción Valdés."[25] The essence of Plácido's poetry—black liberation and freedom from all tyranny—is just as evident today as it was 130 years ago.

Concentrating on Plácido's revolutionary verse, however, fails to give an idea of the enormous range of the poet, who was truly a gifted and keen observer of the society of his time. Various literary historians have classified his poetry differently, some according to form—sonnet, *letrillas*, odes, ballads, *octavas*, *redondillas*, fables, epigrams—some according to content—love poetry, elegiac poetry, patriotic poetry, didactic poetry, improvised festive poetry of occasion, religious poetry, satirical poetry—and some broadly by movement—for example, Romantic. However classified, though, part of his verse that has come down to us, especially some of his poetry of occasion, should never have been published considering its low quality. But even here we should remember that Plácido only published three books of poetry before his death, and much of what we have was left unpublished by Plácido only to be rushed into publication by others after his death.

Plácido made a living with his poetry of occasion, but he was the first to realize that his immortality as a poet would not rest on this laudatory verse. Yet it is this poetry, much of it obviously insincere, that has helped give rise to the range of opinions regarding his merit as a poet and as a person. To some observers Plácido is a "martyr of tyranny"; to others he is a "poor devil." To some critics he is an *inculto*, unlearned improviser, in the pejorative sense; to others he is an accomplished poet; to some he is a mere charlatan, "a worthless quarrelsome mulatto, one given to drink,"[26] and to others he was considered the most outstanding black poet in Cuba until the advent of Nicolás Guillén.

Whatever else he was, there is little doubt that Plácido was a forerunner of Afro-American literature, a black writer who was a victim of racist and political oppression because of the views he held and expressed on black liberation. This poet, who could have passed for white, chose quite pointedly to be a black Cuban. There is very little crisis of conscience in Plácido: he knew who he was and what he wanted to be, and his dedication to purpose often led him away from the dissimulation he practised as survival strategy in life and in literature. Plácido, quite simply, was executed because he forgot to take his own advice outlined very clearly in the following stanzas of the poem "El Hombre y el Canario," where the canary explains why he does not sing overtly of liberty:

Que le adulo en apariencia
Piensa mi dueño, y se hechiza;
Mas mirándolo en conciencia,
Yo engaño al que me esclava,
Por conservar mi existencia

My master thinks I flatter him
But he is under my spell;
When you look at it in all conscience
I deceive the one who enslaves me,
So as to preserve my existence.
(italics mine)

Morir por preocupación
Y sin defensa, es locura,
Suicidarse sin razón:
Vivir y hallar la ocasión
De libertarse, es cordura.[27]

To die of such preoccupation
And without a defense is madness,
It is to commit suicide for no reason:
To live and find the occasion
Of liberating oneself is practical wisdom.

In this "fable" we have Plácido's entire poetic and political stance, his approach.

Stimson is quite right when he speaks of the danger of "allowing admiration of his heroism to enhance the quality of his verse" (p. 143). But we should not ever disconnect his verse from the heroic substance of the man's life, for it is this substance that structures his most meaningful, certainly his most moving, poetry. It is true, as Stimson says, that Plácido does show "inherent genius" and originality in his poems on Cuba's customs and scenery "where he shows himself to be ahead of his times" (p. 144). But he certainly was ahead of his time in other ways as well, and that is why he paid the ultimate price. It is true, as Menéndez y Pelayo has written, "The person who wrote the masterly and beautiful ballad 'Xicotencal,' which Góngora would have been proud to claim, the lovely descriptive sonnet 'La muerte de Gessler,' the delightful rondelet 'La Flor

de la Caña,' and the inspired 'Plegaria,' which he recited on the way
to his execution, need not be a mulatto nor have been shot to death
in order to be remembered by posterity."[28] Nevertheless, he was shot
for being a mulatto and a famous poet besides. Only by merging
these two factors do we appreciate the full impact of his historical
and literary significance.

Stimson is also quite right when he says that "perhaps Plácido
should be classified as a heroic figure rather than a romantic one"
(p. 141). But after making this statement he goes on to give the
wrong reason for considering Plácido heroic, that is, because he
managed to rise above his station in life. While this is true his statement does not go far enough. His statement is true in the same sense
that black writers throughout the literary history of the New World
are heroic; Plácido is hardly the only black writer to rise above an
"oppressive environment." But Plácido the black poet was chosen
for execution partly because of his writings. Even after imprisonment for his writings he, quite heroically, continued to pursue his
ideals of justice for black people. Even under constant surveillance
Plácido continued to act out the heroic role he had chosen for
himself.

It is possible that Plácido had a death wish or that he coveted
martyrdom. We know that he had many opportunities to leave the
country, to go into exile in Mexico as Heredia had done, or to Spain
as Gómez de Avellaneda had done, but even after his several arrests
Plácido never left the island. Martín Morúa Delgado, the black Cuban novelist-politician who worked so hard for integration and national unity—as we shall see in chapter four—in late nineteenth-
century Cuba saw Plácido not as an "enemy of the white race"[29] but
as a patriotic black, like himself, who worked for and gave his life
for the good of all Cubans.

But Plácido's death wish, or martyrdom, is applicable whether he
"poeticized race hatred"[30] or whether he saw himself as a "martyr of
Cuban liberty, of liberty for all the people."[31] It does not matter.
What does matter is that

El poeta no muere;   The poet does not die;
pues del tiempo ignorado   For since time immemorial
la Historia está en su mente   History takes shape in his mind
y la inmortalidad está en sus cantos.[32]   And immortality in his verse.

4

From Antislavery to Antiracism: Martín Morúa Delgado, Black Novelist, Politician, and Critic of Postabolitionist Cuba

> *Being Cuban was more important than being black.*
> Rafael Fermoselle on Martín Morúa
> Delgado, Juan Gualberto Gómez,
> and Campos Marquetti

Martín Morúa Delgado (1856–1910) was the most influential black intellectual in politics—and there were many—of his time. Elected to the Cuban Congress in 1901 and to the Senate in 1902, Morúa even rose to become president of the Senate in 1909, the last black in Cuba to hold that high office. Without question Martín Morúa Delgado was held in high esteem in Cuba, and a measure of that esteem was shown in 1956 when the government gave him official recognition in commemoration of the centenary of his birth. At that time, busts were raised, studies were made, and his complete works were published in five volumes.[1] Morúa has been highly regarded, partly because he was an important novelist, partly because he had a vision of an integrated Cuba, but largely, I believe, because he helped keep blacks under control by sponsoring a controversial law, one that made Morúa a suspect figure in the black community.

These last two points are interrelated, and both are connected to his producing two novels of thesis. As one of the strongest proponents of the integration of blacks into the national life of postabolitionist Cuba, Morúa supported, indeed proposed, the outlawing of political parties based on race, an action designed to force blacks to work within the system for their own good and for the common good of the country. This law, though, had the adverse effect of undermining the emerging black consciousness in postabolitionist Cuba. What is worse, the *Ley Morúa* (in reality an amendment) which was passed in 1910, resulted, two years later, in the massacre of thousands of blacks when it was invoked to help put down a black uprising. Regarding this 1912 race war, Leslie Rout has written: "For the second time since 1844 a presumed Afro-Cuban threat to the status quo had been mercilessly liquidated."[2]

Morúa died on 28 April 1910, two months after presenting his amendment; he did not live to see it passed a few months later, or to see the bloodshed that followed two years later during that racial confrontation, ironically the kind the *Ley Morúa* was designed to avoid. Morúa wanted racial equality and harmony, not race wars. Unlike other influential blacks of the period, Morúa did not believe in the creation of black pressure groups to help bring about that racial equality and harmony. He believed that blacks could prove their worth in the same political arena as whites. Confident of black intelligence and convinced that skin color was an accident of birth, Morúa put great confidence and faith both in the ability of blacks to overcome by working within the system and in the ability of whites to understand and to give blacks a chance.

It was Morúa's spirit of cooperation with white Cubans, together with his unswerving confidence and faith in them and in their political institutions that endeared him more than anything else to his and subsequent generations. But this same spirit supported the ideal of integration and national solidarity at the expense of black separation and solidarity, and some observers believe this helped give rise to much of the neglect—blatant and benign—the black Cuban has experienced in this century. In Cuba, as elsewhere, the ideal of integration has often meant an "intellectual and spiritual arrogance which masquerades as integration,"[3] and exactly that attitude prompted the Cuban Congress to pass a law in 1912—after the black uprising—preventing blacks from becoming president of the republic.[4] Even Morúa, who believed so strongly in the system, would have been hard pressed to justify that law.

Because Morúa opposed "black power" groups, he has been accused by Carlos Moore[5] of having been in the service of the white bourgeosie. But this judgment is perhaps a bit unfair. Though his degree of blackness was suspect by some of the more radical thinkers, Morúa always had the black man and his interests in mind regardless of what some would call his misguided approach. In addition, Morúa was severe in his criticism of those who would abuse and distort the black man and his literary image.[6] He gives through novels a black perspective to the literary treatment of slavery and its aftermath, namely, the lingering evil of racism that pervaded post-abolitionist Cuban society.

Morúa was a journalist like many of the prominent black figures of his time—Rafael Serra, known as the Cuban Booker T. Washington, and Juan Gualberto Gómez, Morúa's major political opponent, to name only two. Journalism was a primary educational force in the black community in postabolitionist Cuba, and there were many journals founded and controlled by blacks. Much of Morúa's complete works (published in 1956) consists of journalistic items that appeared over the years in Cuba and abroad. Morúa, again like several other prominent black figures of his day, spent some time in exile. Along with Antonio Maceo, Rafael Serra, and Juan Gualberto Gómez, Morúa too was suspect for being black and revolutionary, and as was Plácido, they were often under surveillance both by local whites who feared black insurrection in the manner of Haiti, their next-door neighbor, and by those who feared black cooperation in even larger scale independence movements from Spain.

Unlike all of these other end-of-the-century black luminaries, however, Martín Morúa Delgado was also a novelist, and his most substantial and ambitious work was done in this genre. Morúa launched a series of novels which he titled "Cosas de mi tierra," and he completed two in this series before his death, *Sofía* (1891) and *La familia Unzúazu* (1901). These novels are in a real sense extensions of his life as a black leader for they reflect his views on social, political and racial matters. These views, since they are often illustrated with minute, realistic, and detailed descriptions of, for example, medical problems, sicknesses, and prostitution, are often held to be those of a naturalistic writer, perhaps Cuba's first. Also his novels are quite often placed in the tradition of the antislavery novelist, because they do deal with the evils of slavery, as the following description—laced with rhetorical expressions—from *Sofía*, shows:

That plantation, as almost all of them at that time in Cuba, was a terrestial hell, a place of torment where the cries of the victims blended with the imprecations of the victimizers, where the swear words of the condemned were muffled by the sound of the irons that imprisoned them and by the crackling of the whip on their lacerated shoulders.

What suffering that of those poor, wretched souls! What cruelty that of those soulless slave-drivers! What baseness that of the hard-hearted slave-traders! What indignity the tolerance of those inhuman acts! What a curse that which fell upon the indolent society that observed it all, abandoning itself to soft living and laziness, shameful byproducts of a traffic motivated by dishonor and egoism![7]

But by striking primarily against the white Cuban's "imponderable pride of caste, of class, of race" (p. 58), Morúa moves beyond the simple condemnation of slavery as an evil institution to a larger future vision of the role and place of the soon-to-be-liberated black slave in postabolitionist Cuban society. His novels really address the crippling psychological effects of racism, the holdover from slavery that prevented white Cubans from accepting black people without reference to their past. F. Franklin Knight wrote recently that "the slave society in the Americas was essentially a coercive and racist society."[8] Morúa, who knew this as well as anyone, hardly held to the preconceived theory of social class and race held, for example, by Villaverde, whose antislavery novel Cecilia Valdés (1882) Morúa took to task for its restricted view of black people. Morúa saw Villaverde as a typical example of a white who still harbored prejudices against blacks; it is precisely Villaverde's racist approach that Morúa opposed in his own antiracist view. Unlike Cecilia Valdés and other antislavery novels from the nineteenth century, Sofía and La familia Unzúazu were written by a black whose mother had been an African slave.

Morúa's novels, unlike the antislavery novels that preceded him, were published after slavery had been abolished. It is not surprising, therefore, that he chose to turn his attention to the pervasive effects of the system that even after abolition continued to shape public opinion toward blacks. Racism, as an evil inherited from slavery, was much more difficult to regulate, for unlike slavery, "conscious and unconscious feelings of racial superiority"[9] could not simply be abolished. For this reason the challenges facing Morúa as a black writer were greater than those earlier abolitionist writers faced. The institution of slavery had been a large, fixed target easy to attack, but Morúa used that system as a point of departure in his efforts to get the ex-slave to claim his rights under the law, to feel as though he belonged, and to get the ex-slave owner to recognize these rights and to look beyond appearances to see the worth of the individual. These are the points that Morúa drives home, again and again, through a series of ironic devices or twists, first in *Sofía* and later in *La familia Unzúazu*.

Morúa's antislavery novels take their titles from white characters, unlike *Sab*, *Francisco*, and *Cecilia Valdés*, for example, by white antislavery writers whose character-titles are black. Morúa attacks the system by showing the demoralizing and destructive force of slavery on white characters, that is, the Unzúazu family. Also, and perhaps most important, by making the slave Sofía a white girl who was presumed to be black, Morúa shows how silly it is to harbor preconceived notions on race and class. The entire organizing principle of *Sofía* is based on mistaken identity as Morúa sets out to show that there is no such thing as racial inferiority, that slavery is more a result of circumstances of birth, of time, and of situation or environment, but certainly not of race. By placing a white person in a slave situation, Morúa not only shows the preconceived reactions of whites to anyone in that situation, but he shows as well that whites so placed can become as degraded as blacks were made to be.

By organizing his story around the personal history of Sofía, Morúa is able to point an accusing finger toward the larger "infernal system" (p. 163) or society that claims her as a victim. The incest motive, fairly common in nineteenth-century literature dealing with slavery, that contributes to her downfall, is not to be taken sensationally in *Sofía* as it is simply one more by-product of that "age of miserable deceit and inexcusable perfidy" (p. 163). Morúa's accusing finger in *Sofía*, while pointing up the tragedy of slavery and the narrowness of preconceived notions about blacks, does not rule out hope for the future, however, because it is the future Republic and its responsibility to the black that receives repeated emphasis in his novel. Morúa puts this message across primarily through Eladislao Gonzaga, his liberal mouthpiece who often makes such speeches as the following:

> Oh, the blacks! Yes; they will become regenerated the same way and through the same procedure that the whites must undergo for their social perfection, for their moral retraining, for their political education. The black who yesterday cut the sugar cane in our plantations, abandoned to the disgraceful

whip of the field boss, was shielded by the revolution, pro-
tected by the constitution of the young republic, and defended
by Cuban arms until the moment when he is entrusted to the
patronage of the embattled government, with the solemn
promise of conserving his natural rights. The formula is already worked out. The slave of today will be the citizen of
tomorrow. (p. 74)

On the subject of the education of blacks so that they will be
better able to take their rightful roles in society as future citizens,
Morúa again—through Gonzaga—is very explicit in his view that
this important task cannot be left solely to blacks, black societies,
and the black press. The nation has a responsibility in this area to
all its citizens: "Let us confess that the black is an intelligent being
capable of making the same progress as men of any other race. Let
us bear in mind an edifying example: Never has the government or
the country concerned themselves with the educational advancement of the black race—something which I don't even censure of
those who only wished to make of it a race of slaves . . . " (p. 78).

Morúa continues in La familia Unzúazu, his second novel, to focus on the future integration of the black Cuban into the nation's
citizenry. He also continues to rely on the ironic twist. Even in Sofía,
Morúa had carried one of his main points—do not rely on appearances—beyond the death of his heroine by also involving Liberato,
the family coachman, in a case of mistaken identity. He is unjustly
accused of a crime he did not commit by people who thought they
saw him, and in this way the author reiterates the theme that "not
everything which one sees is true" (p. 192). By not having his guilt
proven in Sofía, Morúa sets the stage for the much larger role Liberato is to play in the second novel, where black characters
overshadow the Unzuázu family or what is left of it.

The pivotal action of this bigger and more sluggish second novel
begins with Liberato's rape of Ana María, the head mistress of this
family of "incurable neurotics," [10] and his subsequent flight to the
hills. There he later, and ironically, forms an alliance with Federico,
Ana María's unprincipled, spendthrift brother, to extort the family
fortune from her, with the two of them sharing the payoffs. As it
turns out, Federico is the brains behind this alliance. Liberato, it
develops, and again ironically, despite his ties with a "society of
ñáñigos" whose "reputation for bravery" (p. 145) required each
member to be "fear-inspiring, feared and fearless" (p. 145) despite

his feelings following the rape of being "another man" (p. 146) and despite his magnificent physique, was in reality a pathetic character, weak, submissive, and cowardly. This characterization is hardly surprising since we know that Morúa regarded the society of ñáñigos as "immoral organizations" (p. 144), which in their "malignant ignorance excited the passions and inspired savage hatred . . . " (p. 144). It is Morúa's implication here that these associations that were closer to Africa than to Europe had no place in the New Cuba, in the "new period" (p. 169) toward which Cuba was heading.

Fidelio, perhaps the most significant new character Morúa introduces in this second novel, takes on more than just autobiographical significance. A free black who has numerous similarities with the author, Fidelio was prepared like Morúa to work toward the realization of this New Cuba, and he makes the decision, as Plácido had done in another time, to throw his lot in with the enslaved black and to do this with the "natural revolutionary impulse" (p. 165) that had to become the trademark of the new "Cuban ideal" (p. 168) which has no time for ethnic divisions. Morúa's concern, first raised in Sofía, with "the future of his homeland and the destiny of the race" (p. 176) is expressed through discussions such as the following involving Eladislao Gonzaga, Dr. Alvarado, another new character introduced by Morúa in this second novel, who "had as much concern for the healthy conservation of the human body as for the improvement of the political and social welfare of his country" (pp. 164–165), and Fidelio:

Seven hundred thousand would soon be entering into the world of free men. Was it not wise to concern oneself with those future citizens of the nation? But nothing. In the midst of the greatest indifference, a few education and recreation circles were created in the main cities, with no more inspiration than the desire of a few and the longing of many others to be represented in one way or another; but such circles, directed by people of the colored race, completely inexperienced in a way of life from which they had been excluded by the system, came far from satisfying the needs that existed at the time. Was it not then, a social crime, the abandonment in which they were left by the more illustrious classes of the country? (pp. 303–304)

Strongly influenced by these discussions, Fidelio makes his decision to be useful to his country "by helping the improvement of a race that has been held back" (p. 305). He would do this by opting, as Morúa had done at a crucial point in his development, for journalism as a career. "In the mind of Fidelio that night was born with powerful force the goal to which from then on he subordinated his inclinations: the publication of a newspaper in which he, usually at a loss for words, would expose the world of ideas which had accumulated in his brain" (p. 306).

Fidelio does little in the novel aside from making that decision, but it was for him, as it had been for Morúa, perhaps the most important one in his life. Commitment to all the people, particularly to the under-privileged, which at that time was the enslaved black, was a necessary first step for anyone who genuinely wanted to work for the greater goal of a free Cuba. Martín Morúa Delgado made that commitment, one we should not forget even though it, like the literary blackness expressed in his novels, was overshadowed by the subsequent and more controversial events in his political life discussed at the beginning of this chapter.

Cultural Nationalism and the Emergence of Literary Blackness in Colombia: The Originality of Candelario Obeso

> *Am I not a black man?*
> *I am delighted to be black*
> *and my ugliness is a*
> *joy to me.*
>
> Candelario Obeso

Candelario Obeso (1849–84) is a controversial figure. Part of the controversy surrounds his place of birth, while much of it focuses on his death, which was accidental, some say, or a suicide, according to others. But the controversy that interests me here is the literary one, and it derives from a reluctance in some quarters to accept this black Colombian writer—and the blackness he infused in his late nineteenth century poetry—as the legitimate precursor of *poesía negra* as we know it in the twentieth century. This reluctance, to be sure, comes largely from Cuban nationals[1] who, quite understandably and quite rightly in most cases, see Cuba as preeminent in the field of *poesía negra* and primarily responsible for what we have in this genre, which peaked in the Caribbean in the thirties and forties.

It is clear, however, from reading Obeso's poetry that even before the twentieth century he wanted a "new dignity accorded to the hitherto despised Negro."[2] As early as 1877, the date of publication of his *Cantos populares de mi tierra*, Obeso was according dignity to his black fellow countrymen while advising the local *literati* that a truly national literary identity could be found only in local popular poetry and song. He believed the black was a legitimate literary subject who should be presented authentically, talking his own language, expressing his own thought, and singing his own song.

Long before the "fashion for 'talking real Negro' spread throughout Latin America"[3] Obeso was using authentic black talk in his *Cantos populares de mi tierra* and, unlike that fashion cultivated largely by white writers "who enjoyed playing with these new poetic rhythms,"[4] Obeso was a black writer conscious of his art. He considered it to be a departure from the norm, a distinctive poetry significant in the development of a national literature based on indigenous influences. Black literature to Obeso clearly represented the "true, positive literature" of his country, certainly more so than imitation of foreign models.

Obeso took this position partly because "in popular poetry there is and there always was, and without philosophical advantages, an abundance of delicate sentiment, and many invaluable jewels of beautiful images"[6] but also because the black is truly autonomous to Colombia as this country has a large black population. Leslie Rout recently put the estimated number of blacks, mulattoes, and *zambos* in Colombia at five to six million, and "this easily would give Colombia the largest Spanish-speaking Negroid population."[7]

The emergence of literary blackness—that is, literature with an authentic black sensibility written by blacks—coincided, at least in Colombia, with the emergence of literary Americanism or the preference for native culture, people, and themes over Europe-oriented ones. In this sense *Cantos populares de mi tierra* is as much a native New World-oriented product as is *Martín Fierro*, for this collection of black poems can be placed squarely in that New World tradition where the depiction of *lo autóctono* was to be given priority over the imported.

Obeso promised more "cantos populares," but his short life—he died at the age of thirty-five—prevented him from further developing this genre. Much of his work, however, remains uncollected, and much of it undoubtedly is lost to us, particularly the two novels he reportedly wrote, *La familia Pigmalion* and *Las cosas del mundo*. Some of his work was journalistic, published in newspapers, and some of it was pedagogical: known as a "*schollar* [sic] y poligloto,"[8] he wrote language texts and grammars for French, English, and Italian. These works as well as an arithmetic text were adopted for use in Colombian schools. He also wrote a three-act play, *Secundino el zapatero*, which I understand can be found at the Biblioteca Fernández Madrid in Cartagena.

Obeso was conversant with foreign literatures even though he chose not to emulate them. He made several translations from Longfellow, Hugo, and Musset, for example. He also translated *Othello*, a work—and character—to which he must have felt affinity. In fact, Obeso was known as the Colombian Othello, partly, as we shall discuss, because of his tragic obsession with a white woman. Poet, playwright, novelist, linguist, translator, and scholar, Obeso rose quite high in the military and in the diplomatic service of his country. These accomplishments are all the more remarkable when we realize that as a youth, before winning scholarships to military college, he was largely self-taught and poor, so poor that at times he reportedly had to survive on cups of hot chocolate.

Obeso was multi-talented, but his fame comes largely from three pieces: his pace-setting *Cantos populares de mi tierra*, which draws strongly from the language and the people of the coastal regions of the Atlantic side of Colombia where he grew up; his first work, *Lecturas para tí*, a collection that is part prose and part poetry; and his last work: *Lucha de la vida*, a dramatic and often enigmatic long poem, which is painfully autobiographical in parts. But of these three it is his *Cantos populares de mi tierra* that, on publication, had the same kind of startling impact, for example, as did the publication in 1930 of Nicolás Guillén's *Motivos de son*, another book, this time in twentieth-century Cuba, where blacks appeared for the first time in poetry, talking "real black talk."

The authentic vignettes, or scenes, from black life in these two books are inspired by popular verse rhythms and song forms of their time and place. Although Obeso's *Cantos* are more lyrical and more reminiscent of work songs or leisure songs of working people than are Guillén's *Motivos*, there are striking stylistic similarities, and not just in the phonetic transcription of black speech or black talk. Guillén's *Motivos* or *sones*, like Obeso's *Cantos*, are, for example, variations of the *romance* form, and one of the most obvious variations common to both is the short final line usually pentasyllabic with *agudo* rhyme, the well-known combination that gives *poesía negra* its characteristic beat. The classic example of this is Obeso's much anthologized poem, "Canción del boga ausente." In this justly famous piece the black boatman of the Magdalena river speaks:

Qué trite que etá la noche,
  La noche que trite etá;
No hay en el cielo una etrella
  Remá, remá.

How sad the night is
  How sad is the night;
Not a star in the sky
  Row on, row on.

La negra re mi arma mía,
  Mientra yo brego en la má,
Bañao en suró por ella,
  ¿Qué hará? ¿Que hará?

The black woman of my soul,
  While I struggle at sea,
Drenched, for her, in sweat,
  What will she do? What will she do?

Tar vé por su zambo amao
  Doriente sujpirará,
O tar vé ni me recuerda . . .
  ¡Llorá! ¡Llorá!

Perhaps for her beloved half-breed
  Sufferingly she will sigh
Or perhaps she'll not even remember
    me,
  Oh, to cry, to cry!

. . . .

. . . .

Qué ejcura que etá la noche,
  La noche qué ejcura etá;
Asina ejcura é la ausencia
  Bogá, bogá! . . .[9]

How dark is the night,
  How dark the night is;
Just as dark is absence
  Row on, row on! . . .

These stylistic features are repeated throughout the volume and are found in such poems as "Cuento a mi ejposa," "Arió," and "Canción del pajcaro."

Guillén's *Motivos* on the surface are more humorous than Obeso's *Cantos*, but the latter are more imbued with a nostalgia, a sense of absence and a loneliness brought about by the nature of a work that takes one away from home, and the *Cantos* often points up philosophical conclusions to be drawn from the vignette depicted. This is noticeable, for example, in pieces like "La oberiencia filiá," which concludes "When love strikes the young heart/The obedience of the children comes to an end" (p. 17); or in "Los palomos":

  Siendo probe alimales lo palomos
  Se aprende en ello má que en la j'Ecuela.
  Yo, poc lo meno, en su cocto libro
  Eturio re la vida la maneras . . . ! (p. 16)

  Even though pigeons are just poor animals
  One can learn more from them than at school.
  I, for one, in their learned book
  Study the ways of life . . .

and in "Cuento a mi ejposa":

Si ponemo en agua
  Un granito e sá
Pronto se risuecve
  Con facilirá . . . !

If we put in the water
  A little grain of salt
Soon it would dissolve
  With ease . . . !

Nunca en la mujeres
  Fué efertivo ná;

Never was anything real
  with women;

Toro en ella ej humo,
  Toro farserá . . . !   (p. 19)

Everything with them is like smoke,
  Everything is false . . . !

Despite the foregoing strophe the dominant scene in Obeso's *Cantos* revolves around or involves the family or the *jembra*, at least. Many of the poems are poetic statements of proud, self-sufficient, independent people who derive strength from the family unit or from the need for family attachments. This sentiment is especially apparent in "Canto del Montará":

Eta vira solitaria
  Que aquí llevo,
Con me jembra y con mi s'hijo
  Y mi perros,
No la cambio poc la vira
  Re los pueblos
. . . . (p. 21)

This solitary life
  I lead here
With my woman and my children
  And my dogs,
I would never exchange it
  For life in town
. . . .

and in "Epresión re mí amitá":

Cuando soy un probe negro
Sin má cencia que mi oficio,
No inoro quien se merece
Argún repeto y cariño . . .
Sobre mí tiene er caráter
  Un particulá rominio.

. . . .

Oigame, branco, tar vé
No é bien claro lo que aficmo.

. . . .

Re toro lo grande y bello
Que er mundo encierra, no etimo
Sino ros cosa, que son:
Mi jembra amá y mi arbedrío.
Re aquella ni ar Paire Etecno
Le riera un solo peacito; .

. . . .

Pocque soy rey re mí mimo.

. . . . (pp. 28–29)

Although I am a poor black
With no more knowledge than that of
  my trade,
I give respect and friendship
To those who deserve it . . .
Character has a certain
  Hold on me.

. . . .

Listen, white man, perhaps
It's not very clear what I affirm.

. . . .

Of all the grand and beautiful things
In this world, I cherish
Only two things, which are:
My beloved woman and my free will.
Of the first, not even to God Almighty
Would I give a little piece;

. . . .

Because I am my own master.

. . . .

This poem, as can be seen, also highlights the strong independent nature of a proud people, a characteristic Obeso develops further in the following lines from the same poem:

Amo yo a la libectá   I love liberty
Como er pájaro a su nío,   Like the bird loves its nest,
Como la flore a la lluvia,   Like flowers love rain

. . . .

Y rueño en mi hogá efertivo.   (p. 29)   I am master in my own house.

Another sentiment strongly suggested in these poems is protest. Obeso was, in a sense, a romantic with a sentimental, nostalgic vision of his people. But he was also a keen observer of the "poor black" (p. 24) of the "poor, humble sailor" (p. 31) of the "poor farmer" (p. 34) who lived in poverty, in his "very sad and miserable dwelling" (p. 27) in his "humble ranch" (p. 32). Although much of the literary blackness in this volume is spotted in solitary life situations, there is racial confrontation, or awareness of the heritage of slavery combined with a determination to remain free:

Ya pasó er tiempo   The age of slavery
re loj eclavos;   Is already past
Somo hoy tan libre   Today we are as free
Como lo branco . . .   As the whites . . .
    ("Serenta," p. 32)

This awareness is further emphasized in "Canción del pácjaro":

. . . .
Trite vira é la der probe,   Sad is the life of the poor,
Cuando er rico goza en pá,   While the rich rejoices in peace,
Er probe en er monte sura   The poor sweats in the mountain
    O en la má.   Or at sea.

Er rico poco se efuecza,   The richman makes little effort,
Y nunca le farta ná,   And he never lacks a thing,
Toro lo tiene onde moro   He has everything he needs
    Poc remá.   And then some.

El probe no ejcansa nunca   The poorman can never rest
Pa porese alimentá;   In his search for food;
Hoy carece re pejcao   Today he has no fish
    Leugo é sá.   Tomorrow no salt.

No sé yo la causa re eto,   I don't know the cause of this,
Yo no sé sino aguantá   All I know is how to bear
Eta conrición tan dura   This condition, so difficult
    Y ejgraciá . . . !   And so wretched . . . !
. . . . (p. 39)   . . . .

A similar sentiment of protest against the general conditions of their lives is suggested quite subtly in Nicolás Guillén's *Motivos de son*—a point we will take up again in chapter seven—even though they, like Obeso's *Cantos*, on the surface do not overwhelm with the direct protest statement. It seems appropriate that Nicolás Guillén was one of the first to notice this sentiment or this meaning in Obeso's work. The verses I have quoted are among the ones Nicolás Guillén had in mind when he wrote:

> Obeso was not only a creative artist who wrote in the manner of the black Colombian who heavily populates the Magdalena region. He captured their peculiar rhythm, that of the *cumbia*, which bears resemblance to our *son*. But sometimes he went even further, and left poems that carry a revolutionary sense which, if not manifest in a violent and vindicative manner, is emitted through his expression of the hidden grief the common man suffers in the face of social injustice. . . .
>
> For despite the exalted Colombian cry of "liberalism" in the 19th century, and its vaunted "democracy," Obeso had to react not only against class prejudices, derived from miserable economic conditions, but also against "racial" prejudice against blackness—a prejudice I personally have witnessed—in such cities as Barranquilla and Cartagena. Such prejudices exist in general in all the cities of the capitalist world where an important black population is found, as in Colombia and other areas.[10]

Nicolás Guillén is quite right in seeing the deeper meaning of Obeso's *Cantos populares de mi tierra*. Yet Mónica Mansour is quite wrong in seeing Obeso as an "ivory tower" poet "isolated from the historical and social-economic reality of his country."[11] While there are basic romantic overtones in much of Obeso's work, still his writings tell us much about the black experience in Colombia and about his own black consciousness. He does this from an unmistakable black perspective not only in *Cantos* but in his first book, *Lecturas para tí*, and in his last one, *Lucha de la vida*, as well.

To be sure *Lecturas para tí* are largely love poems or statements in prose that were first published separately in newspapers, but when the author speaks of his "accursed fate," or the "terrible law" that governs his life he gives these statements a racial perspective that goes beyond romantic rhetoric. Obeso was developing and expressing his black pride and his black identity even before his *Can-*

tos, and the following statement shows his acute awareness that blackness in Colombia as elsewhere was a terrible handicap:

> Never have I received affection except from my unfortunate mother. But I felt love, if ever so abstractly, as soon as I entered the world. I was born in an ardent climate and the sun of my country focused on my breast. On various occasions, among some beauties I would encounter, I sought my companion, and at times I thought I found her, but in viewing her closely with the eyes of my soul, I would draw away, happy, whispering: she is not the one. Much time passed by in this fashion, and in my terrible fight with the world, I dedicated myself to my studies, and grew fond of glory. My ragged attire kept me far-removed from people. The dreadful poverty in which I have lived, my sad helplessness, the complexion of my race typical of this climate, rich in many grand qualities, brought upon me tremendous disillusions. (p. 54)

Lecturas para tí has fueled yet another controversy: Obeso's obsession with a married, upperclass, white woman, who reappears, as we shall see, in his last work, *Lucha de la vida.* Much has been made of this unrequited love, of his "unfortunate passion"[12] for a woman whose family "would never have allowed her to marry this black without means or social position."[13] More, in fact, has been made of this episode than of Obeso's later attachment to Zenaida "a girl of the lower classes," who was his "loving companion for fourteen years, right up to the last instant of his existence."[14]

Unrequited or not, Obeso's "obsession" with the white woman ostensibly provided him with an outlet for several philosophical observations that pepper this series of articles, such as: "The worth of a man is in his soul"; "He who is rich is not happy"; "Goodness is the bread of the soul"; "Solitude does not humiliate but ennobles if one suffers with honor." In a diatribe against the rich white nobility, he claims, "their endeavor is to be white, which is to say *pretty . . .* For me, I am delighted to be black and my ugliness is a joy to me. . . . Mankind will be born anew in my race." (pp. 51–52). In a strong statement reminiscent of the dignity of the folk that populate his *Cantos populares de mi tierra,* Obeso writes from his "position" in the "social farces" of life that, "I'm poor and I fear nothing; I envy no one, because my faith is profound." (p. 55).

Lecturas para tí, then, although addressed to "her," seems to be, in a sense, a forum for Obeso to state his claim as a human being with rights to respect despite his poverty and his blackness. This work, in addition, contains some autobiographical passages in prose and in poetry. "Sotto voce," for example, describes his journey to Bogotá from his home village in search of fame and fortune:

> Intacto el corazón, el alma pura
>   Henchida de ternura,
> Y de ilusiones cándidas repleta,
> Abandoné el hogar, me lancé al mundo,
>   Y, niño pudibundo,
> Luché con sus injurias como atleta.
> Lo recuerdo muy bien. Mi noble padre
>   Y mi amorosa madre
> Sólo su santa benedición me dieron
> Entre llanto y congojas . . . De aquel día
>   Mi infantil alegría
> En tristeza los hados convirtieron. (pp. 86–87)

> My heart intact, my soul pure,
>   Swollen with tenderness,
> And filled with naive illusions,
> I abandoned home, and launched myself forth into the world,
>   And, like a modest child, I fought like an athlete against life's
>   injustices.
> I remember it well. My noble father
>   And loving mother
> Gave me only their blessings
> Between cries and anguish . . . From that day
>   My childhood joy
> Was turned by Fate to sadness.

Although *Lecturas para tí* contains autobiographical data, this volume can be read more as a philosophical statement of a spiritual journey the poet had to travel internally to confirm the beliefs that gave him strength as a man, and especially as a black man. *La lucha de la vida*, his last work, however, is more of an outward autobiographical accounting, under the guise of poetic or dramatic fiction. In this work, too, a connection between love and the human condition, and particularly the black condition, is stressed. This connection is unavoidable since the work is structured on Obeso's misfortunes in life and on the impossible love for the white woman.

The protagonist of the poem, a young, poor, black poet, like Obeso, who is a specialist in languages, as was Obeso, is resentful of this well-to-do, married, white woman, as was Obeso, and the reasons that made union with him impossible. The poet in this long, disconnected work meditates on the what-is-life theme, particularly his own life, which because of "a stigma, perhaps" (p. 175) seems to be an existence condemned to suffering. The poem touches on thoughts of suicide. "It is in vain that I try to pursue the struggle" (p. 175) and is in fact laced with references to death, and to his "crushed illusions," his "sufferings," his "pain," his "anguish." These depressing references are contrasted with many memories of a happier time when the poet was young. Nostalgia plays a key role in the poem as the poet, contrasting his present "immense pain" with the past, looks back on that happier time when he, as a youth, heard the river boatmen sing. One of the songs that brings back "very sweet memories" of "those happy days" (p. 129) is Obeso's own "Canción del boga ausente" inserted mid-way in the poem.

The same black sensibility that produced Obeso's authentic black poetry in Cantos populares de mi tierra also produced his pessimistic realization in La lucha de la vida. In that work he is acutely aware of what blackness despite one's accomplishments and worth can do to a man in a racist society. Obeso is the first in a long line of black writers in Colombia to come to this realization. His fellow countrymen Jorge Artel, Arnoldo Palacios, and Manuel Zapata Olivella, for example, continue and up-date this realization in this century by building on Obeso's original understanding of the true nature of race relations in Colombia, which, though often presented by whites as a "nation where the diverse races have become one big happy family"[15] is rarely treated that way by blacks. Obeso's La lucha de la vida shows Obeso's early understanding that in Colombia "for those who cannot become lighter life is hellish."[16] It is this understanding that accounts for the growing disillusion with life so easily traceable in Obeso's prose and poetry. This same understanding intensified the morbid sense of melancholy and despair of his appropriately titled La lucha de la vida.

Despair and melancholy never led him to reject the reality of his blackness. Obeso was racially proud, and he identified with his people and their daily struggles. He despaired more because others looked down on blacks than from a desire to be white. This difference between pride in blackness and cult of whiteness is essentially the difference between Candelario Obeso and Gaspar Octavio Hernández, the Panamanian poet discussed in the next chapter who, weighed down with the reality of his color, sought escape in bohemian living, drinking, and the Modernist aesthetic.

The Black Swan:
Gaspar Octavio Hernández,
Panama's Black Modernist Poet

> No matter how "White" the Black artist's intentions are,
> he cannot exclude absolutely his Black experience.
>
> David Dorsey

> Sometimes a poet in his effort at self-revelation moves
> outside of the immediate concerns of the Black commu-
> nity. . . . Nevertheless, our mere awareness of them as
> Black persons helps to shape our response to the poem,
> whether or not the poet wants us to consider him as other
> than poet pure and simple, or for that matter pure and
> complex.
>
> Stephen Henderson

In the Introduction of this book, I noted the importance of the works of black writers, mostly nineteenth-century ones, who of necessity wrote white but whose works still reflect the "interior drama"[1] that accompanies the realization of being black in a white society. Manzano's poems exemplify this kind of suppressed ethnic affiliation. The works of Gaspar Octavio Hernández (1893–1918), on the surface, seem to have been diverted into directions other than race, or even class for that matter, namely, into a cult of whiteness on the one hand and a cult of nationalism on the other. Yet his literary orientation provides another good example for the black who wrote white. This black Panamanian Modernist poet, whose Modernist aesthetic, as we shall see, is characterized by melancholy, anguish, and despair, created poems and even used white symbols that are open to interpretation based on ethnic affiliation.

There are other black writers in the literary history of Panama:

José Dolores Urriola (1834–1883), known as "The Mulatto Urriola," who was a sharp-tongued improvisor of satirical and epigrammatic verse; Federico Escobar (1861–1912), a humble carpenter known as "The Black Bard," who in his literature perhaps was the most unashamedly black of the Panamanian group and the most straightforward in his approach to himself, to his trade, and to his country; and Cristóbal Martínez known in literary circles as Simón Rivas, who, like his Modernist contemporaries, was fond of "audacious meters" and "innovative forms." Rivas was also called the "Panamanian Poe," partly because of his "fantasies which he called 'nocturnes'."[2] The "Black Swan," however, as Gaspar Octavio Hernández was called, has the most established and best known literary reputation of this group, at least in his country, even though he had the shortest life—he died at the age of 25.

Described by Rogue Javier Laurenza as "the only poet of his generation who displays a bit of literary culture,"[3] Octavio Hernández's name is usually linked with that of Ricardo Miró, Panama's other "National Poet." Miró's son is the author of a very useful article that helped make the work of Octavio Hernández better known. Recalling that he was the "artistic and literary hero of the people, the indisputable intellectual leader of Santa Ana,"[4] the poet's home district, Miró reviews briefly the work of earlier scholars who have written about Octavio Hernández. This discussion included the judgments of Demetrio Korsi, who was a great friend of the Black Swan, a constant companion in drink and in conversation, who earlier than anyone else pinpointed in a very perceptive personality profile the obsession with whiteness that characterized much of the poet's life and work.

Gaspar Octavio Hernández' son too has done his father the honor and the good service of making his works available by collecting and publishing in one volume a fairly complete *Obras selectas*[5] in 1966, which includes prose, poetry, and a good bibliographic listing of works by and about Gaspar Octavio Hernández.

These recent efforts focus deserved attention on the work of this black Modernist poet and, in effect, contribute to "saving from oblivion a work that was already becoming eclipsed in time and space"[6] —in the words of the poet's son.

His writing can be best understood by first studying the man. Ismael García put it quite appropriately when he said of Gaspar Octavio Hernández that "in order to approach this poet's work, we must first pass through the antechamber of his biography, because his life is in a certain way the key to his poetry."[7] Born 4 July 1893 into a poor district of the capital city, Octavio Hernández had a rough youth. With only third grade education, he had to leave school to work in menial jobs after his mother died. He quickly rose through self-effort and a program of self-education to assume the directorship of several literary and political newspapers and to be elected to civic office and to vie with Ricardo Miró for the title of "National Poet." A self-taught man of culture, Octavio Hernández, a founding member of the Unión Intelectual Latinoamericana de Panama, is commemorated today by a bust raised in his memory in Santa Ana Square in Panama City, and a Day of Journalism named in his honor.

This "singer of the national flag," as he was also known, though handicapped by color and his short life, had a remarkable literary reputation as well as one as a heavy drinker and a womanizing bohemian, who had two women pregnant at the same time and joined a local Alcoholics Anonymous Association to curb his drinking.[8]

Judging from biographers, he dedicated himself equally to civic and patriotic duties, to a bohemian existence, and to producing literature. Despite the time and energy spent in pursuit of the latter two, Gaspar the poet was always involved in politics. His political participation and his patriotic writing perhaps were unavoidable because in his lifetime Panama gained independence from Colombia in 1903 and, in what has been called the event of the century, the Panama Canal opened in 1914. The specter of the United States also was becoming one of the concerns that provided issues for much national debate during his youth. The last article he was working on before he died expressed indignation over some foreign businessmen flying flags of their countries and not the Panamanian one on national days. This troubled him as much as the presence of foreign troops in the country and the increasing use of English rather than Castillian in daily social life.

In addition to these factors of a political and patriotic nature, there are other events—some personal tragedies—in his biography that must be brought into focus in any discussion of formative influences that have a bearing on his personality and works. Octavio Hernández was a melancholy poet whose short life was characterized by suffering. The sadness and melancholy that permeated his poetry are not results of mere literary posturing: they are products of the memory of unfortunate experiences, not the least of which was the death of his mother when he was eight years old. We can point also to the suicide of a younger brother followed shortly by the suicide of a second brother who died in his arms. These experiences, plus the ordeal of having another brother allegedly dealing in drugs, combined with his own tuberculosis and his alcoholism, not to mention the reality of his blackness which constantly plagued him, have all helped shape his aesthetic vision, which, it is generally thought, was one of a late romantic, a "delayed romantic" but one who "took advantage of Modernist procedures insofar as versification and style are concerned."[9]

Gaspar Octavio Hernández was both a late romantic and a late Modernist, "a Modernist who arrived with delay" as Max Henríquez Ureña[10] has said. Yet, though his works appeared mainly between 1910 and 1914 and belonged to the third and final wave of Modernist writing in Panama, his verse compositions are characterized by the *afán verbal* generally associated with the early phases of Modernism, by a "variety of meters and strophic combinations,"[11] in short, by all the "tricks of the trade," which Anderson Imbert[12] felt the poet used in his work in his pursuit of the Modernist aesthetic.

His first book, *Melodías del pasado*, published in 1915—his only book of poetry published during his lifetime—has been accurately described, in fact, as a "collection of strange musical sounds, a polychromatic concert of delicate harmony,"[13] a volume full of "mandolin music" and "exotic perfumes." This first book, as with those issued posthumously, including a volume of exquisite prose, conjures up images of "a far-off country of virgins as white as the snow of the mountain range, and always nostalgic, with the nostalgia of impossible loves . . ."[14] The theme of evasion, which these exotic settings and "white virgins" suggest, is not unrelated, as we shall see, to a pervasive tone of grief that also characterizes his work.

Basically, the Modernist aesthetic of Gaspar Octavio Hernández revolves around his escapist tendency, his melancholy, his patriotism, his thematic and technical use of color and his versification, all of which coincide with the Modernist sensibility of the time. Rogelio Sinán, for example, sees this escapist tendency as "one of the essential characteristics of Panamanian poetry."[15] Although Sinán links this "desire of evasion" to the "perennial coming and going of ships" that Panamanians see pass through the Canal daily, in the case of Gaspar Octavio Hernández this theme has more to do with a desire to escape from the racist pressures of society. The poet felt deep within himself that despite his accomplishments society rejected him "because his skin was not white, and because his eyes were not the color of the sea or of the sky."[16] He had, in effect, a desire to escape from his blackness into a world of whiteness "not only because of literary vanity, but also because this escape was the answer to his most intimate and frustrated desires."[17] That is, "to the Modernist, a blond is only a blond to whom one sings because of her beauty. For our poet a blond is a woman whose love it is impossible for him to attain."[18] The poet knew, at any rate, that he was a "social outcast, in spite of his talent,"[19] and it is sad to read reports that despite his accomplishments one of the great sources of pride the poet felt was in his "European" nose.

Demetrio Korsi, we noted earlier, pinpointed this obsession Gaspar Octavio Hernández had with whiteness, and he summarized his revelation in the following passage:

> [Octavio Hernández] loved women, and he loved them with the singular and delectable love of a true poet. He dreamt of oriental harems. For this reason all his poems are saturated with evocations of flesh white as snow, of alabaster bodies, of breasts small and pure as fresh lilies. Blonds attracted him like magnets with supernatural powers; blonds from Scandinavia, blue-eyed ones of German descent, or the spiritual daughters of our beloved Paris. An idealization of whiteness, very lyrical indeed, plucked the chords of his harp, which was always filled with white swans, mother-of-pearl-skinned princesses, immaculate orange blossoms like cotton on branches and perfect ivory . . . [20]

Some examples from his works to illustrate this cult of whiteness would include the following: his long poem "Cristo y la mujer de Sichar,"[21] which, quite appropriately for a religious theme, is filled with things white "as the snow of the mountain of Judea" (p. 44); "Venus del trópico," in which "seated on a rock where moss grows,/ a woman appears singing barcaroles/naked, white and timid" (p. 124); "Visión nupcial. . . .," where his vision is of one "all white, all white/of orange blossoms, jasmin and white lilies" (p. 129); "Afrodita" and her "blond braids" and "rounded marble thighs/which the setting sun accentuated" (p. 141); the "blond cherubs" that populate his exotic "Cuento de hadas" (pp. 142-46); the "buxom blond," the "pregnant white woman" of "Futura" (pp. 262-63). A particularly striking example is "the one with hands as white as snow" of "Floración milagrosa" (pp. 69-70), where the theme of "ideal love," in the sense of both white and unattainable, reaches perhaps its maximum expression, as the sense of frustration which sank the poet deeper and deeper into a state of melancholy becomes significant because it suggests a motif, a melancholic obsession that goes far beyond mere physical possession—we know the poet had white women in his life—to a desire for fulfillment, racial or spiritual, on a higher level. This melancholic longing for a white woman, one characterized by a sense of the unattainable, repeats itself many times in the poet's work, for example in "Profética" (What inaccessible splendours! . . . And how far away . . . /but one day/we will find each other on the same path . . . p. 252), and in "Rima nocturna" (Oh! how alone! . . . How alone! . . . What gloom . . . p. 255).

Melancholy, a key ingredient among the Modernists from Rubén Darío to Juan Ramón Jiménez, is, perhaps, the most characteristic note in the poetry of Gaspar Octavio Hernández. This melancholy, though largely linked to this motif of a "frustrated desire," was also rooted in the personal tragedies of the poet. "Púrpura," "Canción del alma errante," and "Mármol sagrado," for example, deal with the suicide of a younger brother, with his own incurable illness, and with the death of his mother, respectively. The poet not only feels melancholy but sees it everywhere and imposes it on everyone and everything. The biographical poem "Melodías del pasado" (pp. 49-50), filled with "sad notes" and "painful memories" of the past, is especially significant for it reveals his early mood of melancholy during his "bitter childhood." Even then he felt the "virus of human tedium" that an "intense and premature melancholy" had accustomed him to. The "deeply repressed pain" he speaks of in "Havoc" (p. 93), another biographical poem, suggests the quiet desperation of a writer who has internalized the misfortunes that befell him.

This same quiet desperation is seen in "Ego sum," perhaps the poet's most melancholic poem insofar as black ethnic identity confronted with whiteness is concerned:

Ego sum
Ni tez de nácar, ni cabellos de oro
veréis ornar de galas mi figura;

ni la luz del zafir, celeste y pura,
veréis que en mis pupilas atesoro.

Con piel tostada de atezado moro;
con ojos negros de fatal negrura,
del Ancón a la falda verde oscura
nací frente al Pacífico sonoro.

Soy un hijo del Mar . . . Porque en mi alma
hay,—como sobre el mar,—noches de calma,
indefinibles cóleras sin nombre

y un afán de luchar conmigo mismo
cuando en penas reconditas me abismo
pienso que soy un mar trocado en hombre! (p. 111)

Ego sum

Neither pearl-like complexion, nor golden hair
will you see adorning my person;
nor the light of the sapphire, celestial and pure,
will you see in my pupils.

With the dark skin of a tanned Moor;
and with black eyes of fatal darkness,
I was born in the dark green foothills of Ancón
facing the sonorous Pacific.

I am a son of the Sea . . . Because in my soul
there are—as at sea,—nights of calm
and indefinable and nameless anger

And a propensity for inward struggle
as when in profound suffering I sink
I think I am the sea transformed into a man.

In this poem the poet gives us a psychological profile of himself along with a sketch of his physical features. Here, the "sea transformed into a man" refers to the interior drama we spoke of earlier and suggests a black awareness painfully realized in the work of black writers who feel the pressure of whiteness. We see this internalized grief, in the "deeply repressed pain" of "Havoc," and in the "deep sadness" of "Afrodita," and in countless other poems where melancholy is linked to grief. It seems clear that the poet felt, in the words of Thomas Grey, that "melancholy had marked him for his own," and Octavio Hernández even quoted the line (p. 423). The poet also quoted Poe, whose works he knew quite well, and one of the sentences from Poe was, "I do not know in the scale of Verse a higher note than that of Melancholy" (p. 423). Gaspar Octavio Hernández, it seems, tried very hard to live up to this.

The pressures that propelled the poet on the one hand into evasive flights toward whiteness and on the other toward the depths of melancholy, in part because of the futile nature of these flights, are the same pressures that made him opt for a patriotic stance rather than a racial one. He chose the greater glory of a nationalistic identity over a purely ethnic one, certainly over one that was black, considering the low esteem in which blackness was held—even by the poet himself—at that time. Shortly after the turn of the century, patriotism and the destiny of the nation were themes in great abundance in Panamanian literature. The Modernist generation coincided with the beginning of the Republican era in Panama when men of letters from Darío Herrera to Ricardo Miró and Octavio Hernández had ample opportunities to combine patriotic and civic themes with their service to the community and to the nation. Though they wrote "patriotic verses of undeniable poetic merit,"[22] this generation has come in for some severe criticism from Roque Javier Laurenza, who has accused them of "a false, second-hand estheticism"[23] and who believes, in fact, that there was too much verse written in the name of patriotism and that their praise of the new republic was excessive. "The poets," he writes, singling out Miró and Octavio Hernández as the "major gods" of the time, "fulfil rigorously both the role of the flatterer and the flattered."[24]

Obviously not of the same mind, Elsie Alvarado de Ricord[25] sees their work as collectively representing the "literary symbol of our patriotism." She sees poems like "El canto de la bandera" of Octavio Hernández and "Patria" of Ricardo Miró as eloquent expressions of a determined people. It is poems like "El canto de la bandera," "A Panamá," perhaps Octavio Hernández's most famous patriotic poem, and others like his "Alma patria," which he wrote for one of the national days, clearly one of the best expressions of his patriotic fervor, and "Intima," published posthumously in 1918, that gave him yet another title, "poet of the people," which is, in fact, the title of one of the studies dealing with his life and work.[26]

His prose work also contains significant items relevant to the theme of patriotism. "Alrededor de la emancipación" (pp. 285–291), and "El culto del idioma" (pp. 357–359), in which he writes the following strong anti-Yankee words, an early example of reaction against the influx of English in Panama, are but two examples:

> There is no shortage of those who long for the servant's chain and there is an abundance of those who enjoy the greatest

pleasure when they are flatterers of men or of countries. Among these ranks are to be found some South Americans, not a few Antillians of Hispanic descent, who are anxious to North Americanize themselves and, in their eagerness to praise the country of Roosevelt, impudently ignore their mother tongue and brag of expressing themselves in an often incomprehensible, coarse anglo-yankee *patois*.

Let us honor the language! It is a duty which our very dignity as free men imposes upon us. (p. 359)

The word "Yankeemente," a term he coined (p. 401) to denote hypocrisy, also conveys his distrust of the stronger nation to the north.

In "Letras del istmo" (pp. 362–366) the poet calls for more originality in local literary expression, more appreciation for aesthetics, and more artistic sensibility of the kind he himself possessed.

The artistic sensibility of Gaspar Octavio Hernández, in effect, his Modernist aesthetic, can be reduced technically to the same two poles around which Modernist techniques, in general, according to Américo Ferrari, revolve, namely, music and color. Ferrari once defined a Modernist poet as someone who "works like a painter [and] who is at the same time a musician,"[27] and the two keys to an understanding of the Modernist aesthetic of Gaspar Octavio Hernández are precisely *el sentido de color* (usually white) and *la musicalidad* (usually a preponderance of the sonorous *esdrújulo*). Titles alone indicate the importance of color and music. Note, for example, such expressive *modernista* titles of books, sections, and poems as *Melodías del pasado*, "Preludio," "Músicas," "Matices," "Púrpura," "Crepúsculo," "Violeta," "Claroscuro," "Vespertina." His second book of poems is called *La copa de Amatista* and contains poems like "Serenata doliente," and numerous "canciones," among them "Canción del alma errante," "La eterna canción," and "Canción de árboles." His "Poesías dispersas" include "Trova sentimental," "Azul," "Obsidiana," "Canción crepuscular." Prose sections are called "Cromos y esculturas." A short story title becomes almost trite with the name "Oro y perlas."

In great Modernist form the poet makes abundant reference throughout his work to "harmonies," "notes," "mandolins," "pianos," "clarinets," "guitars," "lyres," "harps;" there are "deep vibrations, sweet woman's voices," "sonorous flutes," "timid violins," and especially "mandolins," as in his "Canción del abandonado" which begins:

A los retintines
del tiple sonoro
respondía el coro
de los bandolines.

The chorus of mandolins
answered to the
ringing sound of
the treble guitar.

He goes on:

el tiple tenía las cuerdas de oro
y los bandolines las cuerdas de plata,
y de la juventud éramos tesoro
los que ejecutábamos la serenata. (p. 253)

The guitar had strings of gold
And the mandolin strings of silver,
And those of us who played the serenade
Possessed the treasure of youth.

Needless to say, much of his verse in many ways recalls that of Rubén Darío.

In his pursuit of the Modernist aesthetic, which included a marked preference for the sonnet, Octavio Hernández tried to live up to the well-known dictum, "La musique avant toute chose," especially in the poem "Músicas," in which he repeats throughout it the rhythmically melodic line, "Everything vibrates with music" ("Todo vibra con músicas"), closing with the equally rhythmical, "Lull me with sonorous music" ("Arrúllame con músicas sonoras") (p. 27).

This "sonorous music" is found in much of his verse and derives from the preponderance, as we mentioned earlier and as is noticeable here, of *esdrújulos*, a much used or over-used rhythmic device in Modernist poetry. Octavio Hernández overdoes it with his "young orphan" ("*Huérfana* virgen"), "*pale* sick girl" (*pálida* enferma"), "little *languid* soul" ("almita *languida*"), and his "*limpid* fountain" ("*límpida* fuente"), all found in the same four-verse segment of the poem "Fatum" (p. 117). The poem also contains a rhyme scheme built on what for him was an inevitable use of his key word "melancholy," a word which perhaps reaches its maximum rhythmic expression in the poem on the death of his brother:

Púrpura
Juan, doncel tierno que se adormía
en ilusiones de bien, sintió
que de ignorada melancolía
su joven alma se emponzoñó.
. . . .
y ennoblecido de bizarría
como un gallardo César, cayó.   (p. 71)

Purple
Juan, a tender youth who was slumbering
in illusions of goodness, felt
that by an unknown melancholy
his young soul had been poisoned.
....
and ennobled by these strange happenings
like a graceful Caesar, he fell.

Alternating *llano* and *agudo* rhyme throughout the four strophes of the poem, Octavio Hernández shows that he is equally adept with stress patterns other than the *esdrújulo*. In what is perhaps his most sonorous attempt at verbal music reminiscent of Rubén Darío, he writes in "Balada . . . del campanero de la campana de oro":

> Dí que un bruñido puñal
> de la más bruñida plata, mata
> como un puñal de agata;
> que el metal precioso mata
> cual mata vil mineral. (pp. 171–172)

> Say that a polished dagger
> of the most polished silver, kills
> like a knife of agate;
> precious metal kills
> just as well as base mineral.

This poem is a nice combination of sounds including internal rhyme, even though the verbal music here does seem to be a bit forced.

His other *modernista* obsession, the chromatic one, is largely dominated with allusions to whiteness, since his verse, as we have already pointed out, is filled with *heroínas rubias*, with *ojos azules*, and with *carne de nácar*. His cult of whiteness, which carries with it such typically Modernist meanings as purity, the ideal, and perfection, can, for ethnic and aesthetic contrast, be compared to the presence of blackness in a sense by default in "Claroscuro," where we have one of the very few references, however indirect, the poet makes in his verse to a woman whose skin is not white. He writes:

> Ni albor de mirto, ni matiz de aurora,
> ni palidez de nardo, ni blancura
> de cera encontraréis en la hermosura
> de su faz que a los reyes enamora . . . (p. 74)

> Neither the whiteness of myrtle nor the hue of dawn
> Neither the paleness of spikenard, nor the whiteness
> of wax will you find in the beauty of
> her face which kings have fallen in love with . . .

This poem is remarkably reminiscent in structure to his own self-portrait in "Ego sum" which, as will be recalled, begins:

> Ni tez de nácar, ni cabellos de oro
> veréis ornar de galas mi figura;
> ni la luz del zafir, celeste y pura,
> veréis que en mis pupilas atesoro. (p. 111)

> Neither pearl-like complexion, nor golden hair
> will you see adorning my person;
> nor the light of the sapphire, celestial and pure,
> will you see in my pupils.

Both of these poems suggest blackness by contrast rather than through direct mention, as if the poet could not bring himself to confront it. In both poems references to black ethnic identity are either avoided or oblique ones like "tanned Moor" (p. 111) and "Moorish complexion" (p. 74), respectively.

Even his patriotic verse is marked by the chromatic aspect of the Modernist aesthetic, and his "El canto de la bandera," where he writes

> Bandera de la patria ¡Sube . . . sube!
> hasta perderte en el azul . . .

> Flag of the fatherland, Rise . . . rise!
> out of sight into the azure sky . . .

shows, for example, the importance of the color blue "which he has made a kind of patriotic symbol."[28] Blue, the Modernist color that Octavio Hernández, who can quite rightly be called a "nationalistic Modernist," links "consciously and unconsciously to the notion of country"[29] is given a long poem of its own called simply "Azul," where "Blue, blue, everything is blue" (pp. 208–213)—water, trees, mountains, love, the sky. Perhaps his most striking Modernist "painting," however, can be found in a selection from his prose that begins:

> In lead-colored days, when the atmosphere is a whitish gray and the sea a gray the color of pearl and the Sun, semi-concealed by thick clouds, what seems like shapeless, colorless glass . . . (p. 392)

The richness of the color descriptions of this passage, especially in a segment quoted from Alejandro Sawa, is highly reminiscent of the poet's poem "Azul." Taboga, the island described here, is to the poet the Republic of Panama in miniature. It can be said that his impressionistic description of it and of the surrounding waters and the horizon represent the chromatic aspect of his Modernist aesthetic, in miniature.

Later generations, perhaps seeing such descriptions as too exaggerated, dismiss the work of Gaspar Octavio Hernández and that of some of his contemporaries as too *esteticista*. I would not dismiss his work too lightly, however, because if for no other reason, as a black Modernist poet the ethnic dimension he brings to his work is extremely valuable to those of us who would like as much insight as possible into the aesthetics of the black writer, especially one whose tendency is escapist. His escapism, even his melancholy and his patriotism, are all related to what the poet understood to be his stigma of blackness. Color for him becomes more than literary rhetoric, and melancholy and despair are more than literary themes. It is ethnicity that makes his works and his life more intense. This is so even when, or especially when, we remember that this refined exquisite poet was for the most part alienated or estranged from black society.

Unlike "Plácido," Manzano, Obeso, Morúa and others who had many ties with the black community, Octavio Hernández did not pay court to blackness in his personal life or in his verse. He did not "sing of his race" in his verse partly because blacks—perhaps with not a little envy—saw him as a "strange being" who was wasting his time aspiring to greatness, who cultivated the companionship and friendship of the white literary establishment, and who above all wrote "for white women."[30] These judgments are a little unjust. It is true that overt black awareness is not noticeable in his verse, and indeed Laurenza says "only three times does he mention a woman whose color is not radiantly white."[31] Yet, Octavio Hernández learned of black history in Africa and the Americas through his reading of Padre Sandoval's book, *Naturaleza, Policía Sagrada I Profana, Costumbres I Ritos, Disciplina I Catechismo Evangélico de todos los Etiopes* (1647), which the poet discovered through a Spanish friend and bibliophile. From this work he felt black pride, even though he felt identification only with black kings and nobles of the past.

Consistent with this restricted and selective identification, Gaspar Octavio Hernández felt great admiration for other outstanding blacks of his day, including Edmundo Botello, a journalist poet who wrote on social issues. As a youth he was impressed with Federico

Escobar, whose verses he learned by heart. He delivered a funeral oration on the death of Simón Rivas, and in this impassioned statement he wrote:

> This is an age of injustices and cowardice, where all flying in the sky of Humanity is done by golden eagles; this is an age of injustice and shamelessness, in which animal grease and sheepskin are better appreciated than the book into which a worthwhile writer has poured his thoughts . . . (p. 303)

Had Federico Escobar been white, the poet thought, he would have gone farther. Such "beauty," however, was not to be for the black poet who only wanted to be one figure more on the national literary scene but who was "victim of misfortune from the cradle to the grave, confronted with the egoism of boastful pseudointellectuals." (p. 419)

The introductory paragraph to his piece on Edmundo Botello reads as follows:

> There still persists among some pseudoanthropologists the idea that the black race is a miserable herd of imbeciles, worthy only of living in filthy dwellings beneath the unmerciful African sun, but brilliant models of this race have taken it upon themselves to prove, by their actions, that blacks can achieve in all phases of human progress, and, when the black race develops the great energies with which it is endowed, a great many fools who try to ridicule it will be surprised. (p. 417)

In all of these statements about "superior blacks," Octavio Hernández could well be talking about himself. These are the kinds of realities of the black experience that confronted the black writer in Panama that made ethnicity so significant in the Modernist aesthetic of Octavio Hernández. These are the kinds of experiences that compelled the poet toward escapism, or as Laurenza has said, that compelled the poet to construct his whole literature on a base that is one of complete "self-deception": he strove to obtain in literature the whiteness that was unattainable in life. The ring of falseness and inauthenticity he sees in the poet's work are inevitable results of this unfulfilled or frustrated desire.

Laurenza in this assessment is not far off the mark. Indeed, the poet's whole life-style can be seen as one gigantic self-deception, if we consider his "rare" habits and customs, from the rose petals he drank in his liqueur to the wild and colorful vests he reportedly wore, both seemingly attempts to establish some kind of individual personality to detract from his blackness. Regrettable as it is that Gaspar Octavio Hernández did not become a "standard bearer of black poetry as later on other poets: Jorge Artel, Nicolás Guillén and others, have become,"[32] we should remember, nevertheless, that it is his blackness, his ethnicity or, if you will, his attempt to escape 'from it, that led him into the world of whiteness provided by the Modernist aesthetic. His ethnic identity, ironically, provided him however indirectly with the source of inspiration on which his whole created world unavoidably was based.

Part Two

MAJOR PERIOD, 1922–49

The Turning Point:
The Blackening of Nicolás Guillén
and the Impact of his *Motivos de son*

*I realized that I had to be their friend, their voice, their
leader, their poet.*

Langston Hughes

Nicolás Guillén, like Gaspar Octavio Hernández, had his "white"
stage, but unlike the Afro-Panamanian poet, Guillén has lived long
enough to pass through it and to go on to become the premier black
poet writing in Spanish. Guillén's earlier poetry was definitely nonblack and largely inconsequential, of interest to contemporary readers only as illustrations of his early expertise and technical
domination of traditional Spanish verse forms, particularly those in
vogue during and just after the literary reign of Rubén Darío, and
as contrast they illustrate, as well, how far he has come in the blackening process he underwent from *Cerebro y corazón* (1922) to *Motivos de son* (1930). Before this metamorphosis, Guillén's literary
output in the twenties, with only a very few exceptions, followed
European models. Literary historians who want to "deblacken" him
or turn him into a nonblack poet can find ample evidence in these
adolescent poems to support their view which, as best expressed by
Luis Iñiguez Madrigal,[1] is that Nicolás Guillén is not—nor has he
ever been—a black poet in language, style, or theme. Madrigal has
another view, namely, that Nicolás Guillén is not even a predominantly social poet, but one who writes primarily on "other" themes.
Madrigal can find some evidence in these early poems to support
both his views, as Guillén's pre-*Motivos de son* work is dominated
by such universal or colorless themes as love, death, nature, religion,

and other abstract head and heart ("cerebro y corazón") subjects.

But a turning point came early in Guillén's literary career when he decided to focus his attention on the true black experience in the New World, starting with his native Cuba, where he saw the black as the one most affected by imperialist exploitation and other evils. Refusing to continue to go the way of Gaspar Octavio Hernández, Guillén abandoned the white muse he had followed in his youth and infused his literature with a black sensibility which has permeated his work for more than forty years. A similar black sensibility, as we saw in chapter four, characterized the originality of the black Colombian poet, Candelario Obeso, who had set his sights in the same direction. But Nicolás Guillén represents the major turning point for literary blackness in Latin America. The appearance of his *Motivos de son* in 1930, an authentic literary happening, was upsetting, unsettling and controversial, partly because they broke momentarily with traditional Spanish verse expression and partly because they dealt with authentic black characters, but largely because they brought to literature a new and genuine black concern, perspective, and poetic voice, which even some blacks misunderstood.

The *Motivos de son* had a strong impact on black and white Cubans alike. White readers, after getting over the initial shock of seeing authentic blacks in literature, were pleased to see them appear because, on the surface, Guillén in *Motivos de son* seemed to highlight the comic and picturesque side of the black locked into an uneducated happy-go-lucky lower class image. Black readers were quick to react negatively against the *Motivos de son* largely for the same reason. They were not pleased to see the *negro bembón* given center stage in literature nor were they pleased to see what appeared to be the perpetuation of stereotyped images of the black. Both groups, however, soon came to realize that Guillén's *Motivos de son* went far deeper than racial insult and superficial entertainment. For one thing, both groups began to see in them the unmistakable call to black pride. It was soon recognized that the *Motivos de son* incorporated into formal poetic structure distinctive oral forms from the musical heritage of black people, but popular song and dance forms (the *son*) that were familiar to all Cubans. Black and white Cubans came to understand that Nicolás Guillén was using black talk and black rhythms to set escape motifs like wine, women, and song against a harsh background of unemployment, poverty, prejudice, and misery while making, in effect, a subtle plea for black pride and racial identity as well as for more awareness of social inequities, and of the growing presence of the United States in Cuba.

Although many critics prefer to hasten through this black period in the poet's development, moving on to what they think are his less racial stages, we cannot overestimate the importance of Guillén's work in the late twenties and early thirties. In these years Guillén laid the groundwork that gave his later work meaning and direction, rejecting the white aesthetic whether adhered to by whites, mulattoes, or blacks. It is also during this period that he first declared the black to be as Cuban as anyone else. Guillén attacked in particular during this period the black's own propensity to abrogate his rights by forfeiting them to white Cubans who, though not always backed by law, were willing to take advantage. To Guillén the black's own black phobia, that is his own fear of being black and of identifying with his *son*, his *rumba*, and his *bongó*, was the first obstacle to overcome as he sought ways to restore value to a people long denied it. Rejection of the white aesthetic and a plea for black recognition are really the keys, paradoxically, to his theory of *mulatez*, of a mulatto Cuba. In essence this theory represents the elevation of the black to the level already occupied by whites. Guillén's desire to write Cuban poetry, and not black poetry, is really the culmination of that elevation since Cuban poetry after Guillén can never again mean solely white or European poetry. Moreover, Guillén's subsequent rejection of the term Afro-Cuban paradoxically is the most problack statement he could make. To him the term "Cuban" already includes the "Afro," for the term has come of age and been elevated to the highest degree. Without the black, in other words, there would be no theory of *mulatez*; instead, there would only be white poetry in Cuba. Guillén, then, forces the black man into social recognition, and the white Cuban's acceptance of that theory is in effect a compromise.

Guillén's blackening process, his metamorphosis from a white escapist poet to a black poet, represents a rejection of the white aesthetic in general. More specifically, though, his defiant turnabout can be seen as a black reaction to poetic Negrism, which was a local movement staffed by white intellectuals largely in the Caribbean whose interest in things black in the late twenties and early thirties coincided with the black as *nouvelle vogue* in Europe and America. Rather than associate Guillén with poetic Negrism, we should see his dramatic conversion to blackness in the late twenties and early thirties as a reaction against this white literary fad that was sweeping the world, one Guillén himself defined as

> circumstantial tourism which never penetrated deeply into the human tragedy of race, being more like excursions organized for photographing coconut trees, drums and naked Negroes, whilst there existed the seething drama of the flesh and blood Negro bearing the scars of whiplashes, a Negro now fused with the whites to produce an indelible mulatto imprint on the Cuban social scene.[2]

Guillén writes with characteristic sarcasm in "Pequeña oda a un negro boxeador cubano," the white man

se desnuda	undresses
para tostar su carne al sol	to toast his body in the sun
y busca en Harlem y en La Habana	and seeks in Harlem and Havana
jazz y son.[3]	jazz and *son.*

By drawing directly from the black experience and by giving black reaction to that experience in the *Motivos de son*, Guillén pits the black as speaker from his own environment against the superficial interest in blacks, thus revealing a closeness to the subject, scene, or emotion depicted in each *poema-son* not found in poetic Negrism. It is this closeness, together with Guillén's understanding of his subject, that gives the *Motivos de son* their startling authenticity and Nicolás Guillén the title of authentic black poet.

Guillén lost little time in reaffirming that his conversion to blackness was not a passing fancy. One year later, in *Sóngoro cosongo* (1931), his second volume of black verse, he again set himself apart from the *negrista* craze. In the Prologue to this volume Guillén formulates in unequivocal terms a black credo justifying his new ethnic orientation. He writes, "I am not unaware of the fact that these verses will be repugnant to many persons, because they deal with issues concerning Negroes and the people, but that does not matter to me. Rather, I am happy."[4] Although in this same prologue Guillén talks about "Cuban color" and calls his poems "mulatto verses", we should again remember that this is his way of forcing acceptance of the black as this prologue repeatedly makes reference to the "African shot-in-the-arm" the black presence represents in Cuba. The poems in this volume almost without exception continue to deal with the black experience in Cuba. Just as the semblance of self-mockery and black insult had helped gain respectability among the white *literati* for the *Motivos de son*, so too does his use of the term mulatto (which gives the white a share in blackness) for his black verse, help protect *Sóngoro cosongo* against white backlash.

If anything, the black racial nature of Guillén's poetry intensifies in *Sóngoro cosongo*. The language changes a bit, becoming less colloquial, and the form moves closer to recognizable Spanish verse. The emphasis, though, is the same: black pride, the black experience, and black types continue to dominate his poetry. Guillén continues to introduce the Cuban reader to the black world. But unlike the *Motivos de son* where the black is largely the speaker and singer, in *Sóngoro cosongo* the black, for the most part, is spoken about. The *Motivos de son*, in other words, is closer to black speech and black song (*son*) in poetic form, while *Sóngoro cosongo* is closer in several poems to the Spanish *romance* or ballad form, but with *son* elements. *Sóngoro cosongo* represents growth as Guillén includes variations on the *son* form while enlarging the black world he is introducing by bringing in black folklore, superstitions, even negative types. The black world of the time he represents was not always a pleasant one, but his point is clear: the black has arrived and literature must recognize this fact.

Perhaps the best illustration of this point can be seen in "Llegada" ("The Arrival"), the poem that, significantly, opens this volume. In this lead-off statement which ostensibly describes the arrival of the black as slave to the Island, Guillén repeatedly writes as refrain "¡Aquí estamos!"[5] ("Here we are!") as the poem develops into yet another expression of black racial affirmation. "Pequeña oda a un negro boxeador cubano," which Guillén first published in 1929, one year before the *Motivos de son*, has the same turning-point impact. This poem, like "Mujer nueva" whose black woman figure "trae la palabra inédita"[6] ("brings new knowledge"), is a strong call for racial pride and black identity. To be sure, "Pequeña oda a un negro boxeador cubano" can be read on several levels: (1) as a poem about a black boxer; (2) as a poem where the black boxer acts as symbol for all blacks in struggle; and (3) as a poem about a struggle between nations, more specifically, about impending conflict between Cuba and the United States. But it is the final verse of that poem, where the poet exhorts the black to "hablar en negro de verdad"[7] ("speak in real black talk")—a phrase that certainly refers to more than just black dialect—that underscores the authentic blackening of the poet in this early period. From the black fist of the boxer in "Pequeña oda a un negro boxeador cubano" to the black fist of the slave rower in "Llegada," who has now exchanged his oar for a knife, "apto para las pieles bárbaras"[8] ("appropriate for foreign skins"), there is really very little distance. These three poems, "Pequeña oda a un negro boxeador cubano," "Llegada," and "Mujer nueva," and others in *Sóngoro cosongo* are very black indeed even though they do not contain any of the phonetic speech characteristic of his *Motivos de son*.

In 1934 Guillén published *West Indies Ltd.*, a volume widely hailed as his first volume of social (as opposed to racial) protest poetry. But it is in this volume in which Guillén widens his perspective or attack that he, at the same time, deepens the blackening process begun in the late twenties, crystallized with *Motivos de son* in 1930, and continued in 1931 with *Sóngoro cosongo*. It is evident that Nicolás Guillén focuses as well on the dispossessed white, "Dos niños: uno negro, otro blanco . . . ramos de un mismo árbol de miseria"[9] ("Two children: one black, one white . . . two branches from the same tree of misery"), to illustrate yet another victim, like the black, of United States imperialism in the Antilles, but it would be a mistake to accept that Guillén's concern for the black in this volume is only a symbolic one. The poet continues to depict specific black figures and black folklore, and he also continues his program of instilling black pride in those blacks like Sabás—in a poem of the same name—who continue to go about with their hands out begging rather than shaking the strong black fist, the "puño fuerte elemental y puro"[10] ("fists, pure, unadorned and strong"), of "Nocturno en los muelles," and the "puños los que me das / para rajar los cocos tal como un pequeño dios colérico"[11] ("fists that you give me to slice open coconuts like a small angry god") of "Palabras en el trópico," the lead-off poem in the *West Indies Ltd.* collection. Guillén perhaps more insistently than in his two previous volumes of black verse makes himself the focal character in many of the poems as time and again he emphasizes his own black identity. In "Palabras en el trópico," the poet speaks of his "dark body," his "curly hair." In "Adivinanzas"[12] "the black" becomes "I." Either he or other blacks like "I, Simón Caraballo the black" in "Balada de Simón Caraballo"[13] or "The blacks, working" in "Guadalupe W.I."[14] are the stars. Most importantly in "West Indies Ltd.," the long poem that gives the collection its title, it is clear that Guillén's concerns have moved beyond

Cuba, but it is equally clear that the poet of black pride admonishing Sabás is the same poetic voice speaking at times in the sarcastic tone of an intelligent observer and at other times through the *son* sung at intervals throughout the poem by Juan el Barbero. This is a point the poet does not want the reader to miss, as he closes this poem with the words, "This was written by Nicolás Guillén, *antillano*, in the year nineteen hundred and thirty-four."[15]

Despite Guillén's ever-widening circle of concerns that he has pursued throughout his long career, he has never left the black man behind or out of his poetry. In one of the few published studies of its kind, Constance Sparrow de García Barrio[16] recently traced Guillén's creation of new black characters through his later poetry that includes poems, for example, on such contemporary black figures as Martin Luther King and Angela Davis. In *Tengo* (1964), Guillén, significantly, speaks specifically as a black man in praise of Castro's Cuba where some allege, including Guillén himself, racial identity is no longer important. Throughout his career it has been his insistence on elevating the black that has given his poetry the extra dimension and excitement that makes him a "classic poet" who "has a clear understanding of his art and an absolute control of his technique, as well as something to say."[17] It is this "something to say" that distinguishes his *Motivos de son* and his later poetry from his earlier nonblack work and that sets his verse off from the *negrista* poetry of his white contemporaries. It is also this "something to say" that had a profound effect on Fernando Ortiz, the white Cuban specialist on things black, whose racist research had provided source material and orientation to white *negrista* poets *prior* to Guillén's appearance and domination of the Cuban literary scene in the late twenties and early thirties.

Guillén not only turned himself and *negrista* poetry around but his theory of *mulatez* seems to have been instrumental in turning Ortiz away from a rather clinical examination of the black largely as isolated criminal and slave and more toward the integration of blacks and whites in Cuba, the essence of Ortiz's well-known concept of *cubanidad*, which he developed in the forties. Rather than saying, as G. R. Coulthard has done, that "Guillén's work in many respects appears as an artistic transposition of the ideas of Ortiz,"[18] we should be saying that Ortiz's later work reflects Guillén's ideas on matters of race. Before Guillén's conversion to and insistence on blackness in Cuba, Ortiz was known in part for his *Glosario de*

Afronegrismos (1923), a collection of African words and words that sound African that, because of their rhythmic quality, proved useful to the *negrista* poets. He was known also for what can be called his "unholy trinity," a series of works on "el hampa afro-cubano": *Los negros brujos* (1906), *Los negros esclavos* (1916), and "Los negros curros," a lecture he gave in 1911 whose title he had planned to give to a third volume in the trilogy. This third volume that, according to Alberto Pamies[19] was one of the studies Ortiz was working on at the time of his death in 1959, would have completed the trilogy, but judging from its emphasis on "certain ruffians that *infest* [italics mine] Cuban life"[20]—the definition Ortiz gives for *negros curros*—its publication would have been a retrograde step for Ortiz. The unilateral negativity of that view had been superseded in his work in the *Revista de estudios Afro-Cubanos* (1937–40), in his essay "Por la integración cubana de blancos y negros," in his *Engaño de la raza* (1947), and especially in his "Los factores humanos de la cubanidad," where the antiracist and prointegration stance of Nicolás Guillén are best reflected. Ortiz even co-opts the word *ajiaco* from Guillén's poem "La canción del bongó,"[21] the only real "mulatto verse" in *Sóngoro cosongo*. Ortiz uses this word as the central metaphor for Cuba in his essay, "Los factores humanos de la cubanidad." After the blackening of Nicolás Guillén, Ortiz intensifies his view that "Cuba is an *ajiaco* (stew)."[22] It is also after Guillén that words like *creación mulata* and *música blanquinegra* become a part of Ortiz's repertoire. Before Guillén, in short, Ortiz's emphasis was on the Cuban black, not on the black Cuban or the mulatto Cuban, and on the "Afro" part of the term "Afro-Cuban"—an isolated, negative part at best.

Guillén's decision, then, during the late twenties and early thirties to write as a black about blacks and to blacks, and to whites and mulattoes, too, was an influential one that represented a new departure for himself and for his contemporaries. But what was the immediate impulse that brought him to that new commitment? Literary historians and Nicolás Guillén, too, usually point to a moment in 1930 when the words and rhythm of *negro bembón* came to the poet in a dreamlike trance after which the *Motivos de son* were written, dashed off, as it were, in white hot heat. But what put him in that trance in the first place? Angel Augier[23] in his well-documented background study to Guillén up to 1947 sees the collective unconsciousness at work here. This may well be true, but Guillén's new *racial* plan of attack was more than involuntary. We know that his turning point was inspired in part by his own personal experiences of racism, by his awareness of worsening economic conditions for blacks in Cuba, and by the control of the black literary and cultural image that was being taken over by white intellectuals like Fernando Ortiz and the *negrista* poets. We know also that Guillén had many local black models to emulate, including his father, Lino Dou, Juan Gualberto Gómez, and Gustavo E. Urrutia, the Director of "Ideales de la Raza," the black section of the *Diario de la Marina* where Guillén published much of his first work. But most of all, I believe, the black model or example set by Langston Hughes provided one of the most immediate sparks.

Langston Hughes, the dean of black poets in the United States, was already famous when he made his second trip to Cuba in February 1930. Guillén met Hughes on this trip, showed him around, and as a journalist published an interview he had with him that he called "Conversation with Langston Hughes" on 9 March 1930, in the *Diario de la Marina*. The very next month, on 20 April 1930, Guillén published his *Motivos de son*. For a black writer who had already begun to see that the black problem was really a white problem, the black pride and racial flavor of Langston Hughes' verse and manner had to have an impact on any black, certainly on one who writes. I think what moved Guillén deeper into his blackening process was Langston Hughes' physical or somatic appearance. In Guillén's words, Hughes "looked just like a little Cuban mulatto. One of those dandies who spends all his time organizing little family parties for two dollars a ticket."[24] This description, of course, is negative, but Guillén's appraisal of "this great Black poet," "one of the souls most interested in the black race," is overwhelmingly positive. The impact for Guillén, I believe, comes with the realization that Hughes, a mulatto like himself, could genuinely identify with blacks with a dedication so intense that his only concern "is to study his people, to translate their experience into poetry, to make it known and loved." When Guillén says that Langston Hughes is unique, we have to understand this statement to mean both Hughes' total concern "with everything related to blacks" and the fact that this concern can come from a mulatto.

In this same interview, Guillén says that the Hughes poem containing the words, "I am a Negro / Black as the night is black / Black like the depths of my Africa," makes him feel as though it "springs from the depths of my own soul." Guillén decided shortly after Hughes' departure to inject some authentic blackness into Cuban letters, from the bottom up. He decided, quite simply, that it was time for "The New Negro"[25] to make his appearance in Cuba as well. We should not forget that the twenties had been the decade of the world famous Harlem Renaissance, which influenced just about everybody who adopted a black perspective from that decade on, and Langston Hughes was at the center of that movement from its very beginning. Guillén himself writes about Harlem in an article, "Camino de Harlem," published in 1929, that can be seen as the starting point of his determination to bring to his country a corrective vision regarding Cuba's ethnic composition. It is this new vision that his poetry celebrates with himself at the center as a symbol of the mulatto nature of that ethnic composition. Guillén also was concerned that Cuba avoid taking the negative direction to which "going the way of Harlem" could lead. He did not want black Havana to become as black Harlem had become, a city within a city. He wanted the black recognized but at the same time fully integrated. Nor did he want the black to be a passing fancy, a danger he saw inherent in *negrismo* and perhaps in The Harlem Renaissance, which despite the authentic blackness of Langston Hughes and others, did contain some of the superficiality that white interest and involvement in the movement had fostered. Perhaps more interesting than Guillén's portrait of blacks is his self-portrait as one who resolves in his *son* all the racial and cultural contradictions of a black and white society. His own *mulatez* certainly resolves that conflict. He extends that personal identity through his mulatto verses to his country. That is why I think Langston Hughes' identification with blacks could not go unnoticed by Guillén, especially since the tendency in the Antilles was for mulattoes to identify or to align with whites. Guillén decided, in short, that in Cuba he would bring all the people together—black, white, and mulatto—through his concept of *mulatez*. This is the face Cuba has put on to the world ever since.

It is not surprising, then, that Guillén's conversion to blackness becomes complete shortly after Hughes' departure from the Island. Guillén even deleted an unfavorable reference to Langston Hughes that had appeared in the original 1929 version of his "Pequeña oda a un negro boxeador cubano," one accusing Hughes of being unconcerned about the black boxer.[26] Nor is it surprising to see the *Ltd.*

of Hughes' *Scottsboro Ltd.* (1932) reappear in Guillén's title *West Indies Ltd.* (1934), or to see Guillén try the *son*-form, which sometimes has a blues effect, considering Hughes' earlier success with blues and jazz forms in poetry. One also can see the striking similarity between Guillén's black credo in the prologue to his *Sóngoro cosongo* (1932), especially the part where Guillén says that it does not matter if people are not pleased with what he is doing, and Hughes' own well-known declaration of artistic and racial commitment published five years earlier. He wrote in that piece, "If white people are pleased we are glad. If they are not it doesn't matter . . . If colored people are pleased we are glad. If they are not their displeasure doesn't matter either."[27] Were it not for such credos firmly rooted in black ethnic identity, it is possible that the later revolutionary vision these two poets developed might not have been so intense. Guillén realized, as did Hughes, that "the very root of Fascism grows out of terrain fertilized by racial hatred and the division of men into inferior and superior beings and that he, the Negro, has been assigned the lowest place."[28] It was that indirect vested racial interest that carried them both to Spain to oppose fascism during the Spanish Civil War. The same concern prompts Guillén to care about the dispossessed of whatever color and to oppose what he sees as racist tinged United States imperialism. It is but a small step, then, from Guillén's early black poetry of his *Motivos de son* days— a point I will return to in chapter fourteen—to his current revolutionary poetry. The two are not as mutually exclusive as some would have us think.

I see a compatibility between Guillén poet of negritude and Guillén poet of revolutionary Cuba. Guillén need not have continued with the black talk of the *Motivos de son* to be considered a poet of negritude as Gordon Brotherston[29] and others seem to think. Nor was it necessary for him to abandon the black man to be considered a universal poet. Although Guillén now rejects the term negritude that he insists on seeing in its strictest sense, there can be little doubt that he was just as much a forerunner of the term in its strictest racial sense as he is now a leading exponent of what I have called elsewhere the negritude of synthesis, which is negritude understood in a broader sense that does not reject "a quest for an antiracist, possibly universal culture, 'the culminating point of the dream of every serious advocate of Negritude,' a universal brotherhood in which the black man will establish solidarity with all mankind."[30] The organization of this section on the Major Period reflects the central role Guillén played in the development of black consciousness and black literature in Latin America in the thirties and forties, when—under his influence—the black as author became just as visible as the black as subject. This period is major because of the high visibility given the black as author through the appearance of works like Pilar Barrios' *Piel negra* (1947) and Virginia Brindis de Salas' *Pregón de Marimorena* (1947) in Uruguay, Juan Pablo Sojo's *Nochebuena negra* (1943) in Venezuela. Adalberto Ortiz's *Juyungo* (1943) in Ecuador, and Jorge Artel's *Tambores en la noche* (1940) and Arnoldo Palacios' *Las estrellas son negras* (1949) in Colombia. These works and others such as Guillén's *El son entero* (1947) that follow his initiative of the thirties, made the forties especially a fertile decade for black writers in Latin America.

This, of course, is also the high period of poetic Negrism, or the black as theme in Spanish America. Negritude in the French Caribbean makes its major breakthrough in the late thirties and early forties. The forties especially are an important turning point for the black Brazilian who challenges "whitening" as an official policy. This challenge was led by the black consciousness group that grew up around the Experimental Black Theater, founded in 1944 by Abdias do Nascimento, who became to Brazil in the forties what Guillén had become to Cuba in the thirties: a challenge to the white aesthetic that betrayed the racial and cultural reality of his country. Nascimento, like Guillén, wanted to incorporate the black into the life of the country. He tried to bring about this transformation through the theater where he raised—not unlike Nicolás Guillén—"fists of steel to smash the hypocrisy of the white world,"[31] as he sought to elevate the black up from picturesque, secondary, and superficial parts to authenticity through starring roles. The plays this group put on included Nascimento's own *Sortilégio* (1953), his controversial and covertly racial play that was not performed until 1957. Nascimento continues his single-minded determination to force recognition of the Africanness of Brazilian society, though now from outside his country's repressive regime, as he has lived in the United States for the last few years.

Before the forties black Brazilian authors were known and recognized more for their artistry than for their ethnicity, and many literary historians rank highly Afro-Brazilian authors like Joaquim María Machado de Assis (1839–1908) and Joâo de Cruz e Sousa

(1862–98). This is not to say that ethnicity did not exist earlier in Brazil or that there is no artistry after the forties, only that racial affirmation then was not as dynamic or covertly visible as was the presence of nonblack characters and themes in the novels of Machado de Assis or the predominance of white symbols in the poetry of Cruz e Sousa. There always has been, to be sure, a current of sympathy for blacks running throughout Brazilian literary history from the pens of black and nonblack writers alike. Yet black writers in Brazil before Abdias do Nascimento and his Experimental Black Theater in the forties, as with black writers in Spanish America before Nicolás Guillén, for the most part did not dwell on blackness. Uruguay, close neighbor of Brazil, saw black consciousness developed in the thirties and forties through community organizations, poetry, and the publication of black journals, as we shall see in the following chapter.

The Black Writer, the Black Press, and the Black Diaspora in Uruguay

We have to learn to remember what the clouds cannot forget.

Nicolás Guillén

Black Cubans, particularly in the nineteenth century, used journalism and poetry to carry their ideas to the public. Well-known nineteenth century Afro-Cuban poets like Gabriel de la Concepción Valdés ("Placido"), Juan Francisco Manzano, and Antonio Medina and journalists like Juan Gualberto Gómez, Rafael Serra Montalvo, and Martín Morúa Delgado reached their fellow countrymen through their writings. This tradition continues in the twentieth century with black Cuban poets like Marcelino Arozarena, Regino Pedroso, and of course Nicolás Guillén, the latter well-known as both a poet and a journalist, a fact often overlooked in the English-speaking world.[1]

Journalism and poetry, particularly in the twentieth century, also are the two main vehicles of expression black Uruguayans have used to take their ideas to the public. In fact journalists and poets come together and often represent one and the same group, as black newspapers, magazines, and journals in Uruguay were the main outlet for black writers, many of them directors and collaborators of the publications in which their works appeared. Included in this group, which reached its pinnacle between 1933 and 1948—dates that represent the major period of the life of *Nuestra Raza*, the best known and most stable of the black publications in the country—are Pilar Barrios, the dean of Afro-Uruguayan poets who also played a leading role in the development of the black press of that country, Virginia Brindis de Salas, the leading black poetess in the country, and Juan Julio Arrascaeta, another prominent poet and journalist.

Although not as well known as their Afro-Cuban counterparts, these black figures together with Julio Guadalupe, Iris Cabral, Irica Pérez, Lino Suárez Peña, Isabelino José Gares, and others both associated with and outside the circle of "Nuestra Raza," were the core of much intellectual, social, and political activity in the black community in Uruguay during the thirties and forties. Those years were a thriving and significant period of "dynamic Africanity," of the Black Diaspora in action. Their efforts and achievements are on record in their published books and pamphlets as well as in the pages of black journals like *Nuestra Raza* and *Revista Uruguay*, the second most stable of the black journals at the time; however, the large body of work published by black writers in these black journals has not yet been given the attention it deserves. Any study of the Black Diaspora and the Afro-Latin American author must be based in part on the pages of these journals.

In these journals, blacks largely spoke "as blacks about blacks to blacks." Black writers in Uruguay have always spoken overtly from a racial perspective. Unlike in Panama, for example, where such early black writers as Simón Rivas and Gaspar Octavio Hernández clearly wrote outside the "black collectivity," expressing their ethnicity covertly as a result in personal and nationalistic poetry, the black writer and the black press in Uruguay, whose tradition of black consciousness dates back to the nineteenth century, had a very definite idea of group solidarity and ethnic identity. What can be called "the black absence" in early Panamanian literature, that is, literature by blacks but with no overt "black touch," is not applicable to black Uruguayan literature.

Yet it might come as a surprise to all but the specialist to learn of the activities of this once thriving black cultural, political, and literary center in Uruguay. The general reader would be hard-pressed to find a passing reference to black literary figures in that country in the standard Latin American anthologies and literary histories or even in local publications dealing exclusively with the Uruguayan literary scene.

Although Uruguay is often thought of as one of the white countries in Latin America, blacks have been in that country since slavery times. They were brought in largely through the port of Montevideo, one of the major ports of entry for the slave trade in Latin

America. Blacks also came into Uruguay through Brazil, first as slaves and later as immigrants. Blacks constituted fifty percent of the total population of Uruguay in the nineteenth century, a 'percentage that has dropped radically to less than two percent at the mid-twentieth century point. Yet, although Uruguay is now seen as one of the white countries of Latin America it is misleading to state, as Juan Comas recently did, that Uruguay "has absolutely no black or Indian population,"[2] especially since the same author quoting Rosenblatt puts the black and mulatto population in Uruguay in 1940 at sixty thousand.[3] Black Uruguayans themselves, refusing to become "invisible," strongly objected to references to Uruguay as "a people of Latin origin" with no Indians or blacks. A *Nuestra Raza* editorial published in September 1948 rejected and criticized a foreign broadcast for misrepresenting the country's racial history.

Objection to "invisibility" or omission had been voiced earlier in *Nuestra Raza*, in January 1947, when Alberto Britos, reviewing Emilio Ballagas, *Mapa de la poesía negra americana* (Buenos Aires: Edit. Pleamar, 1946) and José Sanz y Díaz, *Lira negra* (Madrid: Aguilar, 1945), lamented that those responsible for these collections had not taken the care to get their facts straight, writing off as they did the black in Uruguay as nonexistent. It naturally follows that if there are no blacks in Uruguay, then there are no black writers either. To correct that erroneous impression Britos wrote: "And we must also lament the absence [in those anthologies] of black poets like Pilar E. Barrios and Cardoza ... and others like Suárez and Guadalupe. Although they have not yet published their works in book form, the inclusion of these poets would have made such collections more valid" (p. 9). Even earlier, in July 1940, *Nuestra Raza* had objected, in an editorial entitled "Negros de aquí y de allá," to another "slight," this time to an exhibit of Uruguayan books in Río de Janeiro in which "not a single black writer was included" (p. 9).

Black writers in Uruguay have not been limited to creative literature. The enterprising reader, if he is fortunate enough to dig them out, can read historical, sociological and, literary essays by blacks about blacks in Uruguay. Like other blacks in their respective homelands—Juan Pablo Sojo in Venezuela, Quince Duncan in Costa Rica, Armando Fortune in Panama, Manuel Zapata Olivella in Colombia, Adalberto Oritz and Nelson Estupiñán Bass in Ecuador, and Nicomedes Santa Cruz in Peru, to name a few—blacks in Uruguay have written about themselves. The more available studies of the black in Uruguay are by Ildefonso Pereda Valdés, Carlos Rama, and Paulo de Carvalho Neto, but many others exist as well.

Essays by blacks published largely in the thirties and forties include Lino Suárez Peña, "Apuntes y datos referentes a la raza negra en Uruguay," Elemo Cabral, "El negro uruguayo," Marcelino Bottaro, "Rituales y candombes," Isabelino José Gares, "Contribución de la raza negra a la democracia de América," the literary criticism of Julio Guadalupe, the leading "prologuist" and literary historian of the group, and other shorter items he published in *Nuestra Raza* and in other journals over the years.

Uruguay never had twenty-five black periodicals such as existed at one time in Cuba in the latter half of the nineteenth century, but Uruguay did have black periodicals like *La Conservación* and *La Propaganda* in the nineteenth century and *Ecos del Porvenir, La Verdad, La Vanguardia, Nuestra Raza, Revista Uruguay, Rumbos,* and *Revista Bahía—Huland Jack* in this century. As in Cuba, many black organizations served the black community, most of them socially and culturally oriented and most, if not all, of the journals functioned as official organs of these organizations. Ateneo Booker T. Washington, for example, had as its official organ *Rumbos,* in the city of Rocha; the Asociación Cultural de la Raza Negra was associated with *Revista Uruguay*; and C.I.A.P.E.N., the prestigious and sometimes influential Círculo de Intelectuales, Artistas, Periodistas y Escritores Negros in Uruguay which, like the Casa de la Raza earlier, was affiliated with *Nuestra Raza.*

Of all these journals, it was *Nuestra Raza* and the group connected with it that, like Abdias do Nascimento's Experimental Black Theater Group and its journal *Quilombo* in the late forties in Brazil, formed the cultural headquarters of negritude in Uruguay. A prize-winning journal, *Nuestra Raza* published some of the first poems of many of the Afro-Uruguayan writers. *Nuestra Raza,* which ceased to publish in 1948, had the longest life, fifteen years, of the black journals in nineteenth and twentieth-century Uruguay. It was the focal point for black literary expression in the country with its publication of Afro-Uruguayan plays, poetry, short stories, book reviews, and scholarly articles. Its efforts in the thirties and forties in other directions to raise the level of black consciousness in its readers and contributors included support for black political candidates, the formation of a committee for justice in the Scottsboro case, support for an Art and Culture Hour, and calls for a university for blacks. In pursuit of its goal of fostering black consciousness and black pride, the journal devoted much of its space to commentary on black achievements outside the country. Articles abound on international black figures like Nicolás Guillén, Harrison Dillard, Jesús Menéndez, George Washington Carver, Booker T. Washington, Claude MacKay, Joe Louis, Jesse Owens, Langston Hughes, Marian Anderson, Antonio Maceo, Machado de Assis, Paul Robeson, Ethel Waters, René Maran, and Duke Ellington. The work published originated both from within the local black collectivity and from reprints, but in all cases the subject matter dealt with blacks in Uruguay or elsewhere.

The black press in Uruguay, as elsewhere, hoped that by reporting on the accomplishments and achievements of blacks locally and internationally they would raise the level of black awareness in the country and get blacks to organize in concerted efforts to bring about improvements in their lot through pressure group action, particularly in their fight against social injustice, racial stereotypes, and prejudice. The black press believed that by serving as a medium for black literary expression the intellectual and cultural level of the black community would improve. Character improvement was a prime concern to the black press, and for this reason much of their publication was directed toward the moral development of the black youth. Another objective of *Nuestra Raza* was to be "on the side of the people regardless of color." Despite its race orientation, and perhaps as a sign of the times, the black group in Uruguay represents an early example of "class more than race."

The intellectual focus of the journal was to reject the stereotype of the black as inferior. The journal stressed intellectual accomplishments over black achievements in sports and the arts, a preference seen in the numerous laudatory articles on George Washington Carver.

The "Nuestra Raza" group was confronted with a number of familiar problems befalling the race. We mentioned the problem of invisibility. The problem of a name also arose and a tendency among local blacks to refer to themselves as "one of the race" to avoid the use of black was blasted in a March 1945 commentary. The article pointed up the positive black consciousness demonstrated by such international figures as Richard Wright and Nicolás Guillén, who certainly were not reluctant to use the term black. On another occasion, black intellectuals in Uruguay strongly objected to the audacity of a white socialist leader from Argentina who came into the black community and, before a meeting of the Comité Pro Unidad de la Raza Negra (Committee on Black Unity), "in an eloquently improvised speech pointed out the absence of a racial problem in the countries of the Río de la Plata area, declaring himself convinced that in this region there exists no racial prejudice capable of dividing the national conscience." Editorials in the black press were quick to recognize the naïveté in his views.

On other occasions the black press, when dealing with another problem familiar in black history, namely, the white artist in blackface, had to use tact in order not to antagonize their white friends who, unlike some blacks, saw no wrong in whites assuming black roles in the theater. A review article, for example, of a recital by Hugo Devieri and his "partenaire" Goldi Flami, who had performed black literature in blackface, was called "Black art in quotation marks" (*Nuestra Raza*, July 1942, p. 6). *Nuestra Raza* was reluctant to accept wholeheartedly that kind of artificial performance.

The journal did have many white friends, some of whom published in it, including Jorge Amado and Ildefonso Pereda Valdés. The journal's struggles to overcome racist injustices and stereotypes perpetuated against black people inside as well as outside Uruguay led to a polite but running battle even with Pereda Valdés, the recognized white authority on the black in Uruguay. This sometime cultivator of what has been called "false black poetry" managed on occasion to insult blacks by contributing in his false black poetry to the outmoded image of the black as an exotic being (*africanización perpétua* or *perpetual Africanization*, it has been called). Moreover, he sanctioned the exclusion of black Uruguayan journals from a locally held international exhibit of black journals, publications, and artifacts he helped organize.

Black pride was one of the strong points of the journal, and several issues discuss and dismiss literary works such as those of Pereda Valdés that perpetuate stereotyped images of the black. One of these shots aimed at *africanización perpétua* associated with the false black poetry of the white negrista poets was fired by Mario L. Montero in a bold article entitled "We must firmly fight against negrism," and published in May 1946.

Another important statement against *negrista* works came from Isabelino José Gares in "Writers and the black race" (*Nuestra Raza*,

January 1935, pp. 4–5). Gares roundly criticized four white Uruguayan writers for distorting the image of the black of the past and for never dealing with the black "of the new generations." In condemning as guilty Eduardo Diestre, *Buscón, poeta y su teatro,* Ildefonso Pereda Valdés, *Raza negra,* Carlos Reyles, *Gaucho florido,* and Justino Zabala Muñiz, *Crónica de la reja,* Gares writes: "In this country, it has been about half a century since the disappearance of all of those local places where the Congo, Banguelas, and the Magi people, who have left no trace of their atavistic rites and customs, danced the candombe. This does not mean, by any means, that we deny or do not recognize our African origin, of which we are proud, but rather that time marches on and we have been moving ahead with the country" (p. 4). After specifying his charges, using as evidence the works of these authors themselves, he concludes: "I believe that there is an enormous contradiction between historical truth, and that which is written today" (p. 5).

The Círculo de Intelectuales, Periodistas, y Escritores Negros de Uruguay realized it could best advance its interests if all the many and fast proliferating black groups in the country organized for more cohesive and concerted black action. Accordingly, in 1945, a call went out for the formation of a "central coordinating committee for black groups" that would offer strength through unity. To this end, the Comité de Entidades Negras de Uruguay (CENU) was formed. This consolidation, though, came too late to take on a political role, for the Partido Autóctono Negro had dissolved for lack of support in 1937 after its candidate—supported by many black writers of the "Nuestra Raza" group—was roundly defeated. Perhaps because CENU lacked a political cause to absorb its energies, it was plagued by personal jealousies, leadership crises, "endless meetings and discussions," and what has been called "racial egoism"; the coalition eventually dissolved.

Before disbanding, one of the accomplishments of the CENU was to take steps to establish a Black Theater Group, and there was much interest in a continent-wide "Futuro Congreso Latinoamericano de la Raza Negra," in 1945 and 1946. But this, too, came to nothing. Try as they might, the black intellectual community leaders in Uruguay, despite what they saw as a clear need to band together, could never maintain the sustained level of black consciousness and cooperation required to bring the Uruguayan black community together in a permanent organization on the order of the NAACP that, like many other sources of inspiration from the United States, served as a model they emulated.

The use of black models from the United States, the wide publicity given the achievements of international black figures, many of them from the United States, and the constant reporting in the Uruguayan press of black activity in the United States lend credence to St. Clair Drake's[4] theory of a symbolic significance which he believes Afro-Americans have for black Latin Americans. The questions he raises, "What has been the nature of the interaction between the communities of the diaspora and The Homeland and between the various communities and what kind of conscious and deliberate cooperation has taken place?" take on enormous importance when we look at the relationship of Uruguay to the Black Diaspora. St. Clair Drake is correct in saying that the reciprocal relations between Afro-Americans in the United States and black people in the West Indies is a matter of crucial significance to diaspora studies. But the black community in Uruguay also clearly saw itself as part of a Unified Black World. They saw themselves as part of the same Black Diaspora that included the black community in the United States, one they knew even then "represented the largest, most compact, and best organized group in the Hemisphere that considers itself 'black'."[5]

The relationship of the black community in far-off Uruguay to the Black Diaspora is equally significant. A concrete illustration of this unified view of the black world in Uruguay is the name chosen for a local journal, Revista Bahía—Huland Jack, a name taken from the predominantly black state of Brazil and from a black New York politician. There was even a local club named after Booker T. Washington. The Partido Autóctomo Negro was a copy of the Brazilian counterpart of similar name. And in 1948 Ignacio Suárez Peña, Director of Revista Uruguay, was invited to serve on the Board of Directors of the Pan-African Association organized that year in the United States. The Bureau de Informaciones Panamericanas carried in Nuestra Raza was in reality a Bureau de Informaciones Panafricanas, as most of the information disseminated dealt with blacks, largely in the New World.

Uruguayan blacks kept abreast through their journals with black hardships and achievements in other parts of the black World, particularly in the United States. Langston Hughes and Nicolás Guillén, for example, were probably as widely read in Uruguay as in their home countries, and numerous articles on them plus selections from their work appeared in the local black press. In addition to interest in black literature and black figures in science, there was much interest in the black performing arts, in black music, and of course in black sports in the United States. Local black writers like Julio Guadalupe were extremely clear on heroic black participants in the making of the New World as he and others were well informed on the work and history of Plácido, Maceo, Falucho, Toussaint L'Ouverture, Henri Christophe and, closer to home, Ansina, Artiga's reliable companion, after whom a street is named in Uruguay.

The press was not the sole source for black awareness. Blacks from the outside—for example, Marian Anderson—visited Uruguay as well. The two visits that had the most impact—in my opinion—were those of Irene Diggs in 1946, followed the next year by that of Nicolás Guillén. The visit of Nicolás Guillén, widely reported in the black press as well as in the national press, to my knowledge has been chronicled in detail only by Angel Augier in his two-volume biography of the poet. Augier retraces Guillén's path through the many Latin American countries he visited partly on lecture tours, partly to correct proofs, and partly to promote his forthcoming books. Nicolás Guillén was, of course, lionized by the national press, but he made excursions into the black community in Uruguay where his speeches and recitals were well received, as there was much black identification with the Afro-Cuban poet.

Irene Diggs, the eminent professor who was on leave from Atlanta University at the time, while making a research trip through Latin America spent several months studying the black community in Uruguay. Her statements to a foreign press concerning her findings after she left the country aroused much indignation in the black community in Uruguay. The statement provoking the most ire was "The black race in Uruguay in general shows a visible cultural poverty." It was published in the Argentine journal *Qué*, 26 December 1946, and was reported in *Nuestra Raza* in January 1947.

Actually, her outspoken opinion caused resentment in some quarters less for what she said than because she said it, in a sense, behind their backs out of the country. She had talked to the black press and directly to black people through conferences, conversations, and public meetings in Uruguay without stating such views. In a bit of self-criticism, some commentators felt her opinions would have been different and more positive if instead of being lavishly entertained she had been exposed to contacts more befitting and more beneficial to a scholar who had come all that way to do research.

Yet the "Nuestra Raza" group in reprinting her remarks was quick to agree with her overall judgment regarding "cultural poverty" as it related to the journal itself. The previous fourteen years had been spent preaching organization and improvement to the black community during a period when "university graduates isolated themselves and looked on from afar." Echoing the words of their sister magazine *Revista Uruguay, Nuestra Raza* spokesmen wrote in March 1947 that Diggs' opinion "was not far off the mark. She didn't tell us anything we did not already know."

Black intellectuals, then, were aware, as Diggs became aware, that blacks in Uruguay still had a long way to go to overcome their "cultural lack." The Diggs episode also points up the differences between Latin America and the United States in black education. Black institutions and universities do not exist in Uruguay or elsewhere in Latin America. By acknowledging the prevailing official line on race in Latin America that holds that there is no prejudice, discrimination, or segregation and then wondering—aloud, in the Buenos Aires press—why without such barriers blacks there had not progressed more along the lines of the United States, where despite these barriers blacks had achieved, Diggs, in a sense, called attention to the fact that in the United States blacks knew they were separate legally and that they had no choice but to set up separate institutions and universities if they were to have any chance at all for survival. On the other hand, blacks in Uruguay and elsewhere in Latin America had no recourse to these survival outlets because since officially no racial barriers existed then separate facilities were not required. Throughout Latin America, benign neglect and miscegenation led to a false sense of security and a false consciousness in Latin America that, as St. Clair Drake has said, "prevents effective struggle." This absence of struggle in turn minimizes emergence of a Black Aesthetic, at least in the Black Nationalist sense.

Black intellectuals in Uruguay in the forties were unable to pinpoint what they called the "psychological phenomenon that reigns among blacks" that kept the black community in that country from duplicating the positive achievements of their symbolic black brothers in the United States. I do not believe the "Nuestra Raza" group was ever able to understand the problem. Their efforts were hindered by the gradual passing away of prominent members of the group and the subsequent decline of the black press occasioned in part by the deaths of key figures.

Many women were key figures in *Nuestra Raza*. Although many prominent black men of letters were identified with *Nuestra Raza* it was the black woman who was a major contributor, inspiration, and strength behind the journal. Nowhere is woman a better complement to man (to paraphrase Octavio Paz) than in this publishing venture in Uruguay. The dominant figure was María Esperanza Barrios who was founder of the enterprise in 1917 in the first period of the journal and who remained a spiritual force behind the scenes during the second period of *Nuestra Raza* when her brother Pilar took over as director in 1939. It was María Esperanza Barrios who in 1917 "saw in the press a weapon for the social battles an impoverished race must fight."

In the early thirties and forties a surprisingly large number of contributions and editorials were written by promising black female writers like Irica Pérez and Iris Cabral, who were also concerned with raising the cultural and intellectual level of the black community. Many of these women were very outspoken, and their interest in racial and social equality at that time led them as black women, for example, to defend Ethiopia as a black independent State and to challenge the white woman to stand shoulder to shoulder with them in a show of solidarity in public declarations commemorating the centenary of the abolition of slavery. The work of black women in the life of the journal was publicly lauded in an article by Carlos Cardoza Ferreira in October 1944.

After the death of Iris Cabral, "the top woman" and one of the "strongest pillars in the fight for the evolution and improvement of our race," and other collaborators who gave so much of their time and intelligence, the decline of the journal set in. But the impetus had already been given to poets like Pilar Barrios and Virginia Brindis de Salas who emerged in the black community as major literary figures who continued to publish their work, but in book form.

Pilar Barrios can be considered the Dean of black writers in Uruguay, and, together with his family, he was also associated with *Nuestra Raza* from the beginning. Many of his poems were first published in this journal, and it was *Nuestra Raza* that first undertook the publication of his poems in book-length collections. Much of his poetry had the same theme and ideology as found in the jour-

nal: Black pride, liberty, equality, and fraternity are combined in his
poetry with antiwar sentiments, a hatred of injustice and tyranny,
and—a sign of the times—fascism. Barrios' range is wide. The poet
gives encouragement in his verse—as he did in the journal—to
black youth to develop their intellect, ideas, and creativity. There is
praise of the black woman in his poetry, particularly the black
woman as mother, especially in his "Poema de la madre." Black
heroes past and present and other black achievers populate his
poems. Many of his topics have been constant concerns since young
adulthood, and Barrios himself has pointed out in an autobiographical statement and in a published interview that certain interests he showed when he first started to write poetry at the age of
eighteen still appear in his verse.

Of all the black writers in Uruguay, Pilar Barrios is the only one
whose work is relatively available as the three volumes of poetry he
published between 1947 and 1959 were reprinted in one volume by
Kraus Reprint in 1970. This one-volume reprint includes his *Piel
negra, Poesías 1917–1947* (Montevideo, 1947), *Mis cantos* (Montevideo, 1949), and *Campo afuera* (Montevideo, 1959). This "true
pillar of the race as his name indicates" (*Piel negra*, p. 4), regardless
of his range of topics has always kept race and race persecution in
the forefront of his themes. Much of his verse sings of the "intenso
dolor de una raza / que ha sufrido el mayor vilipendio" ["intense
pain of a race / that has suffered the greatest contempt"] ("Mis versos," *Piel negra*, p. 21).

One of the obsessions of the poet, like that of the journal, was the
need to plead recognition for black intelligence, a subject he approaches in "La idea," a poem reminiscent in construction, I believe,
to some of the work of Pablo Neruda. The poet follows up "La
idea" with "Poema de la madre" where he writes that " . . . lo real
y cierto / es que los hijos de la raza blanca / como los hijos de la
raza negra / nacen . . . / llenos de inteligencia y de talento" [" . . .
what is real and certain / is that the sons of the white race / like the
sons of the black race / are born . . . / full of intelligence and talent"]
(*Piel negra*, p. 53). Intelligence is also a concern in "Siembra",
"Siembra bondad, nobleza e idealismo, / riega y siembra la luz, la
inteligencia" ["Sow kindness, nobility and idealism / irrigate and
sow light, intelligence"] (*Piel negra*, p. 99), and again in "¡Negra!"
perhaps his most bitter indictment of society's perpetuation of racism.

Refuting the "myth of the Negro past," Barrio makes perhaps his major statement on the black race, black intelligence, and a world of peace and brotherhood free from prejudice in "La leyenda maldita." He begins by proclaiming, "Raza negra, noble raza; / raza humilde, sana y fuerte" ["Black race, noble race; / humble race, healthy and strong"] and proceeds to trace the black uprooted from Mother Africa "amplio, fértil y ardoroso" ["ample, fertile and hot"] and the planting of the "fatídica leyenda" ["fateful legend"] that branded the black inferior. Barrios shows that the falsehood has persisted despite advances in science that prove the contrary and despite the achievements of the black race itself in such fields as art, music and science. Barrios' message, like that of Senghor, for example, is clear, namely, that the day will come when the black race and the "magnificent lands of Africa" will take their place in the community of men and civilizations.

The poetry of Pilar Barrios, like the journal, was directed to the black youth of the country, an appropriate target for anyone whose concern was for the future of the race. In "Exhortación" he admonishes, "¡Eleva juventud, tu pensamiento! / ... ¡En marcha juventud! ¡siempre optimista! " ["Young people, cultivate your mind / ... Get on the move! And always be optimistic"] (*Piel negra*, p. 103), a theme he repeats in "Raza negra" and in "Tema racial," which he specifically dedicates to young people. He closes this poem with a rousing call to black youth to emulate the "glorious lives" of great black figures.

Some of the names evoked in "Tema racial" also appear in other poems by Barrios who, like the journal, felt a strong affinity to black people in the diaspora. In "Voces" he states pointedly his admiration for Langston Hughes:

Langston Hughes hermano,
hermano de raza
y también por ser hombre
    y humano,
mi admiración te alcanza.
    (*Piel negra*, p. 37)

Langston Hughes you are my brother
because you are black
and also because you are a man
    and a human being,
I admire you.

Unlike Nicolás Guillén, Langston Hughes did not make that long trip to Uruguay even though he did visit many countries in the Hispanic world. Hughes did, however, correspond by letter with Pilar Barrios in an expression of gratitude for the copy of *Piel negra* the black Uruguayan poet sent him.

The only other black writer in the diaspora Barrios devoted a full poem to was Nicolás Guillén. In a poem entitled simply "Nicolás Guillén," Barrios refers to the Afro-Cuban poet's

Voz vigorosa y singular
de América,
con vibraciones saturadas
de Africa.
        (*Piel negra*, p. 68)

Vigorous and singular voice
of America,
with vibrations saturated
with Africa.

The "message of love and of hope" and the "fraternal message" of Nicolás Guillén impressed the Uruguyan poet greatly, coinciding as they did with his own hopes and ideals.

The black New World past, from historical heroes ("Ansina," *Piel negra*, pp. 83–85) to the "unbelievable tragedy" of slavery ("Martirologio," *Piel negra*, pp. 97–98), is ever present in the poetry of Pilar Barrios. There are numerous references to the African past and to the "voices of Africa" in the New World, as in the following poem, "La voz del tamboril," not collected in his books but reprinted in Nestor Ortiz Oderigo, *Aspectos de la cultura africana en el Río de la Plata* (Buenos Aires: Editorial Plus Ultra, 1947):

Suenan los tamboriles
con su ritmo sin par,
y hay mil evocaciones
en su intenso vibrar;
hay rumores de jungla,
luz y ardor tropical;
nostalgias y añoranzas
de la tierra natal.

Son las voces del Africa
condensadas allí,
con sus llantos y ritmos,
su canto y su reír;
como si un gigantesco
y sonoro clarín
volcara la estridencia
de la selva sin fin.   (p. 147)

The little drums resound
with their incomparable rhythm,
and there are a thousand evocations
in their intense vibrations;
there are sounds of the jungle,
light and tropical ardor;
nostalgias and longing
for their native land.

The voices of Africa
are condensed there,
with its cries and rhythms,
its song and laughter;
it is as if a gigantic
and sonorous clarinet
poured out the stridency
of the endless jungle.

This poem, I believe, has more movement and more soft rhythm than any of the poems published in his books. By soft rhythm I mean a musical cadence brought on by Spanish prosody (here a dominant *tipo anapéstico* stress pattern combined with verses of seven syllables—surprisingly—alternating *agudo* rhymes, two features found in Darío's "Sonatina") rather than by the hard driving rhythm of the African or *Poesía negra* beat.

Blackness ("Hombre negro"), slavery ("Esclavitud"), and particularly brotherhood ("Fraternidad") continue to occupy the poet in his second book of poems *Mis cantos*, which he published in 1949, two years after *Piel negra*. One feels that the theme of brotherhood, or "the most lasting kind of solidarity," in particular, is intensified in this volume as the poet, as Martín Morúa Delgado had done, puts more faith in the white man, increasingly depending on the good will of his white brother to bring about change and equal rights for all. Though continuing to be a strong exponent of black identity and black pride, Barrios, nevertheless, does renounce black hatred in favor of a universal solidarity that places him on the side of the oppressed whatever their color, a humanistic vision he had already put across in simple language in his "Hermano blanco."

Shifting his focus almost completely, Barrios published in 1959 *Campo afuera*, a collection of poems written in gaucho dialect that he calls his "homage to the gaucho," who, to the black poet, represents "the maximum custombristic expression of my land" (p. 6). A couple of these poems, nevertheless, are of interest to the black theme; "Yo opino así" (p. 22) in particular emphasizes that there were black gauchos, a fact not widely known. In this poem Barrios, by insisting on one of his central themes, namely, the greatness of the black race and its capacity for intellectual expression, blends gaucho *contrapunteo* with *décima* form and black pride:

. . . .

Soy sí un humilde cantor que no tiene pretenciones pero sí, predilecciones por la raza de color. Raza que tengo el honor y orgullo e' pertenecer, porque creo comprender por lo que he visto y sentido, que ha naide le está prohibido inteligente nacer. (p. 24)	I am indeed a humble singer who has no pretentions but I do have predilections for the colored race. A race to which I have the honor and pride of belonging, because I believe I understand from what I have seen and heard, that there is no law against anyone being born intelligent.

The poems in this collection, written in impeccable gaucho dialect (complete with "bota e potro, chiripá y rebenque" [p. 7]) contrast sharply with his black poems in that nowhere does Barrios in his previous two volumes resort to black dialect. Since he wanted to present the black as an achiever he perhaps tried to stay as far away from the colloquial as possible. The gaucho poems contrasted sharply with his earlier work in form as well as in content because most of his poetry, some of which dates back to Modernism, was written, like much Modernist poetry, largely within the established, traditional forms with very little of the free verse and short lines that characterized Vanguardist poetry. But the long ponderous lines of Barrios with few exceptions generally show little of the multiple play with the established forms that produced the verbal music associated with Rubén Darío and others. Normally putting his points across simply, Barrios occasionally resorts to erudite allusions, some striking of Romantic bombast, such as Febo's awakening ("Mi oración," p. 72) and "la voz del Vesubio . . . las risas del Rin" ["the voice of Vesubio . . . the laughter of the Rhine"] ("Sombras inquietantes," p. 29).

Although he does speak of Febo's "dorados rayos / como un mantón de púrpura" ["golden rays / like a purple cloak"] that cover "las azuladas aguas" ["the azure waters"] (*Nuestra Raza*, Dec. 1940, p. 11), Barrios was not an ardent painter of literary colors. He certainly did not share the cult of whiteness that was the trademark of the Afro-Panamanian Modernist poet Gaspar Octavio Hernández. Pilar Barrios, however, did count on white cooperation in the future world, a hope that makes some of his "brotherhood" poetry appear naïve in its insistent lecturing and preaching of an idealistic gospel. We have to wonder how fruitful was his approach for the black in Uruguay who continued to suffer from indifference, or benign neglect, it is now called.

The poetry of Virginia Brindis de Salas comes closer to shaking the famous black fist. One of the few black women to publish books of poetry in Latin America, Brindis de Salas takes a stronger stance than that of Pilar Barrios. Her poetry, like that of Pilar Barrios, can serve as a thematic model for black literary expression in Latin America as it develops the identification with blackness, the rejection of white racism, and the emphasis on universal solidarity now recognized as central themes of negritude. The black pride she feels and fosters in her people, especially in Uruguay, her acceptance of the black man and his heritage, and her rejection of white supremacy are combined, quite forcefully, with a confidence she has in a future where universal fraternity will reign.

Virginia Brindis de Salas is less accommodating than Pilar Barrios; there is more protest in her poetry. Launching strong attacks against society, Brindis de Salas seems to be prepared to fight to change things. She does not seem willing to wait until the hearts of men change; rather she seems to be prepared to lift a forceful hand to help bring about that change. Though looking to the future she does not forget the past, or more importantly, the present. In general, her poetry has the rhythm and hardness of defiant blackness, and when she resorts to black talk as in "Canto para un muchacho negro americano del sur" it is certainly not for comic effect.

Even her second volume of poetry, *Cien cárceles de amor* (Montevideo, 1949), which contains some love poetry, takes a hard line as, for example, in "Abuelito Mon":

Poco paga el yanqui ya	Little does the Yankee pay now
por este millón de cañas	for these million sugarcanes
que el negro sembró y cortó.	that the black sowed and cut.
Mas no me trago este trago,	But I won't stand for it
porque es trago de sudor. (p. 21)	because it was too hard earned.

And again in "Negro: siempre triste":

Yo negro soy	I am a black
Porque tengo la piel negra	because I have black skin
¡Esclava no! Yo nací de	But I am not a slave! I was
vientre libre. (p. 32)	born of a free womb.

Though this second volume is somewhat more verbose than the first, her poems, unlike those of Pilar Barrios, are compact compositions generally with short, fast moving rhythmical lines with hardly any reliance on regular or traditional forms and rhyme schemes. This freedom is understandable considering the popular and communicative flavor of much of her poetry.

With rare exceptions there was little of the *poesía negra* "black talk" in Afro-Uruguayan verse. The only consistent exception can be found in the poetry of Juan Julio Arrascaeta, who Ildefonso Pereda Valdés finds to be "the most representative poet of his race insofar as negritude is concerned, but not a negritude of social concern, which is not evident in his poetry, but because of the colloquial tendency of his style which reproduces the linguistic habits of his ancestors."[6] Here Pereda Valdés reduces negritude to colloquial black talk as if this black movement had nothing to do with "social concern." It is clear from Pereda Valdés' writings that Arrascaeta is his favorite Uruguayan black poet. It is also clear this preference is because Arrascaeta conforms to what Pereda Valdés believes a black poet should be, namely, one who specializes in what he calls "simplicity and pleasant ingenuousness"[7] which is what this black Uruguayan poet is noted for, especially in the verses Pereda Valdés chooses to highlight, such as Arrascaeta's "Samba bo" which includes such colloquial-sounding speech as

> Samba . . . bé
> Samba . . . bé
> Samba e Catimba.

This excerpt is one of the only two Pereda Valdés cites in his *El negro en el Uruguay*. It is obvious that Pereda Valdés admires the poetry of Arrascaeta as he reserves the largest part of the Uruguayan section of his *Antología de la poesía negra americana* for this poet. Pereda Valdés, overlooking all the poetry of Pilar Barrios and Virginia Brindis de Salas, chose as his other sample to illustrate Afro-Uruguayan poetry a fragment from José Suárez, who "does not direct his black protest against whites or against capitalist oppressors but against his own people."[8] Rougher on his people even than Nicolás Guillén in "Sabás," Suárez writes in this sample:

¡Negro!
Bajo la comba del cielo
¡Densa bruma
dentro de tu cerebro
¡Densa niebla!
Todo delante tu vista . . . !

Black man!
on this earth
you have thick fog
inside your brain
Dense fog!
And with the whole world before
    you . . . !

But like Nicolás Guillén in "Sabás," Suárez seems to crystallize in concrete language the nagging problem confronting the black intellectual in Uruguay who tried to get his people on the move by calling attention to some of the obstacles both personal and institutional that stood in their way.

The only other black poet in Uruguay, in addition to Barrios, Arrascaeta, and Brindis de Salas, to appear in any anthology anywhere is Carlos Cardoza Ferreira, and the one poem that represents his work is his "Canto a Ethiopia." This poem, which begins "Tengo un canto fervoroso, / *Ethiopia*, / para tus hijos indómitos" ["I have a fervent song for you, / *Ethiopia*, / one for your unconquerable sons"], is another sign of the times, and like the Committee Against Fascism formed in the Uruguayan black community during World War Two, it represents another example of black admiration of and identification with Ethiopia's heroic and obstinate stance against first Mussolini and then Hitler's fascism.

There are other black writers in Uruguay, and works by and

about them have appeared in their local black press. Perhaps none of them was more respected and productive than the poet, playwright, and essayist Isabelino José Gares. We have already mentioned his prize-winning study "Contribución de la raza negra a la democracia de América" (1930). We mentioned, too, his article "los escritores y la raza negra" (1935) in which he shows himself to be a responsible and alert guardian of the black man's literary image, too often distorted by white writers. Gares was also a poet, but he was probably better known as a dramatist who, Pereda Valdés tells us, had one of his plays, *El camino de la Redención*, performed at the Teatro Albéniz, 5 October 1935. This play, according to the review of it in *Nuestra Raza*, has an interracial theme.

Earlier that year *Nuestra Raza* had run an article entitled "An hour of pleasant conversation with Isabelino José Gares—a great fighter for the black race" (April 1935), the result of an extensive interview with this "writer, journalist, dramatist" who had published his first theatrical work in 1912. His last play, *La vorágine* (1937), was reviewed in *Nuestra Raza* on 28 February 1937. This play, which deals with the "depopulation of the black race in the rural areas," was published three years before his death.

With his death, as we said earlier, and that of other oustanding blacks, many of them active collaborators in the work of *Nuestra Raza* and other black journals in Uruguay, the presence of this pocket of Africanity was diminished. An editorial in *Nuestra Raza* in March 1942 is a poignant reminder of the neglect they suffered: "The little known influence of the black press in Uruguay, whose existence dates back more than forty years, has still not been assessed. Because of its progressive nature it deserves the attention of the people of this country . . . " (p. 2). We could add to this assessment by reaffirming that the black press and the black author in Uruguay deserve the attention of anyone interested in the Black Diaspora and Afro-Latin American literature.

Juan Pablo Sojo and the
Black Novel in Venezuela

> *The same old story
> and the same old tune
> under
> the Barlovento moon.*
> Nicolás Guillén

The year 1948 marked not only the death of *Nuestra Raza* but also that of Juan Pablo Sojo, the Afro-Venezuelan author who in 1935 came to Caracas from the town of Curiepe with the manuscript of *Nochebuena negra*, which he completed in 1930 at the age of twenty-two, in his possession. Though Sojo did not publish it until 1943, his black novel antedates not only better known black novels in Venezuela, including Arturo Uslar Pietri's *Las lanzas coloradas* (1931), Guillermo Meneses' *Canción de negros* (1934), Rómulo Gallegos' *Pobre negro* (1937), and Ramón Díaz Sánchez's *Cumboto* (1950), but also the high period of *poesía negra* and black literary expression in the thirties and forties when Luis Palés Matos, Nicolás Guillén, and others made black fashionable in the Antilles. It is perhaps understandable that Sojo's *Nochebuena negra* generally has been overlooked because Rómulo Gallegos, the "undoubted king of Venezuelan fiction"[1] dealt with the same Barlovento region in his *Pobre negro*. But Sojo's novel is less exotic and more authentically black than Gallegos', as the view he gives us of the region is that of a black author who writes of lived experiences. The experiences he narrates, including black-white confrontation, miscegenation, the exploitation of black people and black labor, even the way he does it, which includes at times the magical and poetic treatment

of black life and superstition, have become standard fare in Venezuelan literature on black themes. But Sojo's novel generally is free
from the overbearing didactic messages so readily obvious, for example, in *Pobre negro* and in *Cumboto*. This does not mean, however, that *Nochebuena negra* is not polemical. Sojo's novel, however
lyrical, is muted protest against an economic structure that forever
relegates blacks to the bottom where there is little hope for change.

Nocheuena negra is an exposé of the white man's infamous
deeds in the Barlovento region where he came in and enriched himself at the expense of the black man through trickery, treachery,
"legal" expulsion, false documentation, and other criminal acts, including murder. Sojo's novel deals with black peasantry as the author focuses on the *conuqueros*, the peasants of African descent in
Venezuela, whose work as field hands constitutes the backbone of
that country's plantation agriculture. The rural area, not the city, is
the core of this novel, and the hard work required of these peasant
workers "dripping with sweat"[2] under the heavy sacks they carry is,
in fact, not as objectionable to them as are the overbearing, insensitive, and unappreciative white overlords in control of the land.

The novel expresses much black pride among the peasants in their
achievement as farmers working the land. The indictment, though
not an hysterically bitter one, is levelled at the overbearing power,
presence, and privilege of the white landowners who usurped the
holdings of the "poor natives" (p. 306), some of whom were then
forced out and into Caracas where "at least living poorly they will
find more tranquility than dying here" (p. 306). The author emphasizes that life in Caracas was difficult for black men and even worse
for black women (p. 277). The primary focus of the novel is the
"great tragedy of the farm worker" (p. 134), who works from sunup
to sundown "curved like the letter C" (p. 134). A secondary consideration is that nothing changes, and it is this unchanging nature of
the timeless toil involved in a kind of life whose routine stifles initiative and kills ambition for those who want out that blankets the
atmosphere of the area "like a death shroud" (p. 312). In sum, it is
a novel of how blacks were transformed from landowners to peasants working for "The Man."

Nochebuena negra opens with the arrival of Luis Pantoja, nephew
of Don Gisberto, The Man in this novel, who, as an absentee land-
lord, sends his nephew in to administer the plantation and to reduce
the authority of Crisanto Marasma, the old mulatto foreman, who,

together with his workers, had been responsible for the prosperity of the *cacao* crop. But Luis wants even more efficiency and lower salaries for the peasant workers, and we immediately are witness to the confrontation between this tough, unlettered but proud pillar of the black community and the administrative cunning of the relative of the owner. The ensuing confrontation results in a temporary loss of respect for the old man who, forced to accept changes, was held in contempt by the men he commanded, who felt he had sold out. Very little happens during the three-month time span of the novel, for most of the dramatic events had already happened before the novel begins and are retained in the memory of the old man. Other events, equally drastic insofar as character fate is concerned, are summed up in the last chapter which is set ten years after the previous chapter.

Characters appear in the novel fully developed and set in their ways and reputations, particularly old Crisanto, "an honorable and courageous man" (p. 96) who is, in a sense, a modern Afro-Venezuelan *griot*, certainly a village elder who was a living repository or keeper of the secrets and history of the region and the people—black and white—who inhabit it. The obsession he has with passing his knowledge on to his son Pedro, who had left the area but whose impending return shapes the narrative direction for the first half of the novel, makes Sojo's work a novel of ethnic memory sustained by the remembrances first by Crisanto and later by Pedro. In a fascinating chapter " . . . Lo que Crisanto sabía," Sojo narrates how blacks were duped out of their land by whites who played on their superstitions, fears, and beliefs. In that chapter Sojo writes:

> No one in Barvolento knew more stories than Crisanto Marasma. Through his imagination passed the names of all the natives and strangers, their virtues and their miseries, residing in those regions. Only he understood the mute and tragic sufferings of all those untiring arms, of those worn out faces, of those frightened eyes, full of fear and superstition. . . .
>
> Crisanto Marasma sat thinking, thinking with his eyes closed, lulled to sleep by memories and by the deafening roar of the sea, seated like a black patriarch . . . (pp. 73–74).

And this is why Crisanto anxiously awaited the return of his son so that he could tell him the many things he knew about the "kings of cocoa," whose complicated past "is replete with dark tales of spoilage and bloody crimes. He would say: 'My son will know it all . . . ! ' " (p. 99).

Crisanto's "Listen to me, son . . . " were opening words that prefaced the many stories he had to pass on to his son, stories that in the narrating cleared up in his mind "that instinctive hate which he could not himself explain but which he continued to feel for all those men . . . " (p. 165). Ethnic memory was important to Crisanto—and to Pedro—because he did not want history to go on repeating itself, especially where his son was concerned. Crisanto felt an "immense pity" (p. 137) for the other peasants who "had grown old and gray in those farms built with the strength of their own arms" (p. 67). But his primary concern was that things be different for his son, that "those calluses would not harden his son's hands" (p. 134). For this reason Pedro, born the son of day laborers but who wanted no part of that life, left the area, taking steps to break the circle; he would return, however.

Pedro's actual return to his roots, to his *terruño*, together with his impending return and his father's ethnic memory, constitute one of the major organizing principles of the novel. He exists partly as representative of a new generation and partly, through his father, as a link with the past. Pedro, to be sure, was more a dreamer than a militant or rebel, but a thoroughly independent dreamer who believed himself to be "a vindicator of all the miseries that he saw around him" (p. 273). Pedro perhaps can be seen as symbolic Redeemer, or at least one who commiserated as did his father with the hardships of those who were unable to leave the area. Pedro is hardly the fiery dogmatist, and his persuasiveness is more the example he sets than political statement. His role is underplayed in the novel perhaps in keeping with the poetic nature of his presence.

Sojo establishes a very clear contrast between Pedro and Tereso, another black character who, like Pedro, had gone to Caracas but for the wrong reasons. Pedro had gone to prepare himself through education for future service to his community to which he had always planned to return. But Tereso, who rarely gave his *terruño* a second thought, became a dandy who took a *novia* who was "white, as he aspired to be" (p. 149). Once back home, Pedro wants to "stay here always" (p. 274), but for Tereso "there is no place like the capital" (p. 274). Sojo makes it clear that all of the things Tereso holds dear mean nothing to Pedro. Sojo's message emerges from the contrast of the two characters: one must try to better oneself, but one must not lose sight of oneself. Pedro was unwilling, despite his attraction to the white Consuelo, to lose sight of himself completely as he could not forget her spiritual ties with the "kings of cocoa" that he despised.

Consuelo is really the only sympathetic white character in the novel, perhaps because she was willing to take steps to break the circle of opinion that believed a superior position was held by the white race. She tried to take a stand against this tradition and against her family by opting for Pedro and by rejecting a marriage they had prearranged for her with an old colonel. This effort was blocked by her aunt who, with her "prejudices of a landholder," (p. 205) took Consuelo away from the area and out of Pedro's reach, a final reminder that he was not good enough.

Sojo seems to be saying two things with regard to his treatment of their relationship: first, that Pedro, with symbolic reservations conditioned by ethnic memory, resisted "the desire that eats away at every black: to have a white woman" (p. 236)—and again the contrast with Tereso; second, that their inability to relate to each other free from race and class consideration indicates that they are tragic victims of a history that Pedro, through his father, is admonished to remember. The temptation to link these two characters by a force "stronger than their own will" (p. 304) exists but is rejected by the author, and this rejection sets his novel, and Pedro and Consuelo in particular, apart from Gallegos's *Pobre negro* where another Pedro, the mulatto Pedro Miguel, and the white Luisana unite symbolically. Their union, Gallegos makes dogmatically clear, as does Ramón Díaz Sánchez through a similar union in his *Cumboto*, augured well for the future of race relations in the country. But this is a viewpoint Sojo with his inside view and understanding of history is uncertain about.

There are many other characters—black and white—in the novel, among them Emeterio, a proud outspoken black, and his girl friend, Deogracia, a "black Venus" (p. 32), daughter of Crisanto and coveted by Luis Pantoja. Emeterio was one of the black peasants conscripted for army duty with Luis's aid so that the latter could, in Emeterio' absence, better "usurp" his girl friend. There is Lino Bembetoyo, a lively colorful *decimista* with the power—he thought—to cast magic spells. There is, of course, Don Gisberto who "like all masters, was unjust and deaf to reason" (p. 14). Don Gisberto was the first of his line to get rich off black peasant labor. Luis Pantoja, "Luisito," his nephew, is the butt of jokes as the new, inexperienced administrator of the hacienda to the black peasants, but a dangerous joke, for although he was "a sick lad, burnt out and spent by whirlwind affairs and late hours . . . a hopeless case" (p. 42), he was the nephew of Don Gisberto the "absolute master."

Sojo presents the white characters in the novel with understanding. Even when some of them appear as fools or religious fanatics they are believable and not caricatured. Luis, for example, the sickly vice-ridden overbearing white with useful connections to the police, was given the benefit of the doubt even by Emeterio and Crisanto, those most affected by his lust for Deogracia. Lino Bembetoyo, though insulted by Luis' overbearing arrogance, was tolerant of him despite the "mask of civilization" (p. 47) [white education] which he and others like him born "in better economic conditions" (p. 141) used to subjugate blacks. There is some reference in the novel, for contrast, to another white type: those who identify with the area by casting their lot with it; those who till the land and not just exploit the blacks who work it.

Sojo, as we intimated above, is especially adept at setting up contrasts. He works out his indictment through contrast:

> Crisanto had begun to eat his lunch, and watching the workers eat, he began to think of the administrators who, at that same time, were also eating in the office a meal so different from the poor one the workers were eating here on the ground. (p. 64)

And again, this time regarding the forced conscription that befalls the less fortunate:

> Don Luis was relaxing, smoking and drinking brandy. On his bed, an open book. The lastest novel of some French author . . .
>
> At that same hour, huddled in a room where neither light nor air could enter, many men cried silently. . . . Why that evil practice? What had they done? They had not killed or robbed anyone. (p. 76)

A particularly effective contrast is set against the background of La fiesta which takes place while a funeral procession is passing by:

> While Reyes was dying out there on the mountain, his face to

the ground, giving his last kiss to the earth, in the office pious projects were being drawn up and the owners were being praised..., (pp. 165–166)

As its title suggests, *Nochebuena negra* is a religious novel, with such religious observances as Nochebuena and the Semana Santa framing its structure. The contrast between true Christians and hypocrites, perhaps, represents the most important contrast of all since true Christianity is more related to the plight of the poor and "sufferings of the humble" (p. 205).

Carrying biblical significance a bit farther, one is tempted to see in Pedro a kind of Saviour or Messiah, the symbolic Redeemer we mentioned earlier, in the largest sense of the word. In this image of redemption, the novel suggests similarities to *Cane* (1923)—Jean Toomer's black masterpiece that is fast becoming recognized as an American classic. Toomer's work, which includes the poem "Song of the Son," announces the coming or return of a redeeming son or Black Messiah. Further, there are similarities in language, in structure, and especially in subject matter: *Cane* also focuses on black peasantry, but in the American South, where their attachment to the land is as strong as among black peasants in Venezuela. *Cane* also emphasizes like *Nochebuena negra* the importance of remembering the black past, particularly in the New World, so that the New World experience of slavery and oppression will never be repeated.

Just as Jean Toomer was "the first writer of the twenties to delineate Southern Black peasant life perceptively,"[3] so too was Sojo the first black author in Venezuela in the thirties to present rural life. Neither novel presents a "conventional world of Black primitives or exotics."[4] Just as *Cane* is often thought of as a "queer" book,[5] partly because of its enigmatic structure, so too has *Nochebuena negra* been considered an "unusual" novel,[6] partly for the same reason. Though hardly a seemingly disjointed mixture of prose, poetry, and drama to the same extent as *Cane*, *Nochebuena negra* does read at times like a series of short rural sketches. Both novels, however, have thematic unity related in part to the idea of a Second Coming. In addition, Sojo's novel is firmly set in one time and place with continuous characters, even though some drop out along the way.

But more than anything else both novels are richly poetic. Whether cane field or *cacao* field, the imagery often is "boldly sexual."[7] Both writers are remarkably appreciative of nature. Their novels present it as alive with feeling, a nature-setting where women are "ripened too soon," where men are "bent double," with "backs curved like the letter C," where people are born free like nature and bear fruit like nature. Sojo especially, who, as we pointed out, wrote his novel at the young age of twenty-two, hardly passes up an opportunity to single out youthful sexuality as indicated in repeated references to "untouched bodies" and "cursed breasts." Within the span of a few pages Sojo writes, for example, of "rounded breasts of corn anxiously awaiting harvest" (p. 253); of "fruit trees with oranges and other fruit hanging from them like testicles" (p. 259); he sees in nature scenes that remind him of pubic hair and he writes of the "sexuality of flowers" (p. 261). Sexual imagery abounds in *Nochebuena negra*, but the black woman in this novel on the whole is treated with great respect; she is presented as luscious, not lascivious.

However sensuous in his lyrical appreciation of women, *Nochebuena negra* is structured on religious observance, and the larger symbolism of the novel is reinforced in the final pages where Sojo gives the title of his work its true significance, one that goes far beyond festive occasion. The last two chapters in the novel that come before the ten-year hiatus are built around the Nochebuena de San Juan which takes place on 24 June, traditionally the celebration of the Feast of Saint John the Baptist. On this festive day, highlighted by dances, processions, chants, choral singing, and poetry recitation, drums beat into the morning bidding farewell to the day and to the saint that it honors. Sojo, also a folklorist, has led the reader up to these final pages and to this most significant of the religious days of the black in Venezuela.

Realizing that heretofore only lip service has been paid to the aspirations of black people in Venezuela, Sojo, through Pedro's *envoi* to the region in these final pages as he walks through its roads on his second visit back, this time after a ten-year absence, reflects the author's wish that the black, already "thrice denied," will be truly redeemed and that the Despedida de San Juan will, indeed, become the celebration it is supposed to be. Perhaps one of the most important points Sojo makes in the novel is that festival-related music and dancing represent something more than fun and release. Though a Catholic saint is the object of their veneration the African drum dominates the atmosphere, and its significance is multiple. The author earlier in the novel had written that "the infernal *mina* drums resounded furiously to whose beat the shadows of the bad masters danced, those that lashed the defenseless flesh of the good slaves . . . " (p. 188). Here in the final pages the drum functions as the most ethnic of the reminders of the past as it becomes the "ancestral voice" that represents Africa in America, certainly in Barlovento.

It is thematically significant that much of this novel takes place during Semana Santa or the Easter period because the work is built on biblical symbolism like the coming of the "Saviour" or "Redeemer," blacks "thrice denied," and the striking metaphor of the drum defined by Sojo as the "cross of the black Christ." The point here, I believe, is that the black in Venezuela has spent his "Time on the Cross" as this understanding of the black experience in that country ties in with Sojo's expectation that Nochebuena de San Juan should be a meaningful as well as a festive occasion, one that truly bids adieu to the sins of the fathers. The drum in this sense becomes not only a call to ethnic memory but a plea for understanding as well, a plea directed especially to those who pretend not to notice those sins or do not care to.

Nochebuena negra, then, in a larger sense is a plea to Venezuela not to forget the past and that blacks had a hand in building the country. Sojo's admonition is that the country begin to listen to this "desperate, unknown voice" which speaks through the drum to future generations. This drum voice from the past that highlights Nochebuena de San Juan festivities serves as a reminder of the way things were and are as well as a call for an improved future. Central to this improved future is black solidarity, and again it is the drum voice "calling the clan together" (p. 300) that arouses a collective hope. *Nochebuena negra* is a lyrical expression of that hope, which throughout the novel is built, appropriately, on the symbolic representation of the cacao as image of suffering and hope, images Sojo builds up like a lyric refrain, a much used device that helps impose poetic quality on the novel.

Early in the novel, for example, the author establishes in a litany of historical import that "the black man paid in cacao, pounds and pounds of cacao!" (pp. 65–66), and that "each grain of cacao could be a drop of sweat" (p. 67). The author tells us that "cacao is born free, as were our ancestors" (p. 179), and that "the cacao beans, red, are like fists that will protest against iniquity" (p. 68). But the most fruitful use of cacao as symbol, especially as suffering and hope are concerned, is found in the words that close the novel:

Nochebuena negra! The dawning of a better day when men
will be good and growing strong like trees. Then there will be
great harvests and man will no longer have to be curved over
like the letter C burdened down with heavy sacks. . . . Then
the cacao seeds will ripen . . . (pp. 312–313)

Nochebuena negra is a novel of protest on behalf of the black
peasantry in Venezuela, but it is so beautifully crafted that the dogmatic statement can be lost on the reader lulled into admiration by
its overwhelmingly poetic nature. Sojo is no outsider looking in for
his ethnic view reflects the bitter sweetness, the "suffering and song"
(p. 312), of one who loves his region, its land, and its people and
only wishes whites were more tolerant and understanding. The author leaves little doubt where his roots are as he writes into the novel
that it was "written in Curiepe in the year 1930" (p. 313). Sojo's
novel is richly poetic as is Adalberto Ortiz's *Juyungo*, which I shall
discuss in the next chapter, but Sojo's lyricism is never divorced
from context, or from the reality of black life as is sometimes the
case in *Juyungo*. Though ostensibly a poetic novel of black folklore,
Nochebuena negra never strays far from the depiction in one form
or another of black hardship in Venezuela. Indeed, from the hard
work of the black peasants in Venezuela, some of whom "neither
had anything nor even knew why they were born" (p. 306), to the
hardships and hunger of the unemployed black in the Chocó region
in Colombia that we will discuss in Arnoldo Palacios' novels in
chapter eleven, there is but a very small step.

Adalberto Ortiz and
His Black Ecuadorian Classic

> *Every person who writes makes a confession, and that*
> *confession can relate to his experience or to his thinking.*
> *All literature, everything that one writes is, in a way, an*
> *autobiographical statement.*
>
> Adalberto Ortiz

Juan Pablo Sojo waited thirteen years before publishing his *No-chebuena negra* in 1943. That same year saw the appearance of *Juyungo*, perhaps the most widely acclaimed black novel to come out of Latin America. Its author, Adalberto Ortiz, largely on the strength of this prize-winning effort, is considered to be one of the most significant black (mulatto) authors writing in Spanish. Ortiz's story of "a black, an island, and other blacks" is considered to be an achievement in prose that can be likened to Nicolás Guillén's in poetry: both works stand as classic commentaries on the black experience in Latin America. Ortiz brought that black experience to the attention of the world by dealing with it in Ecuador, a country already well-known for its *indigenista* literature.

Ortiz's *Juyungo* is a classic because it underscores the universality of the black experience—racism in Ecuador is little different from any other place. Additionally, he uses that black experience to achieve what seems to be a broader purpose, namely, to show that the "drama of the Ecuadorian black is the same as that of the Indian and of the *cholo*, that is, it is the drama of anybody who is exploited, whatever his race or nationality,"[1] or, in more general terms "to superimpose upon the concern for the suffering of his race the more universal suffering caused by social injustice and war."[2] But, while Ortiz seems to move toward this higher ground there is little doubt that the basic strength of his novel lies in his socio-psychological depiction of black and mulatto characters who must come to terms with racist attitudes in Ecuador.

Juyungo is invaluable for anyone who wants to probe the range of psychological positions that characters along the spectrum of racial color are forced to take in Latin America. Much of the tension in the novel derives from the racial conflict of blacks, whites, mulattoes, mestizoes, and Indians in confrontation with each other and in some singular cases with themselves. The range of ethnic conflict goes from Lastre "ebony on the inside, ebony on the outside"[3] to Max, the mulatto sell-out; from Antonio the mulatto who vacillates to Nelson the light mulatto labor organizer who would rather be blacker. *Juyungo*, I believe, better than any other novel in Latin America illustrates the concepts or parameters of literary blackness discussed in the Introduction to this book. Nowhere are confrontation, dualism, identity, and liberation more in evidence than in this black Ecuadorian novel. This is so in form, character, and theme despite Ortiz's broader purpose, which, ostensibly, was to transcend race.

Ortiz, who has written about his literature, sees *Juyungo* in the following way:

> *Juyungo* deals with the life, from puberty to youth, of a black peasant who dies uselessly in a war. It is the drama of a primitive and wild man who tries to penetrate and understand, in an elemental way, the world in which he happens to live. It is a problem of conflicts between blacks, whites and Indians; it is a case of discovery and identification, that goes from racial hatred to class struggle, from social problems to the fight against injustice. Since it is a work in prose, about black, social, racial and cultural themes, seasoned with folkloric and costumbrist elements, I thought that it would be best to find a style suited to its content, that is to say, to convey, in prose, the rhythm and musicality of Negrist poetry, with a style similar to that which I used in poetry. I believe I have achieved balance, for the most part, especially in the inscriptions "eyes and ears of the jungle." Unfortunately, this form is lost when the book is translated into other languages.[4]

Ortiz has tried to convey in *Juyungo* "the rhythm and musicality of

Negrist poetry" but, though "saturating" his novel with black sounds, his achievement goes beyond stylistic ornamentation in that he has written an epic statement documenting and identifying the predominantly black province of Esmeraldas. There is little doubt that Ortiz is adept at seeing and hearing the sights and sounds of his region that he richly describes. He is a painter as well as a poet, and his experience in these two media is abundantly evident especially in the lyrical "eyes and ears of the jungle" sections he mentions above. But it is the epic sweep of *Juyungo*, a novel of the black man on the move more than his poetic feel for regional language, that gives the novel its power. Ascensión Lastre, the protagonist, is endowed with great strength and valor that he exhibits in battle whether on a personal or a national level. Through his adventures and travels, Lastre raises the novel itself to the status of a national epic in the traditional sense. A champion of justice and liberty, Lastre is an admirable hero who in the end seemingly embodies a national ideal—patriotism. Even though this patriotic ending is problematic, as we shall see, Lastre's central role in the novel—everything for the most part relates to and derives from him—helps make his particular black experience both a regional and a national one.

The epic proportions of the novel are clear, but there are some ambiguities, and the ending is not the only problem. The author's attempts to bridge the gap between novel and poem, between lyric and epic is not a major problem to me. What I am most concerned with in this novel is the author's attempt to bridge the gap between race and class and the difficulties and ambiguities encountered in this attempt. Such problems inevitably arise when a proud black who feels himself inferior to no man, certainly to no white man, learns that not all whites are his enemies. The ambiguities and difficulties in the case of Ascensión Lastre come when Ortiz has his black protagonist attempt to rise above ethnic memory.

But not just the plot as story but the reasons for its structure, the characters' rationale for their behavior, and the author's choice of sequence in his plot are often ambiguous, and these ambiguities with their built-in contradictions are responsible for much of the tension that makes the characters sympathetic, artistic creations. They are responsible, as well, for the fact that the organizing principle of this novel becomes not just blackness but blackness and how to deal with it: not just blackness expressed but blackness confronted. The author never seems to be sure how to deal with Lastre's blackness in relation to his broader purpose. The strong black image he gives Lastre is so strong in fact that the psychological evolution from race to class that we are supposed to be witnessing in the novel never really comes off. Lastre never really puts aside ethnic memory; he certainly does not relegate it to a secondary position.

Several incidents throughout the novel are supposed to reveal three themes to the reader. First there is a proud black's "frenetic rage against . . . all whites" (p. 37) superseded, as we said earlier, by an ability to "love" whites (and hate blacks, I should add, as the novel is supposed to show us that side of the development as well). Second there is a move from race to class illustrated most pointedly and consistently by the person and message of Nelson Díaz, a light-skinned mulatto labor organizer who constantly preached and demonstrated, we are to conclude, by his example, that class solidarity ("class more than race" [p. 97]) was more important than racial pride. Finally, a *rage* eventually not "against the whites, but against injustice" (p. 243), in that broader sense, is revealed.

These incidents or ambiguous structural signposts along the way involve some of the characters, the order or sequence in some cases of their involvement with Lastre, and Lastre's own reaction to them. In this regard the decisive moments in his evolution relate to his love for the white María, his defense of the white Velerio, his affection for the "white" Nelson, his hatred for the black Cocambo and, of course, the war scenes in the final pages of the novel where, perhaps, we have the most ambiguous incidents of all.

The sex role of María is pivotal in the novel and in the evolution of Lastre's development as it gives, perhaps, the strongest impetus to his more tolerant acceptance of whites. After seducing her, his hatred of whites softens, but the act itself proves little in that in the first instance his attraction to and conquest of this white woman was one of black revenge and *macho* bravura. When he applies the often repeated phrase of his famous uncle, "I'm astride the white race" (a reference to the white horse he rode) to his sexual conquest of María, we know that this is not an act of love. While it may have been a satisfying sexual experience, the symbolic and psychological satisfaction he derived from this victory-possession of a white woman was for Lastre, certainly in Fanon's sense, far more significant.

Lastre desired María and took her not because he had lost his

"race hatred" but because she was white and he wanted to "humiliate her sexually" (p. 72). This sexual act is pivotal because immediately after, Lastre again has occasion to "side" with white, namely,
to defend a white enemy who was outnumbered in a fight. But here
again love of whites had nothing to do with Lastre's reaction. This
act, which required standing with the underdog in an unequal fight,
was like the bed act with María, another act of black *macho* bravura. Both incidents are more deeply personal than symbolic illustration, and it is unfortunate that Ortiz's overriding suggestion here
is that this sex act with María becomes magical with the power to
erase not only ethnic memory but the vengeance motif it started out
to be. Even if we accept that encounter as historical cleansing,
María's role at this early point in the novel puts far too much importance on the singular significance of sex. This is the same mistake William Styron makes when he attributes Nat Turner's
rebellious motivation more to a desire for white women than to
Turner's objection to historical oppression based on race. Just as
Turner's desire for reform was more social than sexual, so too
should Lastre's conversion be considered from the same perspective.

Equally ambiguous in Lastre's conversion or development from
hate to love and from race to class is the role of Nelson. One of the
problems with *Juyungo* is that nowhere does the author indicate
that whites have to change. By concentrating on Lastre's evolution,
Ortiz seems to be suggesting that black racism is more of a problem
than white racism. By not making Nelson white he passes up an
excellent opportunity to make his class-more-than-race message
more convincing, because it is Nelson, a light mulatto who is the
prime carrier of this message, whereas historically whites have been
the racist guardians of who gets in, even at the level of proletarian
union. It is clear in the novel that Nelson is a light mulatto and not
white as Ortiz constantly refers to him as "almost white," or "more
or less white," or "very white on the outside." Furthermore, Nelson
identifies with blackness through class, not through race, which
makes his racial role as well as his social role even more ambiguous.

Cocambo becomes as pivotal and influential—and equally un-
convincing—a link in Lastre's development from hate to love and
from race to class as was María, since Lastre's hatred and subsequent murder of this despicable black antagonist is supposed to
show his love more of justice than of race. But this act of color-blind

justice or vengeance proves nothing since Cocambo is hardly a credit even to the human race. Cocambo exists ostensibly to show that blacks too can be bad. But just as Nelson exists to exemplify what should be a white man's message, Cocambo's existence proves just as little because he would be an abnormal case in any color, one who thinks little of raping eleven year-old girls, not to mention his responsibility in the death of Lastre's baby and the resultant insanity of Lastre's wife.

It seems, furthermore, that this act of vengeance should not be used to prove hatred of injustice since the overpowering rage here is that of a father and husband. The hatred and the following act of revenge are personal as were the earlier acts of black *macho* bravura and need not be given a color or used as a springboard to socioeconomic theory. It is unrealistic to imply that in the interest of racial solidarity Lastre should spare Cocambo or overlook his guilt in the tragedy that befell his family simply because Cocambo is black. It is equally unrealistic for this personal act of vengeance to serve as the definitive and climactic factor in Lastre's development away from racial hatred to love of justice. In short, Lastre's discovery that a black like Cocambo can be bad is insufficient justification to erase ethnic memory of an historical past filled with countless acts of oppression based on race. It should be noted, too, that Ortiz absolves Cocambo from blame for his actions because "behind Cocambo there was Mr. Hans and behind Mr. Hans, Mr. Valdez and behind Mr. Valdez, many others . . . " (p. 243). The point here is that Mr. Hans and Mr. Valdez, like the "many others" are all white.

The final pages in the novel are as significant and as ambiguous in the development of its overall structure and of Lastre's psychological perceptions of blackness as have been the pivotal roles of María, Nelson, and Cocambo. In these final pages we find Lastre at the highest elevation in his development away from race hatred as he is on the front lines fighting patriotically for his country in war against Peruvian forces. These final pages can be seen as an irrelevant and unnecessary jab at Peru, a gratuitous addition to an otherwise already well-rounded story. But this ending is important in the development of Lastre, because it shows, in fact, that there has been very little development after all. Only in these pages do we realize the difficulty Ortiz encountered in trying to impose a raceless personality on a proud black character who would not let go of his proud black image. We also see in these final pages the absurdity of a common patriotic front manned only by nonwhites. The following passage sets the tone for this final ambiguity:

> Lastre paid no attention whatsoever to the combat, so as to be able to examine the people around him.
>
> There was Antonio Angulo, pale and ash-colored, as though he were dead, lying face down. Closer up was Nelson Díaz, aiming carefully, serene, with a tuft of hair which the breeze blew lightly, hanging over his temple. . . . Other blacks were shooting farther away. On the other side, he observed the colored highlanders just recently down from the mountains, long-suffering and quiet, mestizos who looked like Cayapa Indians dressed up like soldiers; the whitest and most colored both had a bit of Indian in them. And he, amongst them, fighting for the same reason, perhaps full of the same thoughts, of the same anxieties, of the same desperation. . . . Lastre, the blackest of blacks, was like a brother to those Indians. He had always been around Indians. He spent his whole life among Indians. (pp. 294–95)

The point not to be overlooked here is that there are no whites on the front lines, and this lack of total racial participation does not help Ortiz's theory of class more than race. The all-colored racial composition of the front line forces—on both sides—is as ambiguous as Ortiz's decision to make Nelson a light mulatto rather than white. But these final pages also tell us that Lastre continues to think black and to derive his strength—through his remembrances of his famous black uncle—from his blackness and from his association of the enemy in his mind with *white* exploiters. Lastre goes to war not really out of patriotic fervor but "for himself" (p. 282). He wants to "commit a deed worthy of a Lastre, of a real black" (p. 301). These final pages show, in short, as I said in the Introduction to this book, that Ortiz does have his black priorities straight in *Juyungo* despite himself, and despite the broader purpose of his novel.

Lastre is a "failure" in the class sense because unlike Nelson he could never rise above the personal level in relation to others and to himself. But even Nelson who "did not hate in Valdez the powerful landholder but rather an entire class" understood, nevertheless, "that deep down the problem was one of race . . ." (p. 270). The real strength in *Juyungo*, then, is found in Lastre's inability to put race aside even though Ortiz presents him as a black in evolution towards a consciousness of class. This contradiction underscores the major ambiguity in the novel, one that has been overshadowed by Nelson's survival of the war—the only survivor from Lastre's contingent—ostensibly to continue to bring forth his message of class more than race. It is this strength of blackness in the character of Lastre, too, that separates *Juyungo* from standard proletarian fiction.

Adalberto Ortiz is a mulatto, "son of mulattoes," as he often points out, and despite what he sees as a dichotomy in his literary expression tied to his being "a mixture of blacks and whites"[5] he is partial to blackness in *Juyungo*. This preference is evident despite his intent on the surface seeming to be otherwise, namely, to convert Lastre, to show Antonio to be a "tortured mulatto" caught between two worlds, and to express, through Nelson, a commitment to class. But Antonio, like Lastre, opts for blackness in the final analysis, and even Nelson "would have liked to be blacker" (p. 93). Given the admirably positive and enviable image he endows Lastre with, it is not surprising that Ortiz can write in his poetry that he would rather be more black than white, a statement seemingly resolving his own racial identity.

Ortiz's own literary personality, then, "not very well defined or uniform,"[6] as he writes in a recent edition of his poetry, seems to be imposed on *Juyungo*. Considering his continuing need to express himself on the subject of racial duality, the ambiguity we see in this his first novel should come as no surprise. Ortiz returns to the subject in his poetry, in his essays, and in his latest novel, *El espejo y la ventana* (1967), but it is in *Juyungo*, his black Ecuadorian classic, where we first see him grappling with what can be called an autobiographical dilemma.

Literary Blackness in Colombia:
The Novels of Arnoldo Palacios

> Ports
> *of dark arms opened wide!*
> *Children with swollen bellies*
> *and watchful eyes.*
> *Hunger. Oil. Cattle . . .*
> *And the rower, rows on.*
> Nicolás Guillén

> *To be a Negro in this country and to be relatively con-*
> *scious is to be in a rage almost all the time. So that the*
> *first problem is how to control that rage so that it won't*
> *destroy you.*
> *James Baldwin*

The kind of *rabia* characterizing Ascención Lastre's attitude toward whites found in Adalberto Ortiz's *Juyungo* perhaps reaches its maximum expression in *Las estrellas son negras* (1949) by Arnoldo Palacios. This work illustrates how black rage stemming from unemployment and gnawing hunger, two aspects of the black experience in Colombia, can drive a man to drastic and desperate acts. Reading *Las estrellas son negras* one immediately thinks of such books as *Black Rage* by William H. Grier and Price M. Cobbs, Richard Wright's *American Hunger,* and, of course, *Child of the Dark,* Carolina María de Jesús' diary of her life in the rat-infested slums of São Paulo. *Las estrellas son negras* is particularly reminiscent of this Brazilian book, as the slums of the Chocó region of Colombia that Palacios describes are just as rat-infested, black life is equally bleak, misery and unemployment are just as rampant, and opportunity is nowhere in sight even for a black who, like Irra, Palacios' protagonist, has managed some education. Palacios writes that not only jobs but even "the scholarships were given to whites only,"[1] and Irra like Carolina was the top student in his class.

Like his Brazilian counterpart who felt she was "under the evil eye,"[2] Irra, as the title of Palacios' book implies, felt he was born under "a black star." Reading these two books opens the reader up to extremely harsh experiences not often encountered in Afro-Latin American literature. This is not to say that the black experience they describe is unlike any other, only that their description of it is so much more intimate and deliberately intense. Palacios, in particular, takes us through only one day in the life of Irra, but we know, as Irra knows, that for him and his family "today certainly was not the only day they had to put up with hunger" (p. 45). The following comments about the Brazilian book are equally applicable to *Las estrellas son negras*:

> Carolina is not really the main personage in her diary. It is a bigger character—Hunger. From the first to the last page he appears with an unnerving consistency. The other characters are consequences of this Hunger: alcoholism, prostitution, violence, and murder. The human beings who walk through these pages are real, with their real names, but with slight variations they could be other men who live with Hunger in New York, Buenos Aires, Rome, Calcutta, and elsewhere.[3]

There is little doubt that hunger is really the protagonist of Palacios' book, and the reader is made to feel it. The ever-present absence of food is the controlling force in the narrative as hunger, together with Irra's impatience with it and with the government responsible, is the catalyst for his commitment to do something. One of the options he examines is political assassination. Almost every thought Irra has in the novel is "dominated by hunger eating away the insides of his stomach" (p. 85). The novel is divided into four chapters, and chapter 1, the longest, covering about half of the book, is even entitled "Hunger." It is in this part where hunger is pervasive to the point that the reader is tempted to ask, as does Irra, "How was it possible to go so long without eating?" (p. 31) The verb *chirriar* ("growling"), with its variations, is one of the most used in the novel: "He went on his way and his main problems, hunger and a *growling* stomach, were still with him" (p. 36); "Irra's stomach *growled*, reminding him once again how hungry he was" (p. 41); "hunger once again made his stomach *growl*" (p. 52).

The author's interminable descriptions are not the repetitious ramblings of an immature novelist out for sensationalism or naturalistic effect. What Palacios does is to totally immerse the reader into Irra's surroundings, indeed into his psyche as he suffers those pangs of hunger. Only by sharing his agony are we able to understand the desperation of his misery, the drastic actions he takes to alleviate it, and the authenticity of his despair, for example, when he prays, "Give us, Oh Lord, something to eat today . . . Remember your children, my Lord Jesus Christ. And do not let us perish, drowned in such misery . . . " (p. 40). While taking us through Irra's surroundings and thoughts, the author builds narrative tension based on a growing rage, that, driven by hunger, leads Irra to attempt political assassination in chapter 2, appropriately entitled "Rage."

Chapter 3 "¡Nive!," like chapter 2, allows brief respite from hunger for in these chapters Irra takes steps to "act like a man," first by striking what he thought would be a blow for justice—which the political assassination he had planned would have represented to him—and second by seducing Nive, who was to be his first real *hembra*. Both of these accounts are excellent examples of the author's skill in building the tensions that accompany the decision-making process where psychological and real consequences of decisions have to be considered. There is much psychological wrestling in the novel as Irra is forced to consider a variety of solutions, none of them really viable, to the problem of hunger.

Hunger again takes over in chapter 4, "Luz interior," and becomes the dominant force motivating Irra's immediate thoughts and long-range plans. In this chapter he has to decide whether to go away, to seek relief in a larger city, or to stay with his family and "put up with hunger together" (p. 166), and through it all Irra continues to feel "hunger pains" (p. 158). In this chapter Irra resolves to leave the Chocó in search of "Our Daily Bread" (p. 158); he did not succeed in getting out, however, since he literally missed the boat that was to take him away. His misfortune here, though, was fortuitous as he converts it into an upward turning point in his life.

This turning point, though, to be sure, comes late and after a still proud Irra has suffered through and rejected begging, borrowing, and stealing, as ways to cope with poverty. That is why the only solution he seriously considered was political assassination, and Irra, convinced that "the Government is to blame for all of this hunger," (p. 94) resolved to kill its local representative. Though seemingly on the verge of a nervous breakdown when leaning toward that irrational act, Irra makes good sense when he analyzes the insensitivity of the government to the needs of the poor:

> Bad government was responsible for poverty. All of the politicians he had met were awful. . . .
>
> The government was bad. Government in the hands of the rich who didn't know what it was to suffer from hunger, to have nothing to wear, to walk barefoot or with worn out shoes, to live in a rotten hut. People continued to be anemic. Little children dying left and right. The T. B. pavillion full. How can we expect such people to take an interest in the poor when God himself does not care! Priests do not put up decent temples. (pp. 45–46)

Irra was hardly a politically aware activist. Yet though he had only "a vague idea of what the word 're-vo-lu-ción' meant . . . " (p. 96), because of his unrelenting oppression he had a clearer idea of the need to revolt than someone who had a philosophy of revolution but had never experienced the kind of want and misery that drives men to kill. "He *had* to kill" (p. 96), Irra felt, and that is why he saw murder as a triumphant act of liberation, a blow he would strike for justice on behalf of the poor. With weapon in hand, Irra took almost fiendish delight in his resolve to "fulfill my duty" (p. 58), to make his life "meaningful" (p. 58). But in his blind rage, his dramatic act is not well planned, and as a result he is unable to bring it off. Irra, for example, "had not the slightest idea when the employees [the ones he would have to kill] get off from work" (p. 103). But his failure is really unimportant. What is important was his decision for the first time in his life to "do something," to turn his hunger outward and to use it as a positive, liberating force that would free him from the "futility of his existence" (p. 53).

The government is not the only target in *Las estrellas son negras.* Irra had read of Ku Klux Klan activity in the United States where the black man was also "looked down on by whites" (p. 79). Though basically a deeply religious man who at heart could not kill, Irra felt that priests "deceived and robbed the poor" (p. 84). His greatest wrath was directed toward blacks who, when they got a little ahead, thought they were white and turned their backs on their own people. One of Irra's most humiliating experiences in the novel was caused by the shame he felt when he had to consider begging for continued credit, especially from a black store owner who "felt white" (p. 69) and who had forgotten "how miserable he had been on account of the whites" (p. 69).

In the end Irra does not beg, borrow, steal, kill, leave, or commit suicide, and after eliminating these options he decides to make the most of life in the Chocó. But his decision is not pessimistic resignation. His final commitment to do something derives from a new feeling of self worth, which is a giant step forward for one forced in the past to live like an animal at the bare existence level. Irra decides simply that he is somebody, despite what seemed to be a preordained life of misery. Confidently recognizing his self-worth was the most liberating step he could take. Though hunger and want dominate the protagonist's thoughts and actions, the author makes it clear that "man does not live by bread alone" (p. 80). Palacios also makes it clear that Irra did not hate himself because he was black but only the stigma and the poverty associated with it.

It is the description of this poverty and the unavoidable filth it breeds that makes reading *Las estrellas son negras* an unforgettable experience. Stylistically, Palacios excells in the descriptive details he gives of filth—human, animal, and environmental—and much of the compelling power and emotional impact of his narrative comes from his clinical portrayal of what it means to be black in Colombia. His directness goes beyond his use of the uneducated speech of the people. While there is much phonetically transcribed dialogue, it is the interior thought of Irra looking out on his world that most rivets our attention: "Irra felt the need to defecate. Yes, he had to do it there, turning his back to the river. What! Impossible! The river was full of people swimming. . . . It was a crying shame that his house didn't have a bathroom, not even a rundown one" (p. 38). Palacios returns to this description later on:

> He again felt the need to relieve himself of certain physiological necessities, and he placed himself over a huge crack in the floor, through which the humid earth could be seen. He pulled down his pants and crouched . . . he pushed. Something discharged

loose and landed on the sand below, like soft mud balls. He leaned over and observed the underpinnings of the house dripping with hardening matter and swarming with flies. Irra stood up, took a deep breath, breathing in the foul air in the room, and went to get dressed. (p. 40)

There is very little that is pretty in this novel where people are reduced to eating mud and excrement for survival. Not only rats but chinches, ants, spiders, termites, and other by-products of poverty conditions overrun their living quarters, and basic hygiene does not exist. Palacios does not subdue his description of unrelieved poverty, and like Irra, the reader is forced to experience the bad smells "in his nose, in his eyes, in his ears" (p. 45). The novel is filled with "images of *starvation*" (p. 158), with "*sad* streets" (p. 165) and "*extremely poor* streets" (p. 169), where we see a "*skeletal* face" (p. 169) here, a "*malarial* hut" (p. 177) there as well as an "*unnourished* dog" (p. 47) and a "*hungry, undernourished* boy" (p. 94). Palacios often heightens his descriptions by using graphic adjectives such as these in pairs and in threes, but always with the effect of creating compassion for those involved in the experience he is sharing with the reader.

In a novel where people are no better off than starving animals, it is not surprising to find an analogy like the following:

There in the corner, at the end of the walkway, a black dog wallowed in the dust. It stood up. This long-legged dog, with its big head and droopy ears. His fur had begun to fall off and it didn't seem strong enough to stand up. This dog was thin, hungry and undernourished like the people there, without sap in its system ... Man or dog, it was the same thing, the only difference being that the dog wasn't aware that it was a dog, whereas man suffered from the certainty that he was less than a dog. (p. 47)

This dog, in his desperation, eventually leaps the counter to steal a piece of bread. The entire episode, which Irra observes is a symbolic parallel, of course, to his own desperate situation, as does another description of a crippled beggar forced to drag herself about on all fours through the streets.

But the most significant symbolic parallel, aside from the black stars of the title, certainly the most positive, comes toward the end of the novel when Irra is trying to decide what to do with his life. Having just missed the boat, he witnesses the survival of a river bank hut that resisted the ravages of a rising river:

> The river continued to rise, coming down from its source; it went by yellowish and foamy, carrying roots, branches, tree trunks, and undergrowth. But Irra's gaze was fixed on what was happening with the hut on the opposite side of this rampaging river that went by with the force of the devil, ripping up banana plants and trees planted around the hut. But the hut held on to the earth with its weak supports. The straw roof was shaking as though it were just waking up.
>
> But the besieged walls of the hut held fast, as the waves tried their best to uproot it. Irra closed his fists and gritted his teeth. God! Were there people in the house? Had they managed to get away? And what about the children? The shore was too far away to tell whether those white spots were people swimming, or just white leaves. The river continued to attack the sides of the hut, and the hut held on. How strong that hut was! Yes. Strong. Stronger than a man. The river could carry away a rock, but it could not drag off that hut. The waves uprooted gigantic trees, but that little sickly looking hut challenged their fury. And a poor family lived there, like Irra's. The old man of the house was about ninety years old and could still steer his canoe, and punish the satanic waves with his rebellious paddle. And today's hunger had not weakened him for tomorrow. (pp. 176–177)

It is the survival example of this *choza* that sets off in Irra a burning desire to survive. He would stay and fight: "Everyone did what he could. Irra also would do what he could" (p. 178).

The novel is not a long one; the action is minimal and occurs in approximately a twenty-four hour period in Irra's life. The compactness of the novel enables the author to sustain successfully a narrative account built primarily on hunger as a dominant motif. Further, *Las estrellas son negras* is a very controlled narration about a man in dialogue with himself. Much of the tension in the novel flows from debates he has with himself and with his conscience. Palacios' novel is more than a naturalistic exercise, and this is due in part to the psychological depth he gives his main character, who becomes as real as the miseries, frustrations, and hunger the author describes.

Las estrellas son negras, as a novel of black poverty, inevitably treats the use of drink as an escape from want and grief: "Drink is the only thing that cheers me up" (p. 43); "It is because of my suffering that I get drunk" (p. 43); "Maybe it's better to live drunk than to go about all day with a stomach full of air" (p. 43). It is a novel about unemployment, another affliction of the underprivileged. Unemployment was particularly high in the Chocó region and specifically in Quibdó—the setting for this novel—where work is scarce because "there were no factories nor shops of any kind" (p. 51). The black woman could find work washing "other people's clothing," but Irra could not even get a porter's job "because he was black, and almost all jobs were given to whites, or to boot-licking blacks" (p. 51).

Las estrellas son negras, like *Nochebuena negra* and other black novels on Latin America, is a novel of contrasts. "The whites were employed in the government. They dressed well and smoked quality cigarettes. But the blacks, nothing, Goddamit, nothing! " (p. 44). It is a novel of the haves and the have-nots, of the undernourished, anaemic, and sickly poor "subordinated to those who have" (p. 60). A novel, in short, of the poor who get poorer contrasted with the rich who get richer. But *Las estrellas son negras*, though a depressing novel of black rage is, at the same time, a novel of hope, survival, and spiritual liberation of black people despite the black star they are forced to live under. On another level, Palacios' novel is really concerned with the coming of age of a black individual, a novel of black manhood, and of the responsible action that comes with acquiring a positive self-image.

A message of hope, this time through revolution, is carried in Palacios' other novel, *La selva y la lluvia*, published in 1958, significantly, in Russia, for in this novel he has moved from identifying the problem to offering up a solution to it. The implication here, of course, is that well-planned, coordinated, and concerted mass action is more fruitful than individual and irrational acts of violence (assassination). In this novel the young Pedro José, like Irra, wanted to get out. Even before reaching young manhood Pedro José had begun to feel "an infinite grudge against something which he could not as yet put his finger on."[4] Pedro José was later to learn that this "hatred towards something, towards something he could not put his finger on exactly" (p. 64) should be directed against the Government even though at that point, and given his political innocence, he was not quite certain why.

Palacios in his two novels seems to be approaching the Soviet's definition of literature. "In 1934," according to Jean Franco, "the First All-Union Congress of Soviet Writers attended by foreign intellectuals officially decreed that literature should undertake 'the ideological remoulding and education of the toiling people in the spirit of Socialism.' " [5] She continued that "since the message of Communism was a messianic one, they were to portray not only the misery of the workers but the 'solution' to the misery."[6] Throughout *La selva y la lluvia* we see a growing awareness that mass rebellion is one viable alternative to death by starvation. "If we only had a union," one character says, "it would be more difficult to kick a worker around" (p. 76). Even Irra in *Las estrellas son negras* suspected that mass rebellion by the poor was one way to shake the government from its complacency, and such rebellion should be launched, he thought, "even if lives were lost in the effort" (p. 82). But Irra had no plan.

With the 1917 Russian Revolution as the example, Palacios makes it clear in *La selva y la lluvia* that "in an aware, perfect organization of the workers lies the key to the liberation of the masses" (p. 195). He underscores the kind of alliance required for success:

> Here a union has been founded, but it seems to me that this union isn't working as it should. Strong, united unions would be a powerful help for the guerrilla fighters. . . . and you intellectuals must come here to help us more frequently. . . . Do you get my meaning? (pp. 195–196)

Guerrillas, workers, and intellectuals were to work in unison to bring about a revolution "as never been seen before" (p. 93).

The impact of the Russian Revolution on the Spanish American novel was studied recently by Evelio Echevarría,[7] who believes it important to recognize the debt in themes and style that Spanish American literature owes to Bolshevism—the early stage of the Revolution. He believes this early stage had more influence on revolutionary protest in the Spanish American social novel of the twenties, thirties, and forties than the "highly scientific and technical form of Marxism that came after the Second World War."[8] Palacios' novel, although published in 1958, conforms in style and theme to the "highly propagandistic literature" Echevarría describes.

Overriding any dogma or political propaganda in both *La selva y la lluvia* and *Las estrellas son negras* is the basic idea of social justice for black people. Judging from the detailed examination he makes of the black experience in Colombia, it is clear that Palacios did not have to look to events in Russia to discover that something was wrong in his home town and to realize that "blacks here are born worse off than anyone" (p. 153). Palacios further realizes in both his novels that "if we don't get anywhere through our own effort, no one will give us a hand . . . " (p. 153). Indeed, Palacios expresses in his works a hunger that moves beyond physical want and toward a spiritual liberation—one free from pressures imposed by those responsible for suffering and hunger in the first place.

Part Three
CONTEMPORARY AUTHORS, 1950–

12

Literary Blackness in Colombia:
The Ideological Development of
Manuel Zapata Olivella

*I would send other words to tell, to march, to fight, to
create a sense of the hunger for life that grows in us all, to
keep alive in our hearts a sense of the inexpressible human.*
                                                    Richard Wright

Reference has been made in this study to the symbolic importance
Afro-Americans have for black Latin American writers. It should be
emphasized as we turn to a discussion on contemporary authors
that this symbolic significance has changed over the years. In the
thirties and forties, the black in the United States was the perfect
symbol and victim of United States injustice. But then in the fifties,
sixties, and seventies the black in the United States in his struggle for
racial equality and social justice has come to symbolize and epito-
mize the fight against racism in this hemisphere.

The black Latin Americans' view of Afro-Americans, then, is in-
separably related to their attitude toward the United States. An example of this relationship is the work of Nicolás Guillén. His well-
known "progressive critique"[1] of the United States runs throughout
his poetry, though perhaps finding one of its most famous expressions in *West Indies Ltd.* (1934), where he "combines racial awareness, socialist inclinations, and a violent disgust for the United
States."[2] This symbolic light in which the Afro-American is seen
by Nicolás Guillén was explored recently by Mirian de Costa,[3]
who points out how Guillén used the black American more than
any other to symbolize the double stigma of race and caste. Although she makes no reference, surprisingly, to "¿Qué color?,"

Guillén's poem on the example of Martin Luther King, de Costa does show the poet's concern, like that of other black Latin American writers in the thirties, about the Scottsboro incident. She shows as well the poet's concern about the murder of Emmett Till and about the hard times in Little Rock under then governor Orville Faubus. She mentions Guillén's allusions to Jim Crow and notes his references to the American South and to the Ku Klux Klan in a recent poem on the example of Angela Davis. Her conclusion, not surprisingly, is that "America is represented in Guillén's poetry as the embodiment of materialism, imperialism, neocolonialism, and capitalism; concomitantly, the Afro-American is most often represented as a victim of the system"[4] (p. 13).

Although Nicolás Guillén's progressive critique of the United States continues to dominate much of Afro-Hispanic literature into the fifties, sixties, and seventies, other black Latin American authors, as we shall see in the next few chapters, intensify their own antagonism toward the United States in their literature. These writers include Nelson Estupiñán Bass, Nicomedes Santz Cruz, and Manuel Zapata Olivella, and certainly in one of Zapata Olivella's earlier works, *Corral de negros* (1963), the critique of the United States is harsh. The leitmotif of the novel is Colombian hunger, one of the basic motivating forces shaping *Las estrellas son negras* of Arnoldo Palacios. But Manuel Zapata Olivella moves beyond a portrayal of drastic individual action to alleviate want. He chooses instead to give his novel an ideological framework that preaches responsible planning and organized community protest reminiscent of Civil Rights movements in the sixties in the United States as two means to bring about change and reform. The naturalistic scenes characteristic of Palacios' novels, scenes of debilitating Colombian hunger, misery, and rats, are just as strong in Zapata Olivella's work, though we are not made to live and suffer with the characters on every page. Instead, Zapata Olivella tries to explain "the dialectics of poverty"[5] as his characters act by planning such actions as "a hunger march through the city."[6]

The ideology for change and reform that Zapata Olivella gives the first version of his novel, *Corral de negros*, published and *premiada* in Cuba in 1963 by Casa de las Américas, is just as evident in the second version, first published in Medellín, Colombia, by Editorial Bedout two years later in 1965, this time with a new title *Chambacú, corral de negros*. It is this second version that has since gone through several editions, most recently in 1974. The second version is a greatly improved one stylistically, as is often the case with subsequent editions of works, but—and this is the point I argue in this chapter—changes in this second version go far beyond style and title modification. It would seem, indeed, that this second version represents a departure for Zapata Olivella from the much harder line taken against the United States that characterized the first version, *Corral de negros*, published, significantly, in socialist Cuba.

It is customary to trace an author's ideological development through his chronological output, but rarely does the reader have the opportunity to trace such development through subsequent versions of the same work. Nor does the reader often have the opportunity to read such blatantly antagonistic views from a black Latin American writer toward the United States as those found in—and later excised from—the first version of *Corral de negros*. Racism and discrimination in the United States have been persistent concerns in black Latin American literature, concerns which, together with United States imperialism have, indeed, pervaded much of Latin American literature in general. These preoccupations, in fact, were often inseparable, as seen, for example, in the title *Racism in United States Imperialism*, an important new book by Rubin Francis Weston, subtitled "The Influence of Racial Assumptions on American Foreign Policy, 1893–1946."[7] While using the deeply rooted "assignation of a role of inferiority to the non-Anglo-Saxon element in the United States"[8] as a point of departure, the author shows how racist beliefs influenced America's relations with other countries, particularly how American racial attitudes were exported to Cuba, Haiti, Puerto Rico, and the Dominican Republic, areas that came under the influence of the United States. Anglo-Saxon racism, responsible for many of the inconsistencies the author observed "between America's avowed principles and actual practices led to injustices which questioned the honor and character of the United States."[9] These injustices were obviously observed by black and nonblack Latin Americans and influenced their attitudes toward the United States.

Nelson M. Blake, in a Preface assessing the relevancy and the contribution made by Weston's book, noted that "history always runs the risk of becoming too compartmentalized. The history of

American imperialism has been the concern of diplomatic historians; the history of American race relations that of political and social historians. What tends to get lost"—Blake said—"is the close relationship between the two."[10] What I do in this chapter is to show that literature—certainly in the work of Manuel Zapata Olivella and the two versions of *Corral de negros*—represents an important connection with race relations and political and social history.

The negative image of the United States found, for example, in Cuban revolutionary ideology—the view that it is a "racist and decadent capitalist society that exploits and brutalizes Afro-Americans and all other minorities, as well as the poor and the workers"[11] —has been perpetuated in Latin American literature in general and in the literature by writers of African descent in particular. The image still prevailing in Cuba of the United States as a "racist and inhuman society where American blacks are seen as a *colonized subnation* living in segregated quarters forming colonies of misery in the heart of American affluence,"[12] even if slanted, was not lost on Manuel Zapata Olivella, as the Cuban edition of his *Corral de negros* indicates.

But Zapata Olivella's first vision of the United States did not come from Cuban revolutionary ideology nor even from civil rights headlines that flooded the world press in the early sixties. As his "travelogue" *He visto la noche* indicates, Zapata Olivella had travelled across the United States (and through the South) in the late forties when he had the same trying experiences as black Americans. *Pasión vagabunda* (1948), which relates his pre-United States travels and adventures through Central America and Mexico, recalls an interrogation he underwent because he seemed a suspicious character to "yankee troops" in Panama. In this section entitled "Prisionero de los yanquis,"[13] he had fleeting fears of being shot as a spy. Zapata Olivella also recounts in this book his short career in Guatemala as a boxer under the name "Kid Chambacú." There he fought in the ring to earn money to finance his trek north into Mexico where he worked as a journalist under Martín Luis Guzmán, then Director of *Tiempo*, a prestigious Mexican journal. It is interesting that both *He visto la noche* and *Pasión vagabunda*, which narrate imaginatively a period of his life, are reminiscent of the ageneric structure of Guzmán's own *El águila y la serpiente* (1928).

Even in Zapata Olivella's first novel, *Tierra mojada* (1947), the image of the gringo is negative and tied to the misery of local inhabitants:

> ... not everything is nice in the bay, for there is also poverty. Some day you will come across the mangrove cutters who spend days and weeks cutting along the banks of the river. Then they take it away in boats. The buyers, a bunch of gringoes, who ... pay miserably for the boatfuls of mangrove. ...[14]

In this work, where there is hatred of "the gringos who wear overalls as blue as their eyes,"[15] where hunger and hunger alone drove blacks to work "for the Misters,"[16] Zapata Olivella expressed his vision largely through Marco Olivares, "defender of the poor and of justice."[17] He is a forerunner of Máximo, "Christ Redeemer of the Poor," in *Corral de negros,* who as we shall see, was full of the same kind of "advanced political ideas"[18] that he too, like Marco, tried to "spread among the people of the town."[19] Both Marco with his "desire to write some short stories and accounts of the province"[20] and Máximo, with his political awareness, of course, share an identification with the author who also "stars" in the two autobiographical travel adventures mentioned above.

Other works by Zapata Olivella indicating his continuing awareness of the United States include his collection of stories *¿Quién dió el fusil a Oswald?* (1967), which includes the title story, where he involves the Ku Klux Klan in the Kennedy assassination, and "Un extraño bajo mi piel" set in Atlanta, Georgia, a story in which he satirizes blacks who want to be white. But the hard-line ideological stance toward the United States came in *Corral de negros,* where his main objection, I believe, is to hypocrisy in United States foreign policy, perhaps best illustrated in the following passage, one cut from the second version:

> They arrive with the dollar sign in order to enslave us better. We need tools, not money. They distribute rum and poison minds so as to appear like redeemers. If they really wanted to redeem us, the blacks of Chambacú, they would have started by recognizing the rights of blacks in North America. They want to apply the same law here as there. Why do they come here talking about schools when they refuse Meredith the right

to go to university. They lie. They know they lie. And those fools in Chambacú, bowing down before them, thanking the Lord for their promises. (p. 199)

This passage is followed shortly by another—also removed from the second version—that underscores another primary criticism of the United States, namely, the willingness of that country to work through corrupt local officials in Colombia for the betterment of those who never see the benefits:

The United States is afraid that we and all of Latin America will imitate the socialist revolution in Cuba. They know that the Continent is a dormant volcano that will explode at any moment. And so they rush to plug the top so it won't explode. They affirm that the Alliance for Progress is a plan for our development. A very nice way of putting the fetters back on us. But their propositions are continually failing. Look, if they had found somebody else to tell us their stories, chances are they would have convinced us. But they have to rely on Captain Quiroz, who has always given us a hard time; or shameless people like my brother and that Constantino; or "Carioca" and on Arturo, the "mad one." When did they ever care about the poverty of Chambacú? If now they appear as the saviours, it's because they've received a few dollars to organize the arrival of the Peace Corps . . . the millions of dollars, if they ever do arrive, will remain in the hands of the authorities, who are always interested in getting fat at the expense of us, the underdogs. (p. 200)

These objections and criticisms, even in the first version, are somewhat offset by the slight hope that the United States is sincere and does not always operate in bad faith, but this hope is difficult to sustain in view of the certainty in that first version that "disillusion will come down on anyone who gets carried away with the thought of the Alliance for Progress" (p. 203), a phrase deleted from the second version. The second version also eliminates much of the political rhetoric of Máximo, and these deletions, of course, give the novel more narrative movement as do many other stylistic changes that often involve simple grammatical corrections and preferences, and the shortening of sentences and paragraphs through the elimination of unnecessary words and expressions:

First version	Second version
A hatchet would be just the thing for cutting off the hands of those drummers. There would be silence then. (p. 87)	A hatchet. Chop off their hands. Silence. (p. 75)

Such changes as these undoubtedly sharpen the author's expression and, together with the elimination of much ideological statement are, in truth, attempts to make better art and less propaganda, an option always to be lauded in a creative artist. But we have to keep in mind that in the two versions of *Corral de negros* only one kind of dogmatic statement undergoes modification: Zapata Olivella continues to state a case, and he does this very strongly, but his case in the second version is made less against the United States and more against the local authorities. In the first version there is no question that the United States is the manipulating villain. The entire structure of the novel is framed by United States related events: Part 1, "Las Reclutas," opens with the round-up of black Colombians who, on orders from Washington, are "corralled" for duty in the Korean War; the third and final part, "La Batalla," closes with the arrival of the Alliance for Progress and the Peace Corps.

Most of the changes in Zapata Olivella's attitude toward the United States take place in parts 1 and 3 because these are the sections of the novel where confrontation and foreign manipulation are most felt. Part 2, "El botín," is more internal and local, and changes here primarily involve Inge, the white wife brought into this black community from Sweden by José Raquel, the "black sheep," so to speak, in the novel. Her social consciousness is expanded in preparation for the larger social role she is to play eventually in the community in alliance with other political activists who are determined to follow the example of Máximo, who is killed in part 3. But parts 1 and 3 essentially belong to Máximo who is the obvious spokesman in the community against the hypocrisy, complicity, and duplicity of the United States government, and much of the changes and deletions involve his rhetoric.

One of the first changes in the book is the deletion of the titles of the books Máximo read. The following reference to his reading matter is struck: " 'El Capital,' 'La Revolución y el Estado,' 'Las tácticas Guerrilleras' " (p. 18). Specific and leading references like the following directly accusatory statements (in italics) are repeatedly cut from part 1:

Mama! In any case they'll come for me. They need people like me, cannon fodder, to sacrifice in Korea. *It's an order from the yankee masters!* (p. 18)

and:

He knew where that order came from. *It had Washington written all over it.* (p. 20)

The two passages below can also be compared to see Zapata Olivella's less blatantly accusatory attitude toward the United States in the second version:

First version	Second version
You thought you were a Bolívar and you dared contradict the mandate of the United Nations. *Of the North Americans.* (p. 55)	You have dared to contradict the mandate of the United Nations. (p. 33)

Zapata Olivella continues to delete specific references to the United States in part 3:

First version	Second version
You know very well that *the Government of the United States* is interested in the success of the *Alliance for Progress*. There are millions of dollars for Colombia. But first we must show them what our needs are. Do you understand now? Chambacú is an ideal district. There the *Peace Corps* will see that we need a whole lot to eradicate hunger. (p. 180)	The gringos have millions of dollars for Colombia. But first we must show them what our needs are. Do you understand now? Chambacú is an ideal district. There they will see that we need a whole lot to eradicate hunger. (pp. 134–135)

This more subtle approach in the second version is seen in the passages below, which like the ones above undoubtedly represent stylistic improvement:

First version	Second version
The little banners in the form of a cross decorated the poles of the fence. One striped, white and red, with a starred square. *The Yankee one.* The other, tricolored: yellow, red and blue, the Colombian one. (p. 206)	The little colored banners fastened in a cross. One white and red striped, with a starred square. The other, tricolored: yellow, red and blue. (p. 136)

Not only are specific references to the United States government, to the Alliance for Progress, and to the Peace Corps eliminated, but several references to President Kennedy as well are cut from the second version. Zapata Olivella also removes several favorable references to Cuba from this second version, changes that represent a further softening in attitude toward the United States. But however mild the second version is, Zapata Olivella, largely through the person of Máximo, clearly holds local officials and conditions responsible for the hunger and misery black people suffer in Colombia. This emphasis on the local is the most direct result of his decision to modify his earlier interpretation of the role the United States played. Zapata Olivella seems to suggest that enough mismanagement and mistreatment can be found within the country to sustain a novel of protest. Black people in Colombia need not understand the presence of the United States or the ideology of Cuba to realize the need for change and reform, even revolution, at home.

Perhaps this is why Máximo as a political leader is no less effective in the second version even though much of his speech-making had been cut. In both versions he gives his life attempting to politicize the black community, efforts his followers continue after his death. Though much of his rhetoric is removed, it is significant that the following speech remains untouched in the second version:

> We will defend ourselves! The police are overstepping their bounds here carrying out orders of those who say they are in control of this island. Even the nation has no right here. They know very well that beneath these rice husks and sawdust, there is only black sweat. We didn't come here of our own free will. They've kicked us out of everywhere and now they want to kick us out of this grave we've built here to die badly in.
>
> . . .
>
> They say they will give us other lands, but these are lies. They always make promises. They know our generosity and they exploit it to the maximum. They are aware of our capacity for suffering and they want to make us die of hunger. They confuse our patience with resignation. But enough is enough. We will fight back . . . and we will organize a march through the city to demand our rights! (p. 118)

This speech, one of the most direct calls for civil disobedience in Afro-Latin American literature, by eschewing reference to any imported ideology, further underscores Zapata Olivella's developing conviction that the revolution, when it comes, is to be deeply rooted in local conditions and needs rather than foreign models.

In the second version, where even the new title leaves little doubt that he is talking about Chambacú, Zapata Olivella makes it clear that responsibility for Colombian hunger begins at home where "the rich of Cartagena adore St. Pedro Claver but don't imitate him" (p. 128). The privileges and insensitivities of the local government and the local rich and powerful come to the foreground to take their rightful share of the responsibility as the United States moves more to the background. By rooting his protest in a specific locale, Zapata Olivella refines his ideological stance. He arrives at the universal in that his specific complaint of a specific black community has all the earmarks of universal problems: hunger, hypocrisy, indifference, and corrupt local officials who pocket money designated for the community at large. In other words, in the second version there is more emphasis on the misuse of funds by the entrusted receiver than on the hypocrisy of the giver.

Zapata Olivella might have needed that hard line against the United States in the early sixties to get his novel published and *premiada* in Cuba, but in the second version he need not be so blatantly strident and redundant to make essentially the same point. *Chambacú, corral de negros* continues to stand as a powerful, fast moving, and deeply committed novel of social protest, perhaps the most up-to-date black novel in Latin America insofar as literary blackness and revolutionary zeal are concerned. Through textual revision he has confronted the problem of ideology not by avoiding the issues but by sharpening his approach to them. He has done this not only by lessening social propaganda in favor of a more artistic version where the narration often is more implicit than explicit but also by giving less emphasis to what at that time was an anti-Yankee stance.

These changes obviously enhance the literary value of the second version, but the first version remains an interesting historical document, even though the author himself does not acknowledge its existence in his own listings of his published work. These changes, it should also be remembered, came after the assassination of President Kennedy and coincide with Zapata Olivella's own increased visibility in the United States where he now is widely recognized and respected both as a visiting professor and as an outstanding literary figure, who like other members in his remarkably gifted family, is dedicated to restoring blackness to the Colombian national scene on several fronts. It is likely that his daughter Edelma and his brother Juan Zapata Olivella will become in poetry and in politics respectively as acclaimed and influential as he has become in literature, and as has his sister Delia in dance and folklore.

What all of these changes mean, of course, is that anyone reading the first version, *Corral de negros*, should be aware of the second, *Chambacú, corral de negros,* and vice versa. The nonchanges, on the other hand, mean that Manuel Zapata Olivella, even without the blatant ideology, is just as firm in his conviction that black people in Colombia as elsewhere are prepared to fight and die "for our dignity as human beings," and it is this view that, perhaps, brings him closer to *black* revolutionary thought than to the more Marxist-oriented literature, for example, of Regino Pedroso and Nicolás Guillén in Cuba and Nelson Estupiñán Bass in Ecuador.

Literary Blackness and Third Worldism in Recent Ecuadorian Fiction: The Novels of Nelson Estupiñán Bass

> *You just have to see how they treat the poor! They find it revolting to attend to a poor person! And if he's black, even worse!*
>
> Nelson Estupiñán Bass

> *If you write, my son,*
> ....
> *let your voice reach the poor, and let the poor be reflected through your voice . . .*
>
> Nelson Estupiñán Bass

One of the underlying principles guiding this study has been to illustrate the level of black consciousness in Latin America, where the black writer, even when seeing himself as part of a Unified Black World, often relates his aspirations and ideology to a larger world not limited by race. This tendency is particularly evident in the works of Nelson Estupiñán Bass whose literary blackness is beyond question but who at the same time is quick to identify with the "politically and economically oppressed and exploited . . . segment of mankind"[1] regardless of color. Working outward from the black's "innate desire for liberty"[2] Estupiñán Bass, particularly in *Senderos brillantes* (1974), shows that he is "deeply rooted in the nationalism"[3] of his country. This novel, one of his most recent, is a protest against United States imperialism and implies that "there can be no decolonization without an authentic revolution."[4]

Estupiñán Bass has long been interested in revolution, and his first novel, *Cuando los guayacanes florecían* (1954), tells about the

Concha uprising in Esmeraldas, his home province. This revolt—
early in this century—was led by Coronel Carlos Concha who,
largely through guerrilla warfare and in alliance with black workers, rose up against government forces sent in to quell the mass
movement. *Cuando los guayacanes florecían* is a war novel, and
because of the different racial composition of the antagonists the
events described are similar to the more celebrated race wars that
took place in Cuba in 1844 and in 1912.

His second novel, *El paraíso* (1958), again deals with black uprising in his home province, this time against oppressive, corrupt, and
insensitive local and national government officials. His third novel,
El último río (1966), depicts an extreme case of racial insecurity. By
laying bare the psychological confusion of a brainwashed black, *El
último río* represents a kind of ethnic catharsis for blacks who want
to be white, again in his home province of Esmeraldas. This novel
is a socio-political as well as a psychological tour de force: even the
gringo makes his appearance here involved in racial imperialism
designed to bleach out black people from the province through pre-
meditated cross-breeding. The foreign intervention broached here is
more fully explored eight years later in *Senderos brillantes*.

Estupiñán Bass's earlier novels deal with black protest, rebellion,
and revolution but they turn inward, focusing for the most part on
local affairs like civil war and corrupt officials. *Senderos brillantes*
is more up tempo in that it deals with a contemporary problem in a
Third World context, namely, Yankee imperialism and economic
exploitation of national resources by the United States. To this novel
in particular we can apply phases of Third-World consciousness
recently conceptualized thematically by Q. Troupe and R. Schulte.[5]
These include categories like oppression and protest and their consequences, crisis of identity, and particularly didactic messages,
often humorously related. Troupe and Schulte also have advanced
the notion that "writing from the Third World has very little room
for any subject that is not immediately concerned with the problems
of that world."[6] This notion is highly workable when applied particularly to *Senderos brillantes* where the author addresses the larger
question of "man's true freedom," as Estupiñán Bass writes in the
Dedicatoria to his book, from which racial identity and the rights
of people—black and white—flow.

Nelson Estupiñán Bass is a profoundly humane writer who has
no time for racial hypocrisy, false promises of false leaders, greed,

and narrow minds that try (through the old book burning ritual, for example) to control the mind; no time, in short, for anything with racist or police state overtones that mitigates against the welfare of the people. In *Senderos brillantes* these evils are combined with foreign intervention that brings with it corrupting influences leading to the moral decay of society due to such vices as gambling, drinking, and prostitution, all associated with outside influences that undermine virtues in youth like honesty and hard work.

Even though lyric in quality, utopic in conception, and highly imaginative in elaboration, this novel is the author's strongest antiimperialist, antifascist work to date. Despite its fable-like nature, *Senderos brillantes* is believable because the novelist builds his story on a very real political situation. The resulting effect is the same as a more direct protest statement against the negative forces that threaten individual freedoms. A sententious author who peppers his narration and dialogue with such sayings as "the games of fate are the thermometers of progress"[7] and "there is no work that leaves a bad mark—all work cleanses and ennobles" (p. 132), Estupiñán Bass impresses with his didactic consistency and with a variety of narrative signatures, among them his sense of humor, his creation of believable characters, and his imaginative and refreshing approach to social and political themes. *Senderos brillantes* is especially highlighted by use of excerpts from thirty pages of letters to lead off his novel and by use of a second voice.

This second voice is the author's "other I," which introduces the author as character by giving details of his life so that the reader can see him on his level and on the same level as the other characters in his novel. This device, whose significance lies in its visionary role of chorus-witness rather than in its participation or actions, allows the author to give multi-perspectives and insights to his story as the observations of this second voice, like the story itself, are linked to the history of Calamares (Galápagos), the utopic island whose freedoms are being usurped by Girasol (Ecuador), puppet of The Estados Asociados (the United States of America) which, in the story, makes Calamares its colony over the wishes of the people there.

The two narrative voices come together with parallel reports as the novel closes and they recount the heroic defense of the island against the invasion of foreign troops sent there to put down the rebellion. While serving as a very effective revolutionary voice of the author through its social and political commentary, this "other

I" is, nevertheless, distracting at times. It is written without punctuation, accent marks, or capitalization while alternating in segments lettered from *a* to *z* with or interrupted by (sometimes in mid-sentence or mid-word) regular chapters, themselves numbered backwards from 56 to 1. In short, the author seems to have heeded some of the tongue-in-cheek advice given him by his "other I," who in its introductory statement advises the author that to achieve universal recognition in his literary endeavors he should resort to such "original" techniques as writing the title of the novel backwards, printing the letters upside down, alternating lines, and deliberately ignoring social evils. He does not, of course, ignore the social side, but he does resort to some of the other tricks to get his message across.

Estupiñán Bass, then, establishes contact with his "fictitious" characters through the use of this "other I." He does the same thing with his use of letters from people (characters) who comment on his novel in manuscript form. Some of them condemn it; others praise it. From these letters, written by antagonists and by heroes alike, it is easy to see which characters the author detests and the ones—the organized group of guerrilla fighters, for example—he admires. These letters precede the first chapter of the novel and are significant as they establish an authenticity and reveal to us even before we read the novel what will happen (or has happened). Even the title is explained in these letters by a former student who remembers the words of the author who once had lectured on the theme the title reflects: "I remember that you used to tell us in civics classes that the paths to freedom are always well lighted, even when they seem darkest, and that freedom does not come without hard struggle" (p. 27).

Consistent with his view that the struggle goes beyond race, the author creates as main characters—the prime movers in the fight for freedom—the black Pedro, the white Richard, and the mestizo Granda. There is only one black family in Calamares, and racist ideas on the island are flamed by white foreigners who use race for much of their political intrigue, particualry in the case of the black, Medardo, perhaps the most fascinating character in the novel, who was lynched partly at the instigation of a *gringa* who detested blacks. Despite the gruesomeness of such scenes, when I think of Nelson Estupiñán Bass his humor comes to mind first, which like Third World humor in general (according to Troupe and Schulte) "is used to identify the outrageous assumptions of racism and eco-

nomic exploitation, the hypocrisy of governments, and to strengthen
cheer, and even warn compatriots."[8] Nelson Estupiñán Bass continues in *Senderos brillantes* through purposeful humor to make his
targets cut ridiculous figures.

These targets in *Senderos brillantes*, as in his other novels, are
public officials who usually make fools of themselves through political harangue, a narrative device Estupiñán Bass skillfully uses in
all of his novels. For a novelist constantly dealing with revolution
and mass movements, it is not surprising to see a large number of
his pages given over to the political harangue, which is, of course,
largely designed to agitate those masses to revolt, to avenge, and to
anger. Estupiñán Bass is a master of this device, and he often has
characters, usually antagonists, spout oratorical nonsense spoken
with the conviction of one who takes his listeners for fools but who
is himself one, at least in the eyes of the reader. His novels often rely
on interaction between speaker and listener whose passions and
emotions are gradually manipulated, usually throughout several
pages of the texts.

Estupiñán Bass opens his first novel, *Cuando los guayacanes florecían*, for example, with this kind of repetitive build up:

> You've probably already heard about it . . . !
> You, especially you people . . . !
> You, sons of a province that is the pride of the nation . . . !
> You, the first ones . . . !
> You . . . all of you must avenge the death of General
> Alfaro . . . ![9]

The speaker finishes this segment of his speech with "Long live
Esmeraldas!"[10] followed by response including applause from the
crowd:

> Long live the Liberal Party!
> Long live General Eloy Alfaro!
> Long may he live![11]

The harangue goes on, "Long live the revolution!"[12] and on through
several pages with such exclamations as "Long live liberty!"[13] occasionally interjected. There are many similar examples in his novels,
but the best one of this kind of political harangue is found in the
closing chapter of *El paraíso*, appropriately entitled "The big fake,"
where we have a classic demonstration of public officials cutting

ridiculous figures. I quote only the beginning of one of these speeches as the entire chapter is made up of political harangues, first from the President:

> —People of Esmeraldas! the President began to say. A people of fighters and of heroes. A people of Titans, who always contributed its offerings and its life for the support of liberty, which is the most sublime mark of man. A people of martyrs, of anonymous heroes, who throughout history . . . [14]

The President's speech is followed by a "little speech" from one of his supporters that is even longer. But the true significance of Estupiñán Bass's heavy use of this device is found in the following conversation taking place in the background while these speeches are being made:

> —Have you listened to Chatarra from the beginning?
> —Yes, I heard the big fraud from the start. It's all a pack of lies,—he said with disdain. . . .
> —This has always been our problem: we let ourselves be fooled by words. I can't tell you why, but that whole speech is a lie.[15]

Such speeches, when seen in their true light, become central to the author's vision of his country's ills as they, better than anything else, sharply focus on hypocrisy in government, especially in its leaders who say one thing and do another.

The words "a pack of lies" used above in *El paraíso* and applied to the President's speech reappear in *Senderos brillantes* where the author again sets up a contrast between words and reality, this time between a representative of the Estados Asociados and one of the insurgents from Calamares. Coronel Harry Douglas writes in one of the letters:

> Now the island has changed. It doesn't seem at all like the island of before. Calamares now has canners, airports, piers, schools, sports fields, markets, drinkable water, electricity, paved roads; we found petroleum, tourists come weekly by the hundreds and put money into circulation, and soon we'll have a modern prison, with all the comforts . . . [16]

And the insurgent:

All that the Associated States offered us turned out to be a pack of lies. They've made the island very pretty, but for themselves . . . [17]

There are fewer political harangues in *Senderos brillantes* because Estupiñán Bass modernizes his novel—and his Third World message—with experimental techniques like the use of the letters, the symbolic fable, and the split consciousness of the "other I."

By following his own tongue-in-cheek "recipe," Estupiñán Bass manages to enliven what had become for him basic thematic constants, namely, unrelenting criticism of racial intolerance and exploitation of the poor by the rich and powerful at local, provincial, national, and international levels, and this latter extension is most pointedly summed up by the following from *Senderos brillantes*: "No matter where the poor man goes he cannot escape the grasp of the Associated States."[18] Estupiñán Bass ends this novel with the landing of the marines on the shores of Calamares to put down the uprising, and while this affront to national dignity is unfolding the author's "other I" sends out a call for help that, specifically and significantly, urges "poets, writers and artists"[19] to take up arms.

The scenario Estupiñán Bass develops in his fable is a serious one when we consider the increasing importance of Ecuadorian oil in the world market. The author, in writing elsewhere that "until a short while ago Esmeraldas was an island, the black brother abandoned to his own fate,"[20] underscores what could be a symbolic relationship between this largely black province and the "island" Calamares that becomes in his fiction a colony of the Associated States. Throughout his life Estupiñán Bass's primary concern has been for Esmeraldas, his "black province of Ecuador."[21] Now that the province "has suffered in its own flesh the blows of imperialism"[22] after becoming "the premier petroleum port of Ecuador,"[23] it is to be expected that Estupiñán Bass would combine literary blackness, black pride, and the "fervent passion for liberty"[24] that the black brought with him from Africa, with Third Worldism, not only in his novels, but as we shall see in the next chapter, in his poetry as well.[25]

Folk Forms and Formal Literature:
Revolution and the Black Poet-Singer
in Ecuador, Peru, and Cuba

> *Our work, I imagine, must be, let's say, like a* bambuco
> *that comes from the people and returns whole to the*
> *people.*
>
> Arnoldo Palacios

> A *humanity reaffirmed through a traditional form and*
> *performed as a part of it, is the ultimate revolutionary*
> *demand.*
>
> *Sylvia Wynter*

I prefaced chapter one with the following quotation from Jean
Franco: "No study of Latin American literature, even in the twentieth century, is balanced unless oral performance is taken into account and unless there is some notion of the dialectics of oral and
written literature."[1] I repeat this quotation here to emphasize that
her statement—though her point of reference is the indigenous—
applies equally to the black experience in Latin America where
black Latin American literature often derives from popular oral
forms that are used by the cultured black poet who then returns
them to the people in newer, more formal written versions. As early
as 1771, Johann Gottfried von Herder, a German philosopher and
historian, was saying in his studies of German folksongs that the
formal literature of a country should be built from the ground up,
that is, on the creative accomplishments of its folk.[2] And more recently, and going one step further, Nicomedes Santa Cruz, reacting
against the ostracism of his popular poetry by the white literary
circles in his country, has countered this literary discrimination in

Peru by going so far as to deny that there is any difference between popular and cultured poetry. His view is that "erudite poetry as opposed to popular poetry"[3] does not exist.

The relationship between folk forms and formal literature has become more recognized in recent years, especially by Stephen Henderson who has confirmed that certainly in the United States "there are two traditions or levels of Black poetry—the folk and the formal—which must be seen as a totality, since they often intersect and overlap one another and since the people who create them are one people."[4] Henderson reminds us that as early as 1922 Robert Thomas Kerlin had studied the poetic tradition of the black, outlining the relationship between black folk rhymes, song, and the "sister art of poetry."[5] Henderson's point and that of Kerlin are no less relevant when applied to Latin America where the same two levels of black poetry exist. Latin America, too, has had its share of "black and unknown bards of long ago" whose heritage of song has had no small influence on the formal literature of contemporary black writers. In the polished verse of Nelson Estupiñán Bass in Ecuador, Nicomedes Santa Cruz in Peru, and Nicolás Guillén in Cuba—to take the three most notable examples—we see not only reflections of the "unstudied poetry of the people"[6] but also poetry as "an extension of black music."[7] Poetry as an extension of song means song converted into poetry as well as poetry converted into song.

If we agree with Amiri Baraka who once said, I believe, that the best way to judge blackness in literature is to compare it to the richness and vitality of black music, then music should be the logical culmination of poetry rooted in the oral tradition. Ideal negritude for Senghor is poetry converted into song, which is to him black poetry's ultimate rhythmic and harmonic achievement. Nowhere is this achievement more noteworthy than in Latin America where poetry by Nelson Estupiñán Bass, Nicomedes Santa Cruz, and Nicolás Guillén is rhythmic and harmonic in its own right and in addition has been set to music by various recording artists.

At any rate, "traditionally, the folk ballad usually rhyming abcb in alternating tetrameter and trimeter lines has been thought of as poetry of the people, by the people and for the people,"[8] and either this basic form or variations on it and on the Spanish *romance* form is found, of course, in the *coplas* of El Negrito Poeta and in the *cantos populares* of Candelario Obeso. It is found as well in the *pregones* and *baladas* of Virginia Brindis de Salas, the *contrapunteo* of Nelson Estupiñán Bass, the *décima* of Nicomedes Santa Cruz, the *canción* of Adalberto Ortiz, and the *son* of Nicolás Guillén, to name only a few examples. Nor should we forget *poesía negra* in general where the African sound in speech and musical rhythms combines with Spanish prosody.

Much of the artistic achievement of black poetry in Latin America derives from mastery of Western poetic technique as well as from the use of popular black speech and black music as poetic referents. What I would like to highlight in this chapter, however, is the ideological or revolutionary significance of folk forms in the formal literature of the black poet-singer in Latin America. We should remember in this context that part of the originality of Candelario Obeso in Colombia who was certainly revolutionary in form, as we saw in chapter five, lay in the "revolutionary meaning"—in Nicolás Guillén's words—that Obeso gave to his content as well. Nelson Estupiñán Bass, Nicomedes Santa Cruz, and Nicolás Guillén follow in the tradition of Obeso—and Plácido for that matter—whose popular verse was revolutionary for its time in its intent to get the message across in forms the people could understand and identify with. This closeness makes folk forms and revolutionary consciousness compatible, and it is this compatibility that often converts the popular poet who uses well-known forms into the most revolutionary of poets, a fact that is becoming more recognized even in the poetry of Langston Hughes, often thought to have been less revolutionary than Nicolás Guillén, who is considered to be Hughes' most direct Latin American counterpart.

Nelson Estupiñán Bass, a novelist of revolution as we saw in the previous chapter, is also well known as a poet of revolution. Like Pilar Barrios in Uruguay, Estupiñán Bass also tackles the difficult task of simulating gaucho literature by transforming the popular language and forms of the unlettered *payador negro* into formal literature. Estupiñán Bass does this in *Timarán y Cuabú* (1956), a long gaucho poem where "the verbal battle of two popular poets belonging to different generations"[9] serves to teach political consciousness; this is done without, however, being too dogmatic, that is, without getting too deeply into "the Marxist polemic,"[10] and more importantly, without sacrificing the authenticity of that genre.

Timarán y Cuabú, a "match up between black singers,"[11] is made up, for the most part, of *coplas*, an indispensable form for the literary artist who draws on the popular forms of expression of the people. Estupiñán Bass's book has been called "a book of lyrical poems mixed in with 'committed' poems,"[12] but it is, as well, one long "verbal battle typical of the province of Esmeraldas."[13] In this volume of popular verse Estupiñán Bass abandons for a time the intellectualized free verse that characterized his first volume of poetry, *Canto negro por la luz* (1954), which contains a form of untranslatable and highly stylized verse reaching its maximum expression in the poem "Hombre en la luna":

> Litiasis densa deleterea líquida y licuante
> frágil madrépora tridimensional y tetraedro
> ....
> Nesqua nequaquam niquiscocio nirvana nimbo nomeolvides
> galeotes desorbitados y purpúreos
> ....
> Plúmbea panoplia Penelope
> primigenia píxide pitoche pituitaria
> pin
> pan
> pun
> pun pan pin.[14]

Though his underlying revolutionary message in some of the more intelligible parts of this poem is the same that he develops in *Timarán y Cuabú*, his means certainly were inappropriate for the average man. For this reason it is not surprising that Estupiñán Bass turned to folkloric forms in his formal literature to better "reach the people in their own language."[15] As Jorge Hugo Rengel has pointed out, " 'Canción del niño negro y del incendio' begins this aspect of his great poetry, of his social lyricism, that has already peaked in *Timarán y Cuabú*."[16] The refrain from this poem:

> Negro, negro, renegrido,   Black, black, jet black,
> negro, hermano del carbón,   coal black black,
> negro de negros nacido[17]   black born of blacks

(which leaves little doubt about Estupiñán Bass's degree of blackness) has also been set to music and recorded. Estupiñán Bass, like Obeso before him, immortalizes his own folk-formal creation by inserting "Canción del niño negro del incendio" as a popular song in a subsequent creative work (*El último río*) just as Obeso had done with his "Canción del boga ausente," which he inserted, as we pointed out in chapter five, in his own *Lucha de la vida*.

Estupiñán Bass's identification with the poor, a thematic constant in his prose, is repeatedly emphasized in *Timarán y Cuabú*. Cuabú, in verbal battle with Timarán, says

Soy como el judío errante,	I am like the prodigal son,
no me importan las banderas,	nationalities do not matter to me
pues para los hombres pobres	because for the poor
no se han hecho las fronteras.[18]	there are no national boundaries.

Later in the poem Cuabú again identifies with the poor:

Yo lucho contra los fuertes	I fight against the strong
y aborrezco las fronteras	and I hate national boundaries
porque con sangre de pobres	because those barriers are constructed
se alzaron esas barreras.	with the blood of the poor.
Yo no canto por cantar.	I do not sing just to be singing.
Canto con el corazón,	I sing from the heart,
y quisiera que los pobres	and I want my song
se unieran con mi canción.[19]	to bring poor people together.

Cuabú sums up his argument by calling for revolution:

Pero en días no lejanos	But in the not too distant future
el pueblo habrá de marchar	the people will have to
a las calles a pelear	take to the streets to fight
con el fusil en las manos.[20]	with rifles in their hands.

Estupiñán Bass even includes a verse that points to the revolutionary message of his novel *Senderos brillantes*:

Hay un hermoso sendero	There is a beautiful path
donde está la solución:	where the solution lies:
hacer la revolución	and that path is revolution
de brazo con el obrero.[21]	together with the worker.

Estupiñán Bass is one of the better known poets of revolution in Latin America, and that is why he is one of the notable omissions from Robert Márquez's recent anthology, *Latin American Revolutionary Poetry*; Nicomedes Santa Cruz is another. One of the criticisms—made by Robert Pring-Mill—of this anthology is the glaring omission of such writers as this popular Peruvian poet-singer. Pring-Mill wrote in his review of the book:

> Most of the poets included are intellectuals, or have had at least a middle-class education, whereas with such a genre as this one needs to take into account numerous working-class poets like the Guatemalan Mélinton Salazar or the Peruvian Leoncio Bueno. One must also bear in mind the long tradition

of *campesino* poetry, much of it social in content, usually sung (and often anonymous): the almost universal *décimas*, the Mexican *corridos*, the *tangos* of the River Plate, or the *poesía gauchesca* of the *payadores*. This is important for an understanding of the links between modern social poetry and the *canciones de protesta*, which embrace not only products of popular tradition but the upsurge of works by poet-singers like the Mexican Judity Reyes, Carlos Puebla in Cuba, Atahualpa Yupanqui in Argentina, the Peruvian Nicomedes Santa Cruz, or Uruguayans such as Daniel Viglietti, and Chileans like the Parras or the late Victor Jara.[22]

Nicomedes Santa Cruz who (as if contrasting himself) sees the Chilean Victor Jara as "a revolutionary who sang, not a revolutionary singer,"[23] has assumed the leading role of black popular poet in Peru, where he sees himself closer to the people than what he calls such "elite" writers as Mario Vargas Llosa. Santz Cruz combines literary blackness with the "national tradition of improvising,"[24] making use of among others the *décima* form to explore the black past and to push for the liberation of black people and other oppressed peoples in the world. In "A todo canto de monte," Santa Cruz shows how blacks in Peru took over the *copla* form and gave it a new name:

Su desafío en cuartetas	His challenge in quatrains
sobre un obligado asunto	on an assigned subject
dio margen al contrapunto	gave an opportunity for verbal battle
en muy ingeniosas tretas.	with ingeniously crafty thrusts.
Hábiles negros poetas	Skillful black poets
dieron la copla peruana,	gave us the Peruvian couplet,
. . . .	. . . .
los negros de aquel lugar	and the blacks of that region
llamábanle "Cumanana".[25]	called it "Cumanana".

Santa Cruz has also written what he calls "peasant songs" where a poetic voice spells out innumerable injustices that drive men to revolt:

Para que el usurpador	We water the earth
viva como millonario	with our blood and sweat
regamos el suelo agrario .	so that the usurpers
con nuestra sangre y sudor.	can live like millionaries.
Protegen al vil señor	Murderous officials
funcionarios asesinos,	protect the land owners,

y cercan nuestros destinos
linderos de agudo alambre
donde nos morimos de hambre
millonarios de campesinos . . . [26]

and barbed wire
fence in our destinies
and we peasants die of hunger
millions of us . . .

The role of the *gringo* here, as in the work of Arnoldo Palacios, Manuel Zapata Olivella, Nelson Estupiñán Bass, and Nicolás Guillén, is an unsavory one and he, together with local figures of oppression, becomes a target of revolutionary consciousness:

Donde no hay minas de gringos
   hay tierra de gamonales,
   pagan míseros jornales
. . . .

Where there are no gringo mines,
   there are feudal lands
   where they pay miserable wages
. . . .

In this section, where the poet calls on *campesino, comunero, obrero, andino,* and the young *universitario* to revolt against the "damned oligarchy"[28] whose "cynical arrogance thrives on our ignorance"[29] we have an even more pointed reference to the sinister presence of the United States:

Yo soy revolucionario
porque en este pandemonium
la International Petroleum
no me volvió mercenario.
Y si los ataco a diario
es porque la patria mía
padece la tiranía
de los gobiernos vendidos
a los Estados Unidos
corrompidos por la CIA . . .[30]

I am a revolutionary
because in this mad house
the International Petroleum Co.
did not turn me into a mercenary.
And if I attack them daily
it is because my country
suffers from the tyranny
of governments that sell out
to the United States,
corrupted by the CIA . . .

In a poem published recently in Cuba, Nicomedes Santa Cruz in "canto a Angola" speaks out for revolutionary solidarity between Africa and Latin America against imperialism:

Nuestra victoria es segura,
tan cierta como el mañana
de esta Unidad Africana
que es la esperanza futura.
. . . .
y desde Angola germina
una gran Revolución
que consolida esta unión
con América Latina! . . .[31]

Our victory is certain;
African Unity, the hope
of the future, is as
certain as tomorrow.
. . . .
And the great Revolution
taking root in Angola
will consolidate this union
with Latin America! . . .

Nicomedes Santa Cruz has ranged far and wide through Africa, Peru, and the Third World as he places himself squarely "on the side of the proletariat."[32] With his *décimas*, his *cumananas*, his "country songs," and other poems this black poet-singer popularizes revolutionary consciousness through folk forms and "black rhythms of Peru" as Nicolás Guillén has done in Cuba with his *son*-poem. It is well known that it is the *son* "that really gives Guillén his Cuban dimension, his popular poet image."[33] It is also true that the *son* draws artistically on black speech and black music as poetic sources particularly in *Motivos de son* and other volumes such as *El son entero* and *Cantos para soldados y sones para turistas*, three books by Guillén that specifically carry the word *son* in their titles.

The *son* is a dance "in which the words and music of the people culminate in song,"[34] and this song, in written literature, is usually conveyed through refrain, short final lines, and *agudo* rhyme. As we saw in chapter seven, Guillén first introduced his poetic version of this popular music heard on the streets of Cuba in *Motivos de son* (1930). It is in *Motivos de son*, his first published book of poems where the poet begins to transpose a musical tradition into literary forms, which are themselves later "returned to musical performance only on a formal level."[35] It is there, and not solely with his later more obvious and blatantly anti-imperialist poetry of protest and revolution, that Guillén begins to establish himself as a poet of revolution. Since the poems in this first volume "came from the hot, lively soul of our people,"[36] Guillén's poetry "began to be, from those very first moments, revolutionary poetry,"[37] not by mentioning revolution directly but by "reflecting, offering us and giving back to us the peculiar and essential characteristics of our people."[38] Manuel Navarro Luna, the author of these words, supports the view by referring to Mao Tse Tung, who had said that literature and revolutionary art are the product of the reflection and representation of the life of the people as it takes shape in the minds of revolutionary writers and artists.[39]

Nicolás Guillén, then, was a revolutionary poet or a poet of revolution long before 1959. His poetry over the years, certainly from *West Indies Ltd.* (1934) on, seems to reflect a covert revolutionary sensibility looking or waiting for a revolution to happen. This disposition is most dramatically illustrated by the continuing presence of the "clenched fists" ("Balada de Simón Carballo"), the "vengeful fists" ("West Indies Ltd."), and the "powerful fists" ("Elegía a Jesús Menéndez") that characterized his poetry long before the Black Power salute as we know it today. This is the feeling conveyed by his *Cantos para soldados y sones para turistas* (1937) whose "call to rebellion" in "Diana" again represents the poet as prophet of a revolution to come when time catches up to him. Guillén has always been ahead of his time. Just as his recurring *puños* ("fists") antedate the Black Power salute, his *Cantos para soldados y sones para turistas* reads like a primer for draft evaders and war resisters of the sixties, some of whom felt that as soldiers their guns would be pointed at the wrong enemy. Long before the phrase became popular, Nicolás Guillén was "telling it like it is," perhaps nowhere more explicitly than through the black poetic voice of José Ramón Cantaliso who "les canta liso, muy liso/para que lo entiendan bien" ["gives it to them straight, very straight/so that they do not get it wrong"].[40]

Though a highly cultured poet, adept with the most sophisticated of Spanish verse forms, Guillén, since the publication of *Motivos de son*, has always been conscious of the need to speak to the people through the folk forms they know best: "I don't think we can forget, for the time being, the traditional forms. They're the ones the people know, and therefore, the best means to transmit to them a new preoccupation. . . . It is always best to speak to them in a voice that won't frighten them."[41] Guillén even manages to give his *son* an unmistakable blues voice, for example, in

Ayer vi a un hombre mirando,
mirando el sol que salía;
ayer vi a un hombre mirando,
mirando el sol que salía:
el hombre estaba muy serio,
porque el hombre no veía.[42]

Yesterday I saw a man looking,
looking at the sun coming out;
yesterday I saw a man looking,
looking at the sun coming out:
that man was in a bad way,
because he could not see.

And again, more recently:

Soy como un árbol florido,
que ayer flores no tenía;
soy como un arbol florido
que ayer flores no tenía:
a leer me enseñó el pueblo,
    caramba.
aunque el pueblo,
leer tampoco sabía.[43]

I am like a tree in bloom,
that before had gone to seed;
I am like a tree in bloom,
that before had gone to seed:
I have learned from the people,
    caramba.
even though the people
did not know how to read.

These verses, which illustrate very well the impact of the people in the poet's art and the coming of age of the people through the Revolution, rely on popular folk forms. Guillén's *Elegía a Jesús Me-*

néndez, perhaps, is his most ambitious and multifaceted revolutionary poem. Though constructed on a variety of sophisticated verse forms—and there are segments in prose—the following simple *son*-refrain, also reminiscent in its powerful simplicity to the blues-*son* form mentioned above, is the most hauntingly incorporated:

Pasó una paloma herida,	A wounded dove passed,
volando cerca de mí;	flying close by;
rojo le brillaba el pecho,	its breast shone red,
que yo la ví.[44]	for I saw it.

It is his sophistication with popular folk forms that makes the poetry of Guillén, "Black National Poet of Revolutionary Cuba,"[45] the "perfect revolutionary poetry" that José Antonio Portuondo in the following paragraph correctly thinks it is:

The poetry of Nicolás Guillén exemplifies in a preeminent way the perfect revolutionary poetry. In it the political content forms strophes and verses in accordance with his expressive intention, and the result is a song heard by all, although unconsciously. The revolutionary creator must take into account the necessity and the urgency of presenting the consumer not only a sense of form which he already knows by folkloric tradition or by shallow education, but with the riches of new modes that augment his culture with his own capacity of expression. Repeating every day with all the pretexts of entertaining the people, without any type of precision or artistry, the same simplistic formulas however "popular" they might be, doesn't contribute to the esthetic formation of the masses any more than it favors their ideological vigor.[46]

Echoing these fairly well-known words of Portuondo, Dellita Martin Lowery, in what is no doubt one of the most recent comparative studies of black poets—her comparative subjects are Nicolás Guillén and Langston Hughes—who draw on folk forms for inspiration, has written that Guillén's *rumba* and *son* poems like Hughes' jazz and blues poems "illustrate the poet's efforts to return in a polished form the raw material provided by a culture shared by all Cubans."[47] In her study Lowery shows very well how the oral tradition provided the working material, that is, the forms, musical devices, formulaic patterns, and figurative language characteristic of folk speech for each poet, who, through his own artistic genius recreates them each in his formal written language.[48]

Nicolás Guillén has had the creative genius and longevity to combine folk forms and revolutionary content in his written literature, certainly for a longer period of time than any other black poet-singer in Latin America, without sinning unduly in this combination either on the side of simplistic formula or blatant ideology. Further, by incorporating folk forms from the oral tradition into his formal literature, Nicolás Guillén, like Nelson Estupiñán Bass and Nicomedes Santa Cruz, has shown that the relationship between the oral tradition and the political commitment of Third World writers is not coincidental because that commitment includes "the desire to take poetry away from the academic level and bring it back to the people, to their way of expressing their joys and sorrows, their human concerns."[49] Perhaps in this way the distinction Edouard Glissant[50] makes between free and forced poetics becomes unnecessary since, with this transition or synthesis, the distance between folk or oral forms and formal literature is, through the art of Third World revolutionary writers, eliminated.

Return to the Origins:
The Afro-Costa Rican Literature of Quince Duncan

My only aspiration is to make sure Blacks don't lose their openness and forget their origins.

Langston Hughes

You have to know where you've been before you can get to where you are going.

Willie Ricks

You can't begin to do anything in life until you can own up to your blackness and accept yourself in your blackness and others as they are.

John Conyers

The Experimental Black Theater and other cultural activities fostered by Abdias do Nascimento in Brazil in the forties, fifties, and sixties, the Afro-Colombian dance troupe of Manuel and Delia Zapata Olivella, the Teatro y Danzas Negras of Victoria Santa Cruz in Peru, and more recently the troupe of black Rio de Janeiro dancers choreographed by Isaura de Assis are all attempts to get blacks in Latin America to identify more with their heritage, culture, and history through a return on stage to their origins. Renewing one's strength and reaffirming one's identity through a return to one's origins is repeatedly done by black novelists and poets as well in Latin America, though this return, to be sure, has not always reached all the way back to Africa. Pedro's impending return, a basic thematic and structural feature in Juan Pablo Sojo's *Nochebuena negra*, is from Caracas to Barlovento, his *terruño*. Ascensión Lastre's return is to his blackness, which in the end gives him strength for his final heroic deeds in Adalberto Ortiz's *Juyungo*. Arnoldo Palacios in *Las estrellas son negras* criticized moderately successful blacks who forget their origins "as through they cannot see their black skin with their own eyes" (p. 68). One of the characters in his *La selva y la lluvia*, who had lost his job because he had tried to unionize the workers, consoled his friends by telling them of his decision to return home, to "return to the land from whence I came," to take renewed strength from his roots. Nicolás Guillén, Nelson Estupiñán Bass, and Nicomedes Santa Cruz are constantly refreshing their literary expression by going to the folk forms of their people. Carlos Wilson, the black Panamanian author now based in Los Angeles, California, leaves little doubt what his origins are as he returns regularly to Panama through his literature—discussed in the next chapter—as well as through travel. This return to one's origins characterizes the literature of Costa Rica's Quince Duncan, Wilson's Central American neighbor.

In Panama, Costa Rica, and elsewhere in Central America, black identity and the problem of origin are complicated by a present-day reality that finds the fourth generation Anglo-black alienated or removed several times over from his origin. Unlike the Hispanicized black who was brought in during the colonial days, the Anglo-black in Central America is distant from Africa and from mainstream (white) Central American societies but also from the Hispanicized black himself and from the West Indies as well from where he "was not brought"[1] but rather "was called and came."[2] This present-day reality is further complicated by Costa Rica's attempts "to pass itself off as a 'white' nation."[3]

Fourth generation blacks in Costa Rica—Quince Duncan being one—are "thinking men,"[4] in his words, who are beginning to explore these problems of identity and origin as well as to look critically at their marginality to the larger Costa Rican society. The works of Quince Duncan, the most prolific and the latest black Costa Rican author to explore these problems, deserve our attention, especially since he receives only one single mention—even though he already had four books to his credit—in the recent study by Alvaro Sánchez M. "El negro en la literatura costarricense,"[5] the only one I know of that deals specifically with the black in Costa Rican literature.

Duncan's works, like those of Carlos Wilson, are indispensable for any study of the black in Central American literature. Fundamental for an understanding of his writing is the critical framework set up by Martha K. Cobb,[6] whose concepts of literary blackness discussed in the Introduction are applicable to the works of Duncan. He updates the problem of identity and the divided self, and the structure of his most recent novel *Los cuatro espejos* (1973),[7] with its shifting focus, reflects the tension of duality. The quest for self and the confrontation with self and with the Other, which lead the principal character back to his origin and to a spiritual liberation, formulate an organizing principle that holds the novel together and relate it to the real world outside the fictional one.

This real world is the same one dealt with in part by other Costa Rican authors: Carlos Luis Fallas, for example, in *Mamita Yunai* (1941), perhaps Costa Rica's best known novel; in *Puerto Limón* (1950) and other works by Joaquín Gutiérrez; in some of the stories of Fabián Doblés; and more recently, and with great sensitivity, by Abel Pacheco in *Más abajo de la piel* (1974). While most of these works focus on the social drama of the worker as victim, Duncan focuses on the interior drama of a man in transformation. Just as Fallas wanted to move the public to identify with the worker in his political document, so too does Duncan want blacks to identify with the transformation of his main character in his psychological document that deals first with loss of identity and rejection of origin and later with discovery of identity and acceptance of origin.

Duncan's novel focuses on a black's inner conception and development of self. He is aware of stereotyped thinking underlying white prejudices toward blacks in Costa Rica, and his novel depicts the racism Costa Rican whites inflict on blacks, particularly blacks from the Province of Limón. A timely speech on the black as victim early in the novel serves to summarize his views on the black as alienated from and marginal to Costa Rican society. We see it in the "logical deductions" (p. 104) whites make about blacks they encounter, namely, that all blacks are from Limón and speak bad Spanish. Duncan is adamant on the absurdity of this so-called logical deduction regarding language, and he returns to it in a literary essay, where he writes:

What has happened to us, the blacks of Limón, is that we live in a Latin culture, and our educational background is in English. And you cannot know that from the window of a train. From there, you cannot measure the impact of the Garvey movement in the province, nor can you count the inhabitants of Limón who at the beginning of the century went off to study in Jamaican colleges and returned here to be teachers, practising physicians, etc. From there it is impossible to know of the great exceptions: the late Rev. Ford who graduated from Oxford. P. Harrison, one of the most learned blacks of our country, and undoubtedly one of the most educated people in Costa Rica.

Nor is it at all possible from afar to appreciate the large number of teachers, musicians, etc. that died or live in jail because destiny placed them in an Hispanic Costa Rica that for a long time obstinately denied their worth.[8]

Duncan has his protagonist earn a Ph.D. in English. Awareness of racist behavior is seen in his novel, too, when he shows that blacks are at times served last in stores even though they are there first. He shows how blacks are taunted in schools with shouts like "Hey, Blackey, Blackey don't know nothin'. Don't understand. Blackey only knows about cocoa and bananas" (p. 105), and how blacks are cautioned not to be out late on the streets of San José with the admonition: "Look here, blackey, you're not in Limón. So, watch it" (p. 120).

Such pressures as these, which are backed by a social system for which "white is a symbol of purity, and black a symbol of the despicable and perverse"[9] are of deep concern to the author, who realizes such a system must be subverted. But Duncan aims his message first at blacks because he believes that the black in Costa Rica must begin to accept his origins. For him, salvation lies in "coming to our senses because we've lost ourselves inside, where we have become white men in black skin."[10] But such external pressures as these are related to the inner development of Duncan's protagonist who often felt his own personal dignity threatened by racist humiliations suffered by other less fortunate blacks. In fact, suffering the very humiliations to which the hero thought himself immune helps precipitate his reassessment of his own existence.

This reassessment, together with the psychological trauma that accompanies it, is an excellent account of a black who cannot remain oblivious to the black experience around him, despite his own personal advancement. Duncan's main character came to be aware of what racism in all its forms was doing to him, as all the forms of racism he witnessed were related to his basic problem, namely, his growing estrangement from his blackness, his roots. An analysis by Emile Synder is applicable to Duncan's character who becomes aware that "racism attempts to *disfranchise* a man from his geographical roots, indeed from the earth itself. . . . racism (all forms of racism) attempts to *deterritorialise* its victim who becomes reduced to beg acceptance as an alien or to seek to assimilate in the hope of disappearing from this monstrous illegitimacy fostered upon him."[11]

Nowhere is this assessment more true than in Costa Rica. There alienation—as with assimilation—is a reality that must be faced. For this reason we can say of Duncan's protagonist that at a crucial point in his life he was "condemned to be the spectator of his own painful metamorphosis and to observe with bitterness as his 'I' became more and more 'another'."[12] It is at this point in his life, as he was becoming "a stranger to his tribe, to his religion, to his traditions, and to himself,"[13] that he decides to review his life and the cultural and racial schizophrenia that was splitting him apart. This identity crisis brought on by the contradiction or confrontation between the acculturation or assimilation that he espoused and the alienation that he was beginning to feel is Duncan's treatment of the old cultural hybrid syndrome: "The marginal man caught between two cultures, searching for an identity beyond his grasp."[14] His protagonist no longer loved his present and he turns to the past in order to straighten it out and to get a new perspective on it, on his future, and on the foreign world in which he lives, where he is always looked down on regardless of his achievements. Lewis Nkosi's phrase is very à propos here: "Black consciousness really begins with the shock of discovery that one is not only black but is also *non-white*,"[15] What is more, Duncan's fiction explores this shock of discovery, particularly in *Los cuatro espejos*, whose protagonist is forced into the additional realization that he is *non-white, non-black*, and *non-Hispanic*, a discovery that precipitates the acute identity crisis that had him on the brink of an emotional breakdown.

Charles McForbes is this protagonist and he is a second generation black whose father Pète McForbes, a Jamaican, had settled in Costa Rica to make a new start after the financial ruin of what was once a well-to-do family that had accumulated great wealth through the efforts of Saltimán McForbes, Charles' grandfather. After the death of Lorena Sam, his first wife, who was black, Charles escaped the black world in Limón whose backwardness he thought responsible for her death, using his education and his "light color" to advantage by marrying Ester, a white woman who was antiblack before this marriage, having been reared by a liberal but basically racist father. But Charles, realizing that he would never be able to bury his Limón background, had also begun to realize that he had abandoned that black world and his people.

Finally seeing himself as others saw him, that is, black despite his achievements and his "light color," Charles tried to ward off total emotional breakdown by looking back and confronting his past, including the white family he had married into. Reviewing his life he remembers that his father-in-law was "an animal. An animal of the worst kind." He wonders, "I don't know how I came to get involved with that family. I swear to God I don't know" (p. 76). His lack of a firm identity literally hit him in the face one morning when he awoke and could not see himself in the mirror.

This psychological problem had started the day before when he heard a lecture on blacks in Costa Rica and had intensified afterwards when he was witness to racial affronts to fellow blacks on the streets of San José. The resolution begins only when the protagonist decides to return home to Limón, that is, to his origins, in search of an identity that would replace his present faceless existence. After a period of trying to pull himself together, of wandering the streets searching aimlessly for something that would justify his present existence, Charles opted for a more meaningful "Orphic journey" back in time and space. This use of "Orphic," of course, comes from Sartre, who, in explaining his understanding of black poetry, wrote: "And I shall call this poetry 'Orphic' because the negro's timeless descent into himself makes me think of Orpheus going to claim Eurydice from Pluto."[16] This Orphic option took control of the actions of Duncan's protagonist at one indecisive but crucial moment in his musings, when he subsequently opted to return to Limón.

On this journey back to his province, the author has his protagonist partake of what could be symbolic *yuca con bofe*, in a scene reminiscent of the yam session in Ralph Ellison's *Invisible Man*:

> The old man was trying to tell me something but I hadn't heard.
> Pardon me?
> Do you want some?
> What is it?
> *Yuca con bofe.*
> I haven't had that for years. All right then, I'll take the larg-

est piece there. How much is it?

Three *colones*.

Here.

Thanks, old man.

The old man brought the meat to his mouth and chewed voraciously. As for me, at first I found it repugnant and then nauseating. I put my head out of the window, and, pretending to be taking an interest in the scenery, let my last mouthful drop. The locomotive once again filled the air with its long whistle, and the smell of burned oil contaminated the breeze. (pp. 125–126)

Unlike Ellison's character who readily embraces those yams in a "ceremonial meal" that momentarily reunites him with his people,[17] Charles' distaste for his *yuca con bofe*, a "typical meal of Limón"[18], is symbolic because it shows how far removed from his origins he had become.

Charles continues his journey in search of his identity. On this journey back in time and in space he remembers what in fact had constituted the root of his present identity crisis, namely, the advice his grandfather with his Scottish ancestry had planted in the minds of his children:

I don't want any of you marrying a black woman. Get yourselves a mulatto or an English woman. We've got to rise in color to get ourselves out of this mess we're in. The black, ever since Noah, was condemned to suffer: keep as far away from them as possible. We've got to keep on whitening ourselves; that's the solution, whitening ourselves. (p. 130)

It was this advice that Charles was now beginning to see in perspective, in the black perspective that his father before him, "a black who failed" (p. 131), had come to embrace partly out of his admiration for another proud black called Jakel Duke who "descended from some ashanti king" (p. 46) and who "boasted about being pure African" (p. 46).

Charles, recalling the proud black images of his father and of Jakel Duke, came to realize that not all of his black past had been negative, and thus, he managed to survive his identity crisis. Resolving the duality problem of his protagonist through memory, a key component of survival for one who feels exiled and alienated, the author shows that in Costa Rica, as in the United States, there are at least what Stephen Henderson has called "two levels of ethnic memory"[19], Africa for blacks in both countries, and in the United States the South, a kind of "Down Home" for "transplanted blacks who had gone North for a better life."[20] A third level of ethnic memory, in addition to the Province of Limón, for blacks in Costa Rica who had gone to San José in search of a better life would be, of course, the West Indies. The train trip back, which seemed to the protagonist "a journey through a thousand centuries" (p. 125), and these levels of ethnic memory that helped the protagonist avoid total breakdown constitute in a sense the same Orphic trip that Aimé Césaire made in his *Cahier d'un retour au pays natal.*

By having his protagonist reaffirm his "primary identity" through this Orphic trip, the author has Charles win his battle against total alienation, or the "ultimate madness,"[21] it has been called. The basic message we get from Alex Haley's *Roots*—that we should not forget where we came from and how we got to be where we are,—is to a certain extent the same message we get from Duncan's *Los cuatro espejos.* In fact, by returning to his origins Duncan's protagonist was able to move "from awareness, to revolt, to love,"[22] for in the final analysis, after achieving the "other peace" (p. 150) he sought, he turns his thoughts to "the simple things that erase superficial differences of skin color and reveal the humanity of all. Things which, after all, unite us through God's skin" (p. 153). Just as Ester "had found in his blackness a profound humanity" (p. 101), overcoming as a result her racist background, so too does Charles realize that he had become "a dual being, split between two worlds, trapped between two cultures" (P. 153) for all the wrong reasons.

Once his protagonist achieves the spiritual liberation the journey back afforded him, the author, through what we can call chain imagery-symbolism, moves from "color as a chain holding one back,"[23] where one feels imprisoned or trapped by "black skin, black features and black blood"[24] to a larger conception of *cadenas* as bonds that bind together all mankind, and certainly Charles and Ester, who reject divorce as a way out. Chains, instead of denying one's humanity, are made to express Duncan's understanding of a larger consciousness made possible by being at peace with one's identity.

Duncan reinforces this point in the closing words of the novel:

If you've come for a divorce, she said, forget it.
Is that a threat?
No. I do not want you to leave me. Charles, it is hard for

me to say that.

Yes, it's hard. But do you realize that by chaining me you're chaining yourself?

Charles, she said, her eyes lost in the immensity of the night, we're all chained. They're God's chains. (p. 163)

This conclusion, even in the ties-that-bind imagery, is like Césaire's in his *Cahier* where, at the end of his Orphic journey, he writes:

> bind me, bind me without remorse
> bind me with your vast arms to the luminous day
> bind my black resonance to the very navel of
>   the world
> bind me, bind me bitter fraternity.[25]

Through chain imagery-symbolism and other focal motif devices in the novel (teeth, *yuca con bofe*, the Teatro Nacional, mirrors), with the aid of an internalized narrative flow that allows the reader to get inside the tensions of the dual personality of the protagonist, and through a narrative structure that reflects this tension through constant shifts in focus between the present and the past,—between Costa Rica and Jamaica, and between San José and Limón,—Quince Duncan has shown the importance of origins especially for the new Costa Rican, the English-speaking West Indian and his descendants in Costa Rica.

Quite clearly Duncan wants whites to better understand the identity problem of these descendants. More importantly he wants to move blacks back in the direction of their origin because "the business of their oppressing us is only part of the matter; it's also true that the black oppressed himself" (pp. 34–35). Duncan agrees that a new definition of humanity "is not so much the problem of the whites as the problem of the blacks. For it is blacks who have to smash the system, explode the white man's racist myths that have distorted his humanity for over three hundred years."[26] Duncan agrees that "to achieve this the black man must redefine his reality in his own terms."[27] The Orphic trip, or the journey within, is one way to redefine this reality and to confront the racial, cultural, social, psychological, and political problems of the black in the real world of Costa Rica. This journey is only a first step; however, in Costa Rica as elsewhere, it is perhaps the most important step of all.

16

Ebe Yiye—
"The Future Will Be Better":
An Update on Panama from Black Cubena

> An authentic work always reflects the historical, social
> and economic conditions in which it was conceived and
> written.
>
> Nicolás Guillén

When I discussed Gaspar Octavio Hernández, the "Black Swan," in chapter six, I emphasized that the Panama Canal was a topic of national debate during his lifetime. The Canal issue continues to stir Panamanians as was evident in the 1978 referendum to endorse treaties that will give Panamanians control of it by the turn of the century. This attention coincided with the propitious publication in 1977 of *Cuentos del Negro Cubena* (Guatemala: Editorial Landivar, 1977) and *Pensamientos del Negro Cubena* (Los Angeles, California, 1977) by Carlos Guillermo Wilson, another Afro-Panamanian whose literary debut is timely because the Canal as a theme informs much of his work either implicitly or explicitly. We are fortunate indeed that Wilson has begun to publish at this time because his works provide a welcome perspective, a contemporary black perspective that is often missed in the public discussion on the Canal issue. Wilson considers himself a political writer, and much of his work has been censored in Panama. But the update we get from his stories and poems that have appeared—his two books were published outside of Panama—reveal his determination to tell what he sees as the real story on racial and social justice in his country. Although Hispanicized blacks have a long history in Panama, one that dates back to colonial days and to the nineteenth century when

Panama was known as Colombia's black province, Wilson is primarily concerned with the plight of the "new" black Panamanian, the *chombo*, the black descendant, like himself, of English-speaking West Indians (Wilson prefers the term Afro-Caribbeans) who came in to dig the Canal. Wilson speaks out on behalf of the *chombo*, who was only recently granted the right to Panamanian citizenship and who lives largely a segregated existence in ghettos in Panama and in the Canal Zone.

But Wilson does not limit his concern to the *chombo* or even to Panama. Though born in Panama City, Wilson has lived in the United States and received his doctorate in Hispanic Languages from the University of California at Los Angeles. He has travelled widely in Africa, the West Indies, and the United States, which together with Panama occupy his multiple levels of ethnic memory. Wilson knows who he is and he leaves little doubt what his origins are. In fact, he is one of the first—if not the first—black Latin American authors to take on an African name, a decision that better than anything else underscores the importance he gives to his African origin. *Cubena*, the name he has chosen for himself, is an Hispanicized version of *Kwabena*, the Twi word for Tuesday. Dr. Wilson was born on Tuesday, he tells us, and he has followed the Ashanti custom of giving children the name of the day on which they were born. He has inserted the word *Cubena* at the bottom of a literary shield sketched on the covers of his two books. At the top of that shield, an understanding of which is important for easy access to his literary orientation—and to the meaning of the title of this chapter—are the words, again from Twi, *EBE YIYE*, which means "The Future Will Be Better." Between *EBE YIYE* at the top of the shield and *CUBENA* at the bottom Wilson includes a chain with six links, three stars, an open book, and a turtle with a bee on its back.

The six-linked chain, Wilson has explained, represents the six main African groups that were enslaved in the Americas: Yoruba, Fanti, Ashanti, Congo, Bantu, and Dahomey. The three stars symbolize the three countries where he has roots: Africa, Jamaica, and Panama. The open book dramatizes the way—through education and knowledge—slavery of the mind can be overcome. Finally, the turtle represents the patience and strength of character blacks have had to develop to survive the by-products of those "vulturistic isms"—here symbolized by the bee—I discussed in the Introduction. Wilson continues to emphasize his multiple levels of ethnic

memory as well as his commitment to "peace, love and justice"—
words he includes on the dedication page to his book of poetry—
by dedicating his books to his parents, black Panamanians with
West Indian background, and to "all people of African descent."

I give these details because they highlight the diverse influences
present in his literature and in his quest for black solidarity. He
believes very deeply that an "injustice committed against one is a
threat directed against all," a quotation from Montesquieu that
Cubena uses to lead off "Las Américas," the first section of his *Pensamientos del Negro Cubena.* In this section, the longest in the
book, we are confronted with some of the strongest expressions in
Latin American literature of what it means to be an African in
America, certainly one who clearly feels and acknowledges his African past.

In a poem entitled "In exilium," the first one in this collection,
Cubena, echoing Nicolás Guillén's "El apellido," captures epigram-
matically the ironic lament of the African abroad who is now called ·
something else because his name was lost in transit:

¿Qué desgracia!	How disgraceful!
ASHANTI soy	I am an ASHANTI
y me dicen	and they address me as
Carlos	Carlos
¡Qué insulto!	How insulting!
CONGO soy	I am a CONGOLESE
y me llaman	and they call me
Guillermo	William
¡Qué infamia!	How base! .
YORUBA soy	I am a YORUBA
y me apellidan	and they name me
Wilson. (p. 8)	Wilson.

It is appropriate that Cubena opens with "In exilium," as this
poem sets the tone for this entire first section which, though entitled
"Las Américas," focuses ironically and nostalgically, for the most
part, on "beloved" Africa as Mother Country. Cubena further
dramatizes this nostalgia for Africa by adopting an African word
for it, *cabanga,* in the poem "Cabanga Africana" (p. 11). The irony
of the African in America continues in "Desarraigado" ("Uprooted"), another appropriately entitled poem where this nostalgic
lament shapes the question: "Abuelita africana/¿no me reconoces?"
["African grandmother/do you not recognize me?"] (p. 9).

This nostalgia for Africa does not mean, however, that Cubena is resigned to being a pariah in the country of his birth. His protest ranges from the short, quiet comment on his country's narrow-minded prejudices against the *chombo* in "Dos niños," which does for Panama what Guillén's "Dos niños" has done for Cuba, to his extended blast in "Iratus," which points up the irony of a country constantly complaining of its sovereignty problem while, at the same time, denying citizenship to those born in Panama of West Indian descent. Cubena demands that justice, respect, and dignity be accorded him as an African who, though in America, is still a human being. That these basic needs can be so blatantly denied to the black in America, and particularly to the *chombo* in Panama is an absurdity that Cubena decries. His first work is really a plea for a universal humanistic vision, one which has led him in "Mi raza" to damn political boundaries that type people nationally and racially. Cubena also writes of his humanistic vision in "Amigo":

El mejor amigo del hombre	Man's best friend
no es su hermano.	is not his brother.
¡QUE TRISTE!	It is his dog . . .
es el perro . . . (p. 22)	HOW SAD!

There is rage in Cubena's poems but there is also room for love, and it is the loss of love for one's fellow man in this world that makes much of his poetry a lament. Although he closes his collection of poetry with a group of love poems in a section entitled "Amor," a kind of geographical exploration of love in the manner of Rubén Darío's poem "Divagación," the power of this first collection comes from his wide-ranging attacks on racism. His onslaught is present in such poems as "Invitación," where Cubena updates Regino Pedroso's "Hermano negro" by inviting his black brothers

en Bahia	in Bahia
Palenque o Colón	Palenque or Colón
enmudece un poco	to soften the
tu bongo	drumbeat and
imita elritmo	to imitate
GUERRILLERO	the WAR-LIKE rhythm
de Bayano, Benkos	of Bayano, Benkos
y Cudjoe (p. 30)	and Cudjoe

It also is found in the combative verse he hurls against the Ku Klux Klan in the United States and against the white rulers of Rhodesia and South Africa. In "Chimurenga," the lead-off poem in the second section, "Africa," of this poetry collection, Cubena illustrates that he sees not only the Paradise Lost that was ancient Africa, but also Africa today, which he characterizes as an "infierno de mis primos" ["my cousins' hell"] (p. 32) in places like Rhodesia and South Africa, and tomorrow's Africa where *chimurenga* (Bantu word for war of liberation) will be fought. In this second section of his book, Cubena has moved from nostalgia for Africa to empathy with present day Africa, with his "African friend," his "African cousin," his "African brother."

Cubena's verse, belying the quiet demeanor of the man, literally shouts at the reader. It is filled with capitalized words, and many of his already powerful lines are punctuated with exclamation marks. There is an abundance of sarcastic questions heavy with irony that some whites would be hard pressed to answer. Cubena uses the diminutive pejoratively to insult and to belittle: "*hombrecitos* criminales" (p. 37), "*ratoncito* portugués" (p. 37), "coloso del norte/repleto de *hombrecitos*" (p. 24) ["colossus of the north/full of *little men*"]. Though many aspects of his literature—the many whips, the "flood of whiplashes" (p. 11), for example, in his verse—remind us of Nicolás Guillén, Cubena's poetry is fresh, original, highly inventive, and especially visual in his graphic layout of the printed word. He writes such self-explanatory formations into his poetry as the following:

NAZARENO
L
A
S

ESPINAS Y LA CORONA

L

A

C
R
U
Z (p. 26)

and

No queremos	K	K	K
	o	o	r
	c	l	i
	a	a	n
			g
			a (p. 19)

In a poem entitled "Definición" he graphically poses the question:

¿Qué es un	What is a
12	12
N	N
E	E
9—NEGRO—3	9—NEGRO—3
R	R
O	O
6	6

His answer is:

una bomba de tiempo	a time bomb
tic-tac-tic-tac-tic-tac	tic-tac-tic-tac-tic-tac
tik-tak-tik-tak-tik-tak	tik-tak-tik-tak-tik-tak
TIC-TAC-TIC-TAK-TIK-TAK . . .	TIC-TAC-TIC-TAK-TIK-TAK . . .

one he applies to "Gringolandia" as well as to "Pañalandia" (p. 29). Like Vallejo, Wilson rivets our attention by confronting the reader with words written in reverse:

> ACIREMA
> ACIRFA DUS
> AMANAP   (p. 26)

In the manner of Nicolás Guillén, he runs words together that so joined they tell condensed stories: "golpesinsultosycadenas" (p. 12), "triangulihispanoamericano" (p. 14). AMERSUDPANRIAFRICA-MACA (p. 26), "Lamialatuyaolacolorada" (p. 21). Again, like Nicolás Guillén, Cubena has already become adept at the art of repetitive build-up where poetry becomes song through a litany of chant. He uses this technique very effectively in "Carifesta 1976"

Encadenados llegaron . . .	They came in chains . . .
. . . .	. . . .
mis antepasados	my ancestors
. . . .	. . . .
como sardinas en lata	like sardines in tin cans
encadenados	in chains
en navíos negreros	in slave boats
encadenados	in chains
. . . .	. . . .
encadenados	in chains
mis antepasados	my ancestors
encadenados	in chains
arrancados de la cuna	torn from their place of birth
encadenados (p. 27)	in chains

Wilson again uses repetition for incantatory effect in "Usutu" (Zulu war cry), which begins with

> Usutu
> corre ... albino ... corre ...
> usutu

and ends with three lines of, "usutuusutuusutuusutuusutuusutu" (p. 34), as he converts the poem itself into a war cry.

Cubena's poetry, then, relies in part on graphic inventiveness to hold the reader's attention. But his prose is another matter, for Cubena's stories are creating a new kind of literary expression that already has been defined by Adalberto Ortiz, Wilson tells me, as "tremendismo negrista." His stories are intentionally shocking. They are shocking because they are built for the most part around excessive violence, sexual abuse (even on dead bodies), prostitution, incest, lesbianism, homosexuality, gang rape, and murder. Just as he shows how hunger and poverty grow out of substandard living conditions, so too is Cubena careful to show how perverse, deviant, and contemptible behavior of whites toward nonwhites is an outgrowth of the sickness of racism. If the single biggest irony in his poetry is the black uprooted from "beloved" Africa and implanted in racist America, then the overriding irony in his stories is the realization that blacks in Panama are excluded from the mainstream of a country they in large measure helped to build.

"Tremenismo negrista" is evident in the first paragraph of the first story, "Carbón y leche," where Cubena's preference for the adjective ending in -oso, that Arnoldo Palacios used so effectively in *Las estrellas son negras* to emphasize *asqueroso* conditions in Colombia, paints a depressing picture of filth, poverty, and hunger in Panama. *Mocosos, piojosos, andrajosos,* and *apestoso* appear in the first three lines of this story which is characterized by violence, sexual abuse, and starving children forced to feed on dog vomit to survive. Cubena has even gone beyond the limits reached by Palacios in showing the extremes to which hunger can drive a starving human being. His second story, "El niño de harina," shows another extreme to which the by-products of white racism can drive a person; a young school boy dusts himself regularly with white flour, his pathetic attempt to escape the stigma of blackness. In "El quilombo" Cubena again illustrates the pervasive racial discrimination in Panama directed against blacks from academic ranks to particular prostitutes who do not go to bed with blacks, certainly not with *chombos*. The pathology of racial prejudice in "Luna de miel" drives a white family to absurd lengths to preserve its racial exclusiveness. This story also puts into perspective the historical role of the black West Indian's involvement in the construction of the Canal:

> In those days, blacks sweated like hell from sunup to sundown in that hot tropical climate, earning ten cents an hour while the illiterate North Americans from Alabama and Georgia, like Mister Boss, were paid twenty dollars an hour. The majority of the North Americans were "water boys" for the black workers. (p. 30)

White insolence based on the assumption of white superiority and disrespect for those who are not white appear in "La tercera ilusión" and "Depósito de cadáveres," stories that deal respectively with a white homosexual and an Indian victim of a judicial double standard. "Depósito de cadáveres" illustrates as well Cubena's penchant for drawing political analogies in his stories that reveal his suspicion and awareness of the United States. He writes that "they took control of that poor Indian body and soul, 'in perpetuity' like they had already done with Panamanian sovereignty" (p. 49). The same message is even blunter in "Martes de Carnaval," for example, where we witness the gang rape and murder of a young Panamanian girl by characters whose names are Richard Nixon, Edgar Hoover, and John Mitchell. Carrying this heavy analogy a bit further, the assault takes place in a "white house" where the girl had come to work as a maid.

In "El bombero," one of his best stories, Cubena shifts the locale to the United States, to the Ku Klux Klan in "Kalifornia, Kalabama y Killinois" and in particular to Sam Wallace, a KKK leader who likes to firebomb black churches. Cubena's characterization of Wallace as a person who has "a bird brain in an ox's body" (p. 65) helps explain the perverse satisfaction Wallace derives from such nefarious deeds. This KKK bomber is known as "Uncle Sam," and in another heavy bit of irony and word play his life is saved in the end from a fire of his own setting by a fireman who is black.

Much of Cubena's work has obvious autobiographical overtones, especially "La depravada," where a young Cubena is the protagonist. In this story a white *compañera* breaks off a relationship, to the great satisfaction of her mother who looked with disfavor on that relationship, but not, it is implied, on her daughter's lesbian attachment with a partner of her own race that followed her break-up with the distinguished black Dr. Cubena. Cubena is again pro-tagonist in "La fiesta," which like "El bombero," is set in the United States. The story opens with Cubena polishing off an autobio-graphical novel that, like Wilson's own autobiographical novel he has in preparation, is to be called "Chombo." In this story the author with gentle humor chides customs of some of his American associates, while at the same time showing off, as he does in several of his stories, his erudition of which he is justly proud. "La abuelita africana" returns to Panama to give another update on the contem-porary black in that country, this time through the character of a ninety-three-year-old black woman accused of murdering the grandson of a former master. Cubena, in the manner of Nelson Estupiñán Bass, makes his white targets cut ridiculous figures as he points up how the Panamanian judicial system makes a mockery of the court when it comes to dispensing justice to nonwhites. "La abuelita africana" is one of Cubena's more ambitious stories tech-nically with flashbacks, interpolated poems—some in an African language—and simultaneous narration that tells two stories that are related but separate in time and space.

In "La familia," Cubena comes full circle as he returns in this story, the last one in the collection, to the depressing economic situa-tion of a contemporary black family in Panama whose poverty and hunger are reminiscent of the equally depressing economic plight of the black family in "Carbón y leche," the opening story in the col-lection. In this last story Cubena paints a fuller picture of misery and suffering than in other stories. Particularly graphic are scenes of the one bed *cuartucho* without electric lights that houses and sleeps the family with its six children "undernourished, painfully feeble and very thin . . . deathly thin, whose arms and legs are cov-ered with festering sores" (p. 87), and everywhere there are the "pu-trid odors from the 'rat-infested' black ghetto" (p. 90). The human condition in this squalor is tragic: there is the father with his "hun-gry lips" (p. 85), his "hands, calloused and deformed" (p. 86), whose spirit like his shoes has been worn down looking for work no one will give him because of his color ("We don't want blacks here," p. 86), and the "desperate" (p. 91) mother with her "ex-hausted . . . drawn face, her body bent over with premature aging" (p. 91), fired from her maid's job, accused of having stolen dog food to feed her starving children, a desperate act of a desperate mother, but one that does not match her final act of desperation—the mercy killing of her six children and her suicide as the only way to escape from the New World racial injustice. In this story Cubena joins together the two main themes or ironies that give strength to his literary expression: an indignant eye on the present plight of a people reduced to a slave existence in Panama and a solemn respect for his African origin—the six black Panamanian children in this story are named Yoruba, Fanti, Ashanti, Bantu, Congo, and Dahomey. Also in this final story we are reminded of the importance Cubena gives to women. In his stories they are visible in roles ranging from the most noble to the most depraved. Black women particularly are depicted in authentic characterizations that go beyond the black woman as sexual animal. In such stories as "La familia" the black woman is shown as strong, determined, and concerned with survival.

Carlos Guillermo "Cubena" Wilson is an excellent storyteller who brings the reader quickly to the central focus of his tales, which almost always are on black awareness. If graphic inventiveness characterizes much of his poetry his stories are characterized by and punctuated with a final punch line worth almost as much as the entire story in its telling intensity. Cubena is gifted as well with a sententious style much in the manner of Nelson Estupiñán Bass and Candelario Obeso, two other black authors whose proverbial statements and homespun wisdom enrich their erudite expression. In addition, Cubena's style is further characterized by the Panamanian flavor he gives to his Spanish which itself includes many words of African influence or origin. *Chombo*, for example, a pejorative term applied to blacks of West Indian descent in Panama, is one of the most obvious localisms used. And there are others: *bembón* (bemba) "big lipped," *burundanga* "delicacy," *calungo* "hairless," *canyac* "marihuana," *cuzcú* "nappy hair," *chichi* "baby," to name only a few. Local flavor is captured too by Cubena's use of Panamanian terms for food (*guandú, angú, guacho, bollo sancocho, carimañola*) dances (tamborito, cumbia), drinks (*chicheme*, guaro) and children's games (*mirón-mirón, florón*).

In his update on Panama, Black Cubena, much like Guillén's Juan Ramón Cantaliso who sings *sones* tourists cannot dance to, gives us a side of his country in prose and in poetry that is not pretty, and this is true whether he is giving historical perspective or a view of Panama today. In his first two books Wilson has raised black consciousness to a new level of intensity. Though he paints a depressing picture of the present plight of black people in Panama, Black Cubena is optimistic that the future will be better, or at least his by-line could mean that it cannot get any worse.

Conclusion:
Prospects for a Black Aesthetic in Latin America

*Let us unite people of the Third World and make it the
First World.*

Nicomedes Santa Cruz

*The black can never put aside his consciousness of race.
Class consciousness is very important but the black must
hold on to his own psychology.*

Nelson Estupiñán Bass

In the Introduction, I stated my acceptance of a distinction between a poetry of the Black Experience and a poetry of the Black
Aesthetic. I used the definition of the former to characterize black
literature in general in Latin America, where a negritude of synthesis
(cultural and biological), *mestizaje*, and class solidarity have perhaps understandably slowed down any widespread move toward a
literature of a Black Aesthetic in the fullest United States Black Nationalist sense as Addison Gayle Jr., Amiri Baraka, and Don Lee,
for example, understand it.

I should point out here, however, that it is not improbable for a
literature of the Black Aesthetic to develop in Latin America. Despite
the *mestizaje* or *mulatez* dimension of the black experience in Latin
America, there are "persisting black communities in Cuba, Colombia, Venezuela, Ecuador, Brazil and the Dominican Republic, some
of which think of themselves as part of the Black World and some
of which don't."[1] It is to these groups and to the mixed blood groups
who do not deplore their African ancestry that we must look if we
are to find the highest level of black consciousness, in effect, a "su-
pra-ethnic Pan African consciousness"[2] that is, together with a tra-

191

dition of a literature of the Black Experience to build on, prerequisite for the development in Latin America of a black aesthetic in the strictest sense.

For that development to come to pass, however, the false consciousness we spoke of in chapter eight created by the widespread process of *mestizaje* would have to be dissipated. This false consciousness, according to St. Clair Drake,[3] has enabled those in power to use divide and rule along the spectrum of racial color in Latin America. The dissipation of this false consciousness and its replacement by a full-blown Black Aesthetic would mean that the black component of the "creative dialogue between Africa and Europe,"[4] as Ian Smart defines the *mulatez* factor, would have to control or monopolize the dialogue. Should that happen it could well turn out that *mulatez* or *mestizaje* in Latin America, as Smart has intimated, "may not be the ingenious solution it appears to be, but rather an ingenuous avoidance of the basic issue"[5] that, I might add, involves making a fundamental or precise racial choice. Understood in this sense dearyanization, or freedom from a deliberate whitening process, becomes the ultimate liberation for blacks in Latin America. It becomes, as well, a first step in the direction of a Black Aesthetic, as necessary a first step for blacks in Latin America as de-Americanization would be for blacks in the United States.

Furthermore, for a literature of the Black Aesthetic to develop in Latin America, black writers there would have to extricate themselves from the humanistic vision that characterizes with few exceptions much of Afro-Latin American literature. They would have to adopt the *poetic hatred* that seems to characterize "The New Poetry of Black Hate"[6] written by blacks in the United States since the late fifties that has risen concomitantly with the New Black Aesthetic. I do not see this happening, however, even though continued racial assertion and more aggressive, even if not militant, attitudes by the black in Latin America are inevitable.

We have already seen some assertiveness in Afro-Latin American literature, particularly in the combative, cutting poetry of Nicolás Guillén, where the black man and his literary image continue to concern the poet, a concern, to be sure, that has never been incompatible, as I pointed out in chapter seven and again in chapter fourteen, with his reputation "as an artist who surpasses the narrow limits of black poetry; as a Cuban, American, and universal poet."[7] This quotation, however, erroneously implies that there is nothing

universal about the black experience and the treatment of it in literature. Nicolás Guillén, perhaps the black writer in Latin America
with the most Marxist, Third World orientation, has always had,
like Nelson Estupiñán Bass, Nicomedes Santa Cruz, Arnoldo Palacios, Adalberto Ortiz, and Manuel Zapata Olivella, his First (or
Black) World-Third World priorities straight: like the others, he has
never abandoned the black man despite other directions his literature has taken.

Though his poetry was one of the first in this century to raise the
Black Power salute and although it "hits, explodes, screams, like the
poetry of Black American poets of the late Sixties and early Seventies,"[8] Guillén's poems are largely written from a Third World perspective against Yankee imperialism perhaps because he has always
seen that racism against blacks and colonialist oppression go hand
in hand. His kind of *poetic anger*, if not *poetic hatred*, common to
Pablo Neruda, César Vallejo, David Diop, and René Depestre, it has
been said, unites such Third World writers "at a universal level, free
of racial or regional prejudice."[9]

We should remember, too, that Amiri Baraka—the prime force
behind a Black Aesthetic in the strict United States Black Nationalist
sense—in moving even beyond the Third World has gone from
black nationalism to socialist revolution, a change in ideology that
places him closer to Nicolás Guillén. Neither writer, though, abandons the black struggle; both men continue to have at heart Black
Liberation, but a liberation from a double oppression, namely, from
oppression suffered as black people as well as from the "class
oppression of workers in relationship to the capitalist."[10] "The duality
of this oppression," Baraka writes, "and the twin aspects of our
struggle must be understood if we are to struggle with the intensity
our liberation demands."[11]

The bond that drew W.E.B. Dubois, pioneer in Pan-Africanism,
to Africa had at its essence the social heritage of slavery, discrimination, and insult.[12] Though he extended his common heritage of
suffering to a wider unity of the oppressed outside the African-Afro-
American continuum his love for justice always had black pride and
black liberation at its core. This order of priorities continues to be
true of Pan-Africanism, for, as an "impulse generated by blacks of
the diaspora"[13] Pan-Africanism has, according to Richard A. Long,
given rise to two myths: a *myth of combat* and a *myth of becoming*.
"The myth of combat," he writes, "is directed against the white Eu-

ropean hegemony of the postmedieval world. The myth of becoming is an idyllic myth of a peaceful world in which full political rights would be enjoyed by all black people, and is based upon the assumption that black people, at least, would never interfere with the enjoyment of political rights of people of different color."[14]

Not only Nicolás Guillén but other black Cubans, even the more militant ones who want to keep African culture separate, do not, we are told, find Socialism irrelevant to the black struggle. Elizabeth Southerland,[15] who tells us this, has made a further interesting point. She argues that just as some militant blacks are looking beyond "strict skin analysis—the view that blacks are oppressed solely because of their color—so too must whites, if racism and unconscious racist values and myths are to be truly rooted out, look beyond "pure class analysis"—the view that blacks are simply one more element among the oppressed millions, by chance black, and that racism automatically disappears when exploitation ends.

But as Southerland says, "only a combination of the two analyses can explain the total reality of racism and point the way to full liberation."[16] This kind of combination, she adds, would be "a truly dialectical *revolutionary* analysis in Cuba, one that could benefit and educate not just Cuba but the entire continent."[17] Indeed, should such a combination become a reality in Latin America a Black Aesthetic or Black Nationalism in the strict United States Black Power sense as a political imperative might not be necessary. Once Black or First World thought is seen in this light, neither Third Worldism nor identification with the world-wide proletariat need be incompatible with a Black Aesthetic should it develop in Latin America. Perhaps the we-they dichotomy Sylvia Wynter[18] sees resolved in the oneness of ethnopoetics can have its most fruitful socio-historical meaning in the coming together of First World-Third World peoples. Roberto Fernández Retamar[19] may well prove right when he says that Latin America, certainly its revolutionary figures (the Ariels), must identify with Caliban (the slave) and not with Prospero (the oppressor).

Nevertheless, whatever alliances blacks make in Latin America and elsewhere they will always have in common what has been called "their precarious, their unutterably painful relation to the white world."[20] For this reason we can raise the question, what will happen if black writers in Latin America take up the challenge of Abdias do Nascimento, perhaps the leading spokesman for a Black

Aesthetic in Latin America, who, tired of "inactive and passive people who go on accepting the situation," told the black man in his native Brazil that he must "take a position?"[21] Even Sartre, who developed an elaborate theory that saw negritude renouncing itself and pride in color, leaves open the following general question: "What will happen if, casting off his negritude for the sake of the Revolution, the black man no longer wishes to consider himself only a part of the proletariat?"[22]

I began this book with one set of questions, and from the set I am now raising in closing, the most important are the following: What impact will the current phase of the black liberation struggle in the United States, successor to the old Civil Rights movements, have in the future on the development of a Black Aesthetic in Latin America? What effect will the black sixties and the black seventies in the United States, which have been called "without a doubt the most profound and meaningful period of this century for black Americans,"[23] have in the future on the prevailing acceptance in Latin America of the official line on race that holds the black Latin American to be well off, miscegenated, and because of these factors unenthusiastic about negritude and all that the concept implies?

What will be the impact of Alex Haley's book *Roots* after it is translated and disseminated in Latin America? What would happen if Don Lee's "worldview," or the psychological unification of black people the world over into an international black community or black nation, which he proposes in his *From Plan to Planet* catches on in Latin America? What will happen in the wake of the "conscious and deliberate" cooperation now taking place between "the communities of the Diaspora and the Homeland and between the various communities"[24] illustrated by the First Afro-Hispanic Congress held in Cali, Colombia, in August 1977, where interaction among blacks from Anglo-America, Latin America, and Africa assures such cooperation in the future?

Finally, we certainly should not overlook the impact of FESTAC 77 (the Second World Black African Festival of Arts and Culture), where black dancers even from the Cuban contingent "punched the air with Black Power salutes."[25] This Festival, held in Lagos, Nigeria, in January and February of 1977, has been called "the biggest and most significant gathering of black people in the history of the world."[26] Nicolás Guillén, among other blacks from Latin America, attended that gathering, where the "powerful idea"[27] that "there is a black nation, a black world"[28] and indeed, the idea of Black World as First World, were reasserted.

With all of this before us and with acceptance of one's African-in-Dispersion identity being brought to bear on the black Latin American writer who more now than ever before is being confronted with the pressures of a rising international black consciousness, there is no question that in the future increased identification with such concepts as Black World, First World, Africanity, Negritude, Pan-Africanism, and the Black Diaspora will continue to develop in Latin America based on a relationship of color among people of African descent whatever their location in the world. Whether this development will lead outspoken old guard leaders like Brazil's Abdias do Nascimento and Solano Trinidade and the younger black writers in Latin America—Antonio Preciado in Ecuador, Quince Duncan in Costa Rica, Carlos Wilson in Panama, Edelma Zapata Olivella in Colombia, to name only a few—into a Black Aesthetic in the strictest United States Black Nationalist or Black Power sense, only time will tell.

It already seems clear, though, insofar as Cuba is concerned, that if even black militants are accepting the position on race put forward by the government which is buttressed by the support of such well-known black literary figures in Cuba as Nicolás Guillén, Marcelino Arozarena, Nancy Morejón, Manuel Granados, and René Depestre, other lesser-known black Cuban writers such as Eugenio Hernández, Carlos Moore, and Wilfredo Carbonell—who want to think "racial blackness as a value beyond the limits of folklore"[29] — will continue to have trouble getting their work published, performed, and reissued in Cuba because of the Cuban fear of what has been called a black "separatist pull based on United States models,"[30] a problem Carlos Wilson also encountered recently in Panama.

Anani Dzidzienyo implied not long ago that such difficulties are not limited to Cuba or to Panama. Commenting on the "we are all one people" syndrome in Latin America and on the difficulties such black writers as Abdias do Nascimento of Brazil, Nicomedes Santa Cruz of Peru, and Manuel Zapata Olivella of Colombia have had in expressing their "dynamic Africanity," Anani Dzidzienyo wrote that "the spectre of Americanization in the sense of injecting what is perceived as the North American racial antagonisms of Black Power with its concomitant hatred and violence"[31] elicits heated argument in Latin America "because of a fundamental principle which in Latin America appears to equate the assertion of dynamic Africanity with real or implied denationalization."[32]

As long as that equation is accepted in Latin America, prospects there for a Black Aesthetic in the strictest sense will not be very good. But continued reliance on that equation and insistence on the other equation, namely, that one equates racial sameness with racial equality, could paradoxically provide the spark. Perhaps that is what Marvin Harris[33] had in mind when he said that a Black Power movement in Latin America will emerge certainly in Brazil despite all the claims that given time and more miscegenation alleged racial disabilities will disappear.

But all we can say with any degree of certainty is that for now there is little black literature in Latin America that specifically supports black nationalism and a concomitant militancy. There is, nevertheless, much authentic black literature written there, one drawn from oral tradition, group solidarity and identity, black consciousness, commonality of experience,[34] and black protest. This literature written by blacks is clearly distinguishable in theme, focus, and purpose from black literature written by nonblack authors. Recognizing this distinction and the ethnicity factor that underscores it is very important, especially in Latin America.

Notes

Introduction

1. Sandra Govan, "The Poetry of Black Experience as Counterpoint to the Poetry of the Black Aesthetic," *Negro American Literature Forum for School and University Teachers*, no. 8 (Winter 1974): 288–292, a journal that in 1978 became the *Black American Literature Forum*.

2. Jerry W. Ward, "Speculations about Contemporary Black Literature," in *The Contemporary Literary Scene*, ed. Frank McGill (Englewood Cliffs, N.J.: Salem Press, 1973), p. 79.

3. Antonio Olliz Boyd, "The Concept of Black Esthetics as seen in Selected Works of three Latin American Writers: Machado de Assis, Nicolás Guillén and Adalberto Ortiz" (Ph.D. diss., Stanford University, 1975). Doris J. Turner, "Symbols in Two Afro-Brazilian Literary Works: *Juliabá* and *Sortilégio*," in *Teaching Latin American Studies*, ed. Miriam Willsford and J. Doyle Casteel (Gainesville, Florida: Latin American Studies Association, 1977), pp. 41–58.

4. Ibid., p. 22.

5. Eugene Perkins, "The Changing Status of Black Writers," *Black World*, June 1970: 95.

6. Boyd, "The Concept of Black Esthetics," p. 30.

7. Jahnheinz Jahn, *A History of Neo-African Literature* (London: Faber & Faber Ltd., 1968).

8. Ibid., pp. 222–223.

9. Martha K. Cobb, "The Black Experience in the Poetry of Nicolás Guillén, Jacques Roumain, Langston Hughes," (Ph.D. diss. The Catholic University of America, 1974).

10. Ibid., p. 15.

11. Richard A. Preto-Rodas, *Negritude as a Theme in the Poetry of the Portuguese Speaking World* (Gainesville: University of Florida Press, 1970), p. 17.

12. Stephen Henderson, *Understanding the New Black Poetry* (New York: Morrow, 1973), p. 7.

13. Angela Gilliam, "Black and White in Latin America," *Présence Africaine*, no. 92 (1964): 61–73.

14. S. Washington Ba, *The Concept of Negritude in the Poetry of Léopold Sédar Senghor* (Princeton, New Jersey: Princeton University Press, 1964), p. 160.

15. Anani Dzidzienyo, "Afro-Brazilians, other Afro-Latin Americans and Africanity: Frozen and Dynamic," (Paper read at the Eighth Annual Meeting of the African Heritage Studies Association, 23 April 1976 in Atlanta, Georgia), p. 1.

16. J. Mbelolo Ya Mpiku, "From one Mystification to Another: 'Negritude' and 'Negraille' in 'Le Devoir de Violence'," *Review of National Literatures* 2, no. 2 (Fall 1971): 136.

17. Gastón Baquero, *Darío, Cernuda y otros temas poéticos* (Madrid: Editora Nacional, 1969), p. 213.

18. Don L. Lee, *Dynamite Voices* (Detroit, Michigan: Broadside Press, 1971), p. 23.

19. Maurice Lubin, "Jean Brière and his Work," *Black World*, January 1973:44.

20. Leopold Sédar Senghor, "The Problematics of Negritude," *Black World*, August 1971: 14–15.

21. Leonard E. Barrett, *Soul-Force: African Heritage in Afro-American Religion* (Garden City, New York: Doubleday, 1974), p. 1.

22. Cobb, "The Black Experience," pp. 7–10.

23. Richard Wright, "Introduction: Blueprint for Negro Writing," in *The Black Aesthetic*, ed. Addison Gayle, Jr. (Garden City, New York: Doubleday & Co., 1971), pp. 341–342.

24. George Kent, *Blackness and the Adventure of Western Culture* (Chicago, Illinois: Third World Press, 1972), p. 17.

25. Julian Mayfield, "You Touch my Black Aesthetic and I'll Touch Yours," in *The Black Aesthetic*, p. 26.

26. Ibid., p. 26.

27. "Orphée Noir" was first published as the preface to Leopold Sédar Senghor's *Anthologie de la nouvelle poésie nègre et malgache de langue française* (Paris, 1948). It has been translated into English by John Mac-Combie and published in *The Massachusetts Review* 6 no. 1 (1964–65): 13–52, and reference in this chapter is made to this English version.

28. Richard L. Jackson, *The Black Image in Latin American Literature* (Albuquerque: University of New Mexico Press, 1976), p. 130.

29. By Richard A. Preto-Rodas in his commentary on Rosa Valdés-Cruz's paper, "El negrigenismo en la narrativa ecuatoriana," at the LASA/ASA panel on Africa in Latin America, Houston, Texas, 3 November 1977.

30. Wilfred Cartey, Introduction to *Negritude: Black Poetry from Africa and the Caribbean*, ed. and trans. Norman R. Shapiro (New York: October House, Inc., 1970), p. 35.

31. Leopold Sédar Senghor, "Address . . . Doctor *Honoris Causa*," University of Vermont, 13 June 1971, pp. 5–6. Reported in Ba, *The Concept of Negritude*, p. 180.

32. Frederic M. Litto, "Some Notes on Brazil's Black Theatre," in *The Black Writer in Africa and the Americas*, ed. Lloyd W. Brown (Los Angeles: Hennessey & Ingolls, Inc., 1973), p. 218.

33. See Julia Fields in *The New Black Poetry*, ed. Clarence Major (New York: International Publishers, 1965), p. 140.

34. Perkins, "The Changing Status," p. 18.

35. Lloyd Brown, Introduction to *The Black Writer in Africa and the Americas*, p. 8.

36. See *Alcheringa: Ethnopoetics. A First International Symposium*, ed. Michel Benamou and Jerome Rothenberg (Boston: Boston University, 1976).

37. Frank Fanon, "Racism and Culture," in *Black Poets and Prophets*, Eds. Woodie King and Earl Anthony (New York: New American Library, 1972), p. 25.

38. Abraham Chapman, "Concepts of the Black Aesthetic in Contemporary Black Literature," in *The Black Writer in Africa and the Americas*, p. 40.

39. Kent, *Blackness*, p. 112.

40. Elizabeth Southerland, *The Youngest Revolution* (New York: The Dial Press, 1970), p. 162.

41. *Black Homeland/Black Diaspora: Cross-Currents of the African Relationship*, ed. Jacob Drachler (Port Washington, N.Y.: Kennikat Press, 1975), p. 13.

42. Ibid., p. 134.

43. Ibid.

Chapter 1

1. See Roger Bastide, "Three Kinds of Folklore," in *African Civilizations in the New World*, trans. Peter Green (New York: Harper & Row, Publishers, 1971), pp. 171–193.

2. *The Book of Negro Folklore*, ed. Langston Hughes and Anna Bontemps (New York: Dodd, Mead & Co., 1959), p. viii.

3. Sterling Brown, "Negro Folk Expression," *Phylon* 11, no. 4 (1950): 322.

4. Ibid.

5. Ibid.

6. *The Book of Negro Folklore*, p. ix.

7. Fernando Ortiz, Prologue to Cabrera, *Cuentos negros de Cuba* (La Habana, 1940).

8. Hilda Perera, *Idapo: El sincretismo en los cuentos negros de Lydia Cabrera* (Miami: Ediciones Universal, 1971); Rosa M. Valdés-Cruz, *Lo ancestral africana en la narrativa de Lydia Cabrera* (Barcelona: Editorial Vosgos, 1974); Josefina Inclán, *Ayapá y otras Otán Iyebiyé de Lydia Cabrera (notas y comentarios)* (Miami: Ediciones Universal, 1976). Also see *Homenaje a Lydia Cabrera*, ed. Reinaldo Sánchez, et al. (Miami: Ediciones Universal, 1978).

9. Perera, *Idapo*, p. 110.

10. Ibid., p. 70.

11. Valdés-Cruz, *Lo ancestral africano*, p. 104, where she points out that Lydia Cabrera calls them "transposiciones," in Lydia Cabrera, *Ayapá: Cuentos de jicotea* (Miami: Ediciones Universal, 1971), p. 18.

12. Cabrera, *Cuentos negros de Cuba* (Madrid, 1972), pp. 58–59.

13. *Por qué . . . cuentos negros de Cuba* (Madrid, 1972), p. 17.

14. Perera, *Idapo*, p. 96.

15. Ibid., p. 74.

16. Ibid.

17. Ibid.

18. Ibid., p. 21.

19. Lydia Cabrera, *Ayapá: cuentos de jicotea* (Miami: Ediciones Universal, 1971). See pages 10–11 of her introduction to this collection for her reasoning on this subject. This introduction is informative though loaded with racist stereotypes (for example, "any black is an actor and possesses an innate sense of rhythm and animation" (p. 14); " . . . laughs showing all his teeth and rolls his eyes . . . " (p. 16); "What white woman has not heard some time her black cook seriously scolding her pots and pans?" (p. 16); " . . . the colored nursemaid who looked after him during his childhood, the one who because her kindness and self-sacrificing tenderness was for him another mother, capable of all sacrifices" (p. 15).)

20. Valdés-Cruz, *Lo ancestral africano*, p. 58.

21. Ibid., p. 59.

22. Lydia Cabrera, *El monte* (Miami, Ediciones Universal, 1971), p. 10.

23. See ibid., pp. 181–183.

24. This tale, which Guirao collected "from the oral tradition in the Provincia de Oriente, Cuba," is reprinted by Enrique Noble in *Literatura afro-hispanoamericana* (Toronto: Xerox College Publishing, 1973), pp. 128–129.

25. José Antonio Portuondo, *Cuentos cubanos contemporáneos* (México: Editorial Leyenda, 1946), pp. 191–192.

26. Nicolás Guillén, *Prosa de prisa* (Buenos Aires: Editorial Hernández, 1968), p. 172.

27. Reprinted in Denys Cuche, *Poder blanco y resistencia negra en el Perú* (Lima: Instituto Nacional de Cultura, 1975), pp. 112–114.

28. Paulo de Carvalho-Neto, *El folklore de las luchas sociales* (México: Siglo XXI Editores, 1973), p. 118.

29. Arthur Ramos, *The Negro in Brazil* (1939), reprinted in Nora Seljan, "Negro Popular Poetry in Brazil," *African Forum* 2, no. 4 (Spring 1967): 55.

30. Ibid.

31. Sterling Stuckey, "Through the Prism of Folklore: The Black Ethos in Slavery," *The Massachusetts Review*, 9 (1968): 435.

32. Richard K. Barksdale, "Black America and the Mask of Comedy," in *The Comic Imagination in American Literature*, ed. Louis D. Rubin, Jr. (New Jersey: Rutgers University Press, 1973), p. 349.

33. Ibid., p. 353.

34. Ibid., p. 351.

35. Mildred Hill, "Common Folklore Features in African and American Literature," *Southern Folklore Quarterly*, 39 (June 1975): 123.

36. Stuckey, "Through the Prism," p. 434.

37. Bastide, "Three Kinds of Folklore," p. 187.

38. Carvalho-Neto, *El folklore*, p. 64.

39. Quoted in ibid., pp. 30–31.

40. Paulo de Carvalho-Neto, "Historia del folklore de las luchas sociales en América Latina," *Cuadernos Americanos*, 189 (July–August 1973); 134.

41. See Edouard Glissant in "Free and Forced Poetics," in *Alcheringa: Ethnopoetics. A First International Symposium*, ed. Michel Benamou and Jerome Rothenberg (Boston: Boston University, 1976), p. 98.

42. Ibid., p. 135.

43. Ibid., p. 136.

44. "El negro en la poesía folklórica americana," in *Miscelánea de estudios dedicada a Fernando Ortiz*, 1 (Havana: García, 1955), pp. 82–106.

45. Nelson Estupiñán Bass, "Apuntes sobre el negro de Esmeraldas en la literatura ecuatoriana," *Norte*, no. 5 (September–October 1967): 103.

46. Ibid.

47. Jean Franco, "Criticism and Literature within the Context of a Dependent Culture," *Occasional Papers*, no. 16 (New York University: Ibero-American Language and Area Center, 1975), p. 5.

48. Ibid.

49. Ibid.

50. Rubén M. Campos, "La tradición del Negrito Poeta," *El folklore literario de México* (México: Publicaciones de la Secretaria de Educación Pública, 1929), p. 101.

51. Ibid., p. 104.

52. Nicolás León, *El Negrito Poeta Mexicano y sus populares versos* (México: Imprenta del Museo Nacional, 1912), p. 229.

53. Houston A. Baker, Jr., "Black Folklore and the Black American Literary Tradition," in his *Long Black Song: Essays in Black American Literature and Culture* (Charlottesville: The University Press of Virginia, 1972), p. 20.

54. In Ildefonso Pereda Valdés, *El negro en el Uruguay* (Montevideo: Revista del Instituto Histórico y Geográfico del Uruguay, 25, 1965), p. 148.

Chapter 2

1. See Ivan Schulman, "The Portrait of the Slave: Ideology and Aesthetics in the Cuban Anti-Slavery Novel" (Paper delivered at the New York Academy of Sciences International Meeting on Plantation Societies, May 1976).

2. Francisco Calcagno, *Poetas de color*, 3rd ed. (La Habana, 1887), p. 94.

3. Juan Francisco Manzano, *Autobiografía, cartas y versos*, con un estudio preliminar por José L. Franco (La Habana: Municipio de La Habana, 1937), p. 92.

4. *Orbita de la poesía afrocubana 1928–37 (Antología)*, Selección, notas biográficas y vocabulario por Ramón Guirao (La Habana: Ucar, García y Cía., 1938), p. 43.

5. Manzano, *Autobiografía, cartas y versos*, p. 84.

6. Juan Francisco Manzano, *Autobiografía de un esclavo*, Introdución, notas y actualización del texto de Ivan Schulman (Madrid: Ediciones Guadarrama, S.A., 1975).

7. See Russell C. Brignano, *Black Americans in Autobiography: An Annotated Bibliography of Autobiographies and Autobiographical Books Written Since the Civil War* (Durham, North Carolina: Duke University Press, 1974).

8. Jean Franco calls *Biografía de un cimarrón*, put together by Miguel Barnet from interviews with his ex-slave subject, "imaginative documentary writing," a documentary type, she says, that has already been given literary respectability by Norman Mailer, William Styron, and Truman Capote (see Jean Franco, "Literature in the Revolution," *Twentieth Century*, no. 1039/40 (1968–69): 64.

9. R. Anthony Castagnaro, *The Early Spanish American Novel* (New York: Las Americas Publishing Co., 1971), p. 158.

10. César Leante, "Dos obras antiesclavistas cubanas," *Cuadernos Americanos*, 4 (July–August 1976): 177.

11. Schulman, "The Portrait of the Slave," p. 13.

12. Ibid.

13. Calcagno, *Poetas de color*, p. 71.

14. Domingo del Monte, *Escritos* (La Habana: Cultural, 1929), 1, p. 44. Reprinted in Schulman, *Juan Francisco Manzano*, pp. 37–38.

15. Francisco Calcagno, fragment of the nineteenth-century novel *Romualdo, uno de tantos*, published in *Islas* (Cuba), no. 44 (January–February 1973): 107–108. Reprinted in Schulman, *Juan Francisco Manzano*, p. 30.

16. Calcagno, *Poetas de color*, p. 60.

17. Ibid., p. 62.

18. Ibid., p. 52.

19. Ibid., p. 62.

20. Reproduced in Calcagno, *Poetas de color*, p. 82.

21. Schulman, *Juan Francisco Manzano*, p. 47.

22. Reprinted in Calcagno, *Poetas de color*, p. 76.

23. Ivan Schulman, *Juan Francisco Manzano*, p. 47.

24. Leante, "Dos obras anti esclavistas," p. 185.

25. Jean Starobinski, "The Style of Autobiography," in *Literary Style: A Symposium*, ed. Semour Chatman (London: Oxford University Press, 1971), p. 289.

26. Ibid., p. 290.

27. Catharine R. Stimpson, "Black Culture/White Teacher," in *New Perspectives on Black Studies*, ed. John W. Blassingame (Urbana: University of Illinois Press, 1971), p. 181.

28. Saundra Towns, "Black Autobiography and the Dilemma of Western Artistic Tradition," *Black Books Bulletin*, 1975: 17–23.

29. Juan Francisco Manzano, *Zafira* (La Habana: Consejo Nacional de Cultura, 1962), p. 37.

30. Ibid., p. 110.

31. Ibid., p. 129.

Chapter 3

1. See, for example, the ten essays in *Neither Slave nor Free: The Freedman of African Descent in the Slave Societies of the New World*, ed. David W. Cohen and Jack P. Greene (Baltimore: The Johns Hopkins University Press, 1972).

2. Frederick P. Bowser, "Colonial Spanish America," in *Neither Slave nor Free*, p. 19.

3. Franklin W. Knight, "Cuba," in *Neither Slave nor Free*, p. 281.

4. Leonardo Guinán Peralta, "La defensa de los esclavos," in his *Ensayos y conferencias* (S. de Cuba: Editora del Consejo Nacional de Universidades, 1964), p. 75.

5. José Antonio Saco, cited in Peralta, "La defensa," p. 78.

6. Bowser, "Colonial Spanish America," p. 49.

7. Quoted in Fernando Romero, "José Manuel Valdés, gran mulato del Perú," *Revista Bimestre Cubana* 48, no. 2 (March–April 1939): 192–193.

8. Ibid., p. 195.

9. Ibid., p. 198.

10 Ibid., p. 188.

11. Ibid., p. 189.

12. Cohen and Greene, *Neither Slave nor Free*, p. 16.

13. Knight, "Cuba," p. 282.

14. Ibid., p. 292.

15. Francisco Calcagno, *Poetas de color* (La Habana, 1887), p. 105.

16. José Luis Cano, "Quintana: Poeta Político," *Insula*, no. 284–85(1970): 22–23.

17. Martha K. Cobb, "Plácido: The Poet-Hero," *Negro History Bulletin*, 38 (April 1975): 374.

18. *Poesías selectas de Plácido*, Introducción por A.M. Eligio de la Puente (Havana: Editorial Cultural, 1930), p. 1.

19. *Poesías completas de Plácido*, 3rd ed. (Paris: Librería española de Mme C. Schmitz e hijo, 1862), p. 401.

20. *Poesías selectas de Plácido*, p. 300.

21. Lola de la Torriente, "Plácido, un poeta víctima del prejuicio racial," *Bohemia*, no. 15 (24 June 1966): 102.

22. Ibid.

23. *Poesías completas de Plácido*, p. 403.

24. Ibid., p. xl.

25. Cited in C.A. Cervantes, "Bibliografía Placidiana," *Revista Cubana*, 8 (1937): 183.

26. Calcagno, *Poetas de color*, p. 27.

27. *Poesías completas de Plácido*, p. 400.

28. *Historia de la poesía hispanoamericana*, vol. 2 (Santander: Consejo Superior de Investigaciones Científicas, 1948), p. xxxv.

29. Martín Morúa Delgado, "Ensayo político o Cuba y la raza de color," *Obras completas de Martín Morúa Delgado*, Vol. 3 (La Habana: Edición de la Comisión Nacional del Centenario de Martín Morúa Delgado, 1957), p. 82.

30. Ibid.

31. Ibid., p. 81.

32. *Poesías selectas de Plácido*, p. 129

Chapter 4

1. Martín Morúa Delgado, *Obras completas*. Introducción de Alberto Baeza Flores (La Habana, Cuba: Edición de la Comisión Nacional del Centenario de Martín Morúa Delgado, 1957).

2. Leslie B. Rout, Jr., *The African Experience in Spanish America, 1502 to the Present Day* (Cambridge: Cambridge University Press, 1976), p. 304.

3. Stephen E. Henderson, "'Survival Motion': A Study of the Black Writer and the Black Revolution in America," in Mercer Cook and Stephen E. Henderson, *The Militant Black Writer in Africa and the United States* (Madison, Wisconsin: The University of Wisconsin Press, 1969), p. 72.

4. M.A. Pérez Medina, "The Situation of the Negro in Cuba," *Negro*, ed. Nancy Cunard (New York: Negro Universities Press, 1931–33), p. 481.

5. Carlos Moore, "Cuba: the Untold Story," *Présence Africaine* 24, no. 52 (1964): 198.

6. See his celebrated article, "Las novelas del Sr. Villaverde," in *Obras completas*, vol. 5., pp. 17–51.

7. Martín Morúa Delgado, *Sofía* (La Habana, Cuba: Instituto Cubano del Libro, 1972), p. 22.

8. Franklin W. Knight, "Cuba," in *Neither Slave nor Free: The Freedman of African Descent in the Slave Societies of the New World*, ed. David W. Cohen and Jack P. Greene (Baltimore: The Johns Hopkins University Press, 1972), p. 281.

9. Charles Boxer, *Race Relations in the Portuguese Colonial Empire* (Oxford: Clarendon Press, 1963), p. 56.

10. Quotations are taken from Martín Morúa Delgado, *La familia Unzúazu*, in *Obras completas*, Vol. 2, p. 140.

Chapter 5

1. See, for example, Hortensia Ruiz del Vizo, *Poesía negra del Caribe y otras áreas* (Miami, Florida: Ediciones Universal, 1971), p. 121.

2. Jean Franco, *The Modern Culture of Latin America: Society and the Artist* (Middlesex, England: Penguin Books, 1967), p. 131.

3. Ibid., p. 132.

4. Ibid.

5. Candelario Obeso, *Cantos populares de mi tierra* (Bogotá: Biblioteca Popular de Cultura Colombiana, 1956), p. 13.

6. Ibid., p. 12.

7. Rout, *The African Experience*, p. 375.

8. Donaldo Bossa Herazo, in Vicente Caraballo, *El negro Obeso (Apuntes biográficos), y Escritos varios* (Bogotá: Editorial ABC, 1943), p. 81.

9. Obeso, *Cantos populares de mi tierra*, pp. 17–18.

10. Nicolás Guillén, "Sobre Candelario Obeso," *Granma* (Havana) 12 June 1966, reprinted in Mónica Mansour, *La poesía negrista* (México: Ediciones Era, 1973), pp. 83–84.

11. Mansour, *La poesía negrista*, p. 84.

12. Caraballo, *El negro Obeso*, p. 29.

13. Ibid., p. 28.

14. Ibid., p. 30.

15. Rout, *The African Experience*, p. 244.

16. Ibid., p. 245.

Chapter 6

1. Abdias do Nascimento, "The Negro Theater in Brazil," *African Forum* 2, no. 4 (Spring 1967): 43.

2. Ricardo Miró, *La literatura panameña* (Panama: Imprenta Nacional, 1946), p. 136.

3. Roque Javier Laurenza, *Los poetas de la generación republicana* (Panama: Ediciones del Grupo "Pasaje," 1933), p. 109.

4. Ricardo Miró, "Volviendo a Gaspar Octavio," *Lotería*, no. 37 (1968): 51.

5. Gaspar Octavio Hernández, *Obras selectas*. Compilación, introducción, notas y bibliografía de Octavio Augusto Hernández (Panamá, R. de Panamá, 1966).

6. Octavio Hernández, *Obras selectas*, p. 54.

7. Ismael García S., *Historia de la literatura panameña* (México: Universidad Nacional Autónoma de México, 1964), p. 68.

8. Concha Peña, *Gaspar Octavio Hernández, Poeta del pueblo* (Panamá, 1953), p. 183.

9. García S., *Historia de la literatura*, p. 70.

10. Max Henríquez Ureña, *Breve historia del modernismo* (México: Fondo de Cultura Económica, 1954), p. 417.

11. Henríquez Ureña, *Breve historia*, p. 417.

12. Enrique Anderson Imbert, *Spanish American Literature: A History*, trans. John V. Falconieri (Detroit: Wayne State University, 1963), p. 471.

13. Octavio Hernández, *Obras selectas*, p. 523.

14. In Peña, *Gaspar Octavio Hernández* p. 103.

15. Rogelio Sinán, "La poesía panameña," *Cuadernos Americanos*, 120 (1962): 52.

16. Demetrio Korsi, "Elegía en prosa del poeta," in Octavio Hernández, *Obras selectas*, p. 105.

17. Sinán, "La poesía panameña," p. 54.

18. Yolanda López de Berbey, "Gaspar Octavio Hernández (Apuntes biográficos y críticos)," disertación presentada a la Facultad de Filosofía, Letras y Educación de la Universidad

de Panamá como requisito parcial para optar el título de Profesora de Segunda Enseñanza con especialización en español. Panamá, 1960, p. 73.

19. Demetrio Korsi, "Elegía en prosa," p. 105.

20. Ibid., pp. 102–103.

21. Octavio Hernández, *Obras selectas*, pp. 33–46. All subsequent page numbers of quotations from the poet's work are taken from this edition.

22. Javier Laurenza, *Los poetas*, p. 18.

23. Ibid. p. 19.

24. Ibid., p. 20.

25. Elsie Alvarado de Ricord, "El sentimiento patriótico en la poesía panameña," *Lotería*, no. 72 (1961): 39–44.

26. Peña, *Gaspar Octavio Hernández*.

27. Américo Ferrari, *El universo poético de César Vallejo* (Caracas: Monte Avila Editores, 1972), p. 214.

28. López de Berbey, "Gaspar Octavio Hernández," p. 56.

29. Ibid.

30. Peña, *Gaspar Octavio Hernández*, p. 44.

31. Javier Laurenza, *Los poetas*, p. 101.

32. López de Berbey, "Gaspar Octavio Hernández," p. 69.

Chapter 7

1. See his Introduction to his edition of Guillén's poetry. Nicolás Guillén, *Summa poética* (Madrid: Ediciones Cátedra, 1976), pp. 13–45.

2. Nicolás Guillén, *Prosa de prisa: 1929–1972*, vol. 1 (La Habana: Editorial de Arte y Literatura, 1975), pp. 99–100. Trans. J.A. George Irish and reprinted in, "Nicolás Guillén's Position on Race: A Reappraisal," *Revista/Review Interamericana* 4, no. 3 (Fall 1976): 339.

3. Nicolás Guillén, *Obra poética*, vol. 1 (La Habana: Editorial de Arte y Literatura, 1974), p. 120.

4. See J.A. Irish, "Nicolás Guillén's Position," p. 338.

5. Guillén, *Obra poética*, vol. 1, pp. 115–116.

6. Ibid., p. 120.

7. Ibid.

8. Ibid., p. 115.

9. Ibid., p. 152.

10. Ibid., p. 142.

11. Ibid., p. 136.

12. Ibid., p. 145.

13. Ibid., pp. 152–155.

14. Ibid., p. 171.

15. Ibid., p. 170.

16. Constance Sparrow de García Barrio, "The Image of the Black Man in the Poetry of Nicolás Guillén," in *Blacks in Hispanic Literature: Critical Essays*, ed. Miriam De Costa (Port Washington, N.Y.: Kennikat Press, 1977), pp. 105–113.

17. Arturo Torres Rioseco, *The Epic of Latin American Literature* (Berkeley and Los Angeles: University of California Press, 1959), p. 129.

18. G.R. Coulthard, *Race and Colour in Caribbean Literature* (London: Oxford University Press, 1962), pp. 36–37.

19. See His Prólogo to Fernando Ortiz, *Los negros brujos* (Miami, Florida: Ediciones Universal, 1973), p. xiii.

20. Ibid., p. xxii.

21. Guillén, *Obra poética*, p. 118.

22. Fernando Ortiz, "Los factores humanos de la cubanidad," *Revista Bimestre Cubana* 45, no. 2 (1940): 11.

23. Angel Augier, *Nicolás Guillén, notas para un estudio biográfico crítico* (La Habana: Universidad Central de Las Villas, vol. 1, 1962), p. 107.

24. Nicolás Guillén, "Conversación con Langston Hughes," *Diario de la Marina* 98, no. 68 (March 1930): 6. Trans. Edward J. Mullen and reprinted in *Caliban: A Journal of New World Thought and Writing*, 2 (Fall–Winter 1976): 123.

25. From the volume *The New Negro*, ed. Alain Locke (1925; reprint ed., New York: Atheneum, 1968).

26. See Guillén, *Obras poéticas*, p. 487.

27. Langston Hughes, "The Negro Artist and the Racial Mountain," *The Nation*, 23 June 1926, pp. 692–94.

28. Nicolás Guillén, *Prosa de prisa* (La Habana, 1975), p. 85. Trans. J.A. George Irish and reprinted in "The Revolutionary Focus of Guillén's Journalism," *Caribbean Quarterly* 22, no. 4 (Dec. 1976): 77.

29. Gordon Brotherston, *Latin American Poetry: Origins and Presence* (Cambridge: Cambridge University Press, 1975), pp. 22–23.

30. Richard L. Jackson, *The Black Image in Latin American Literature* (Albuquerque: University of New Mexico Press, 1976), pp. 92–93.

31. Abdias do Nascimento, *Sortilégio*, in *Dramas para Negros e Prólogo para Blancos* (Rio de Janeiro: Edição do teatro Experimental do negro, 1961), pp. 195–197. Trans. Doris J. Turner and reprinted in "Symbols in two Afro-Brazilian Literary Works: *Jubiabá* and *Sortilégio*," in *Teaching Latin American Studies*, ed. Miriam Willsford and J. Doyle Castell (Gainesville, Florida: Latin American Studies Association, 1977), p. 58.

Chapter 8

1. Robert Márquez and David Arthur McMurray plan a volume of Guillén's prose in English translation to be titled *Racism, Culture and Revolution: The Prose Writings of Nicolás Guillén*.

2. Juan Comas, *Antropología de los pueblos iberoamericanos* (Barcelona: Editorial Labor, S.A., 1974), p. 159.

3. Ibid., p. 132.

4. St. Clair Drake, "The Black Diaspora in Pan-African Perspective," *The Black Scholar* 7, no. 1 (September 1975): 2–14.

5. Ibid., p. 2.

6. Ildefonso Pereda Valdés, *El negro en el Uruguay* (Montevideo: Revista del Instituto Histórico y Geográfico del Uruguay, 1965), p. 211.

7. Ibid.

8. Ibid., p. 212.

Chapter 9

1. Kessel Schwartz, *A New History of Spanish American Fiction*, vol. 2 (Coral Gables, Florida: University of Miami Press, 1971), p. 72.

2. Juan Pablo Sojo, *Nochebuena negra* (Caracas: Monte Avila Editores, 1972), p. 152.

3. Jean Toomer, *Cane*, Introduction by Darwin T. Turner (New York: Liveright, 1975), p. xx.

4. Ibid.

5. Jean Toomer, *Cane*, Introduction by Anna Bontemps (New York: Harper & Row, 1969), p. x.

6. Schwartz, *A New History*, p. 120.

7. Odette C. Martin, "*Cane*: Method and Myth," *Obsidian* 2, no. 1 (Spring 1976): 12.

Chapter 10

1. Fernando Alegría, *Novelistas contemporáneos hispanoamericanos* (Boston: D.C. Heath, 1964), p. 213.
2. Enrique Anderson Imbert, *Spanish American Literature, A History*, trans. John Falconieri (Detroit: Wayne State University Press, 1969), vol. 2, p. 728.
3. Adalberto Ortiz, *Juyungo* (Quito: Editorial Casa de la Cultura Ecuatoriana, 1957), p. 275.
4. Adalberto Ortiz, "Negritude in Latin American Culture," in *Blacks in Hispanic Literature*, ed. Miriam de Costa (Port Washington, N.Y.: Kennikat Press, 1977), p. 81.
5. Adalberto Ortiz, "Negritude in Latin American Culture," p. 80.
6. Adalberto Ortiz, *Fórmulas, El vigilante insepulto, Tierra, son y tambor* (Quito: Editorial Casa de la Cultura Ecuatoriana, 1973), p. 83.

Chapter 11

1. Arnoldo Palacios, *Las estrellas son negras* (Bogotá: Editorial Revista Colombiana Ltda., 1971), p. 52.
2. *Child of the Dark: The Diary of Carolina María de Jesús*, trans. David St. Clair (New York: E.P. Dutton Co. Ltd., 1962), p. 20.
3. Ibid., p. 16.
4. Arnoldo Palacios, *La selva y la lluvia* (Moscow: Ediciones en lenguas extranjeras, 1958), p. 12.
5. Jean Franco, *The Modern Culture of Latin America: Society and the Artist* (Middlesex, England: Penguin Books, Ltd., 1970), pp. 157–158.
6. Ibid., p. 158.
7. Evelio Echevarría, "Bolshevism and the Spanish American Social Novel," *Latin American Literary Review* 4, no. 8 (Spring–Summer, 1976): 90.
8. Ibid., p. 90.

Chapter 12

1. *Man-Making Words: Selected Poems of Nicolás Guillén*, trans. Robert Márquez and David Arthur McMurray (Amherst: The University of Massachusetts Press, 1972), p. xiii.
2. Lemuel Johnson, *The Devil, the Gargoyle and the Buffoon: The Negro as Metaphor in Western Literature* (Port Washington, New York: Kennikat Press, 1971), p. 137.
3. Mirian de Costa, "Nicolás Guillén and his Poetry for Afro-Americans," *Black World* 22, no. 11 (September 1973): 12–16.
4. Ibid., p. 13.
5. Manuel Zapata Olivella, *Chambacú, corral de negros* (Medellín: Editorial Bedout, 1974), p. 110.
6. Manuel Zapata Olivella, *Corral de negros* (La Habana, Cuba: Casa de las Américas, 1963), p. 223.
7. Rubin Francis Weston, *Racism in United States Imperialism* (Columbia: University of South Carolina Press, 1972).
8. Nelson M. Blake, Preface to *Racism in United States Imperialism*, p. xiv.
9. Weston, *Racism*, p. 262.
10. Blake, Preface to *Racism*, p. x.
11. Begnino E. Aguirre, "Differential Migration of Cuban Social Races," *Latin American Research Review* 10, no. 1 (1976): 113.
12. Ibid.
13. Manuel Zapata Olivella, *Pasión vagabunda* (Bogotá: Editorial Santa Fé, 1949), pp. 64–75.

14. Manuel Zapata Olivella, *Tierra mojada* (Madrid: Editorial Bullón, 1964), pp. 49–50.
15. Ibid., p. 68.
16. Ibid.
17. Ibid., p. 64.
18. Ibid., p. 165.
19. Ibid.
20. Ibid., p. 171.

Chapter 13

1. *Giant Talk: An Anthology of Third World Writings*, ed. Quincy Troupe and Rainer Schulte (New York: Vintage Books, 1975), p. xxiii..
2. Jorge Hugo Rengel, "Nelson Estupiñán Bass y la poesía negra ecuatoriana," Introduction to Nelson Estupiñán Bass, *Canto negro por la luz* (Esmeraldas, Ecuador: Ediciones del Núcleo Provincial de Esmeraldas de la Casa de la Cultura Ecuatoriana, 1954), p. 7.
3. *Giant Talk*, p. xxiv.
4. Ibid., p. xxix.
5. Ibid., p. xxiv.
6. Ibid., p. xxxvii.
7. Nelson Estupiñán Bass, *Senderos brillantes* (Quito, Ecuador: Editorial Casa de la Cultura Ecuatoriana, 1974), p. 36.
8. *Giant Talk*, p. xxxviii.
9. Nelson Estupiñán Bass, *Cuando los guayacanes florecían* (Quito, Ecuador: Editorial Casa de la Cultura Ecuatoriana, 1954), pp. 16–17.
10. Ibid., p. 17.
11. Ibid.
12. Ibid., p. 20.
13. Ibid., p. 26.
14. Nelson Estupiñán Bass, *El paraíso* (Quito, Ecuador: Editorial Casa de la Cultura Ecuatoriana, 1958), p. 297.
15. Ibid., p. 300.
16. Estupiñán Bass, *Senderos brillantes*, p. 18.
17. Ibid., p. 19.
18. Ibid., p. 212.
19. Ibid., p. 299.
20. Nelson Estupiñán Bass, "Apuntes sobre el negro de Esmeraldas en la literatura ecuatoriana," *Norte* 7, no. 5 (September–October 1967): 104.
21. Ibid., p. 103.
22. Manuel Agustín Aguirre, Preface to *Senderos brillantes*, p. 10.
23. Ibid.
24. Nelson Estupiñán Bass, "Apuntes sobre el negro de Esmeraldas," p. 104.
25. The year 1978 has been a busy one for Nelson Estupiñán Bass as he has just completed three new books which are in varying stages of publication: two novels—*Las puertas del verano* and *Toque de queda*—and *El desempate*, his second book of poetry "for the people", which is, in effect, a continuation of his *Timarán y Cuabú*. Preliminary indications are that with his two new novels (and with *Senderos brillantes* [1974]) the black novel in Latin America is entering a new phase of experimental fiction, one that I will explore in a future study.

Chapter 14

1. Jean Franco, "Latin American Literature in a Social Context," *Association of Departments of Foreign Languages*, 7 (March 1976): 33.

2. In Dellita Martin Lowery, "Selected Poems of Nicolás Guillén and Langston Hughes: Their use of Western Folk Music Genres" (Ph.D. diss., The Ohio State University, 1975), p. 9

3. Nicomedes Santa Cruz, *Décimas y poemas, Antología* (Lima, Perú: Campodónico Ediciones S.A., 1971), p. 15.

4. Stephen Henderson, "Saturation. Progress Report on a Theory of Black Poetry," *Black World*, June 1975: 5.

5. Robert T. Kerlin, *Negro Poets and their Poems* (Washington, D.C.: Associated Publishers, Inc., 1935), p. 7.

6. Ibid., p. 18.

7. Don L. Lee, "Toward a Definition: Black Poetry of the Sixties (After Leroi Jones)," in *The Black Aesthetic*, ed. Addison Gayle, Jr. (Garden City, New York: Doubleday & Co., Inc., 1971), p. 247.

8. Bernard W. Bell, "Contemporary Afro-American Poetry as Folk Art," *Black World*, March 1973: 23.

9. Helcías Martín Góngora, "Nelson Estupiñán: El último río," *Boletín Cultural y Bibliográfico* 10, no. 2 (1967): 356.

10. Ibid.

11. *Diccionario de la literatura latinoamericana: Ecuador* (Washington, D.C.: Unión Panamericana, 1962), p. 121.

12. Ibid.

13. Ibid.

14. Nelson Estupiñán Bass, *Canto negro por la luz* (Esmeraldas, Ecuador: Ediciones del Núcleo Provincial de Esmeraldas de la Casa de la Cultura Ecuatoriana, 1954), pp. 65–66.

15. Hugo Rengel in Estupiñán Bass, *Canto negro por la luz*, p. 16.

16. Ibid.

17. Ibid., p. 50.

18. Nelson Estupiñán Bass, *Timarán y Cuabú: Cuaderno de Poesía para el Pueblo* (Quito, Ecuador: Editorial Casa de la Cultura Ecuatoriana, 1956), p. 9.

19. Ibid., pp. 13–14.

20. Ibid., p. 92.

21. Ibid., p. 93.

22. Robert Pring-Mill, "The Poetry of Protest," *Times Literary Supplement*, 6 August 1976: 994.

23. "Habla el peruano Nicomedes Santa Cruz," *Siempre*, no. 1103 (14 August 1974): 39.

24. Teresa C. Salas and Henry J. Richards, "Nicomedes Santa Cruz y la Poesía de su conciencia de negritud," *Cuadernos Americanos*, 202 (September–October, 1975): 183.

25. Santa Cruz, *Décimas y poemas, antología*, p. 20.

26. Ibid., p. 25.

27. Ibid., p. 28.

28. Ibid., p. 31.

29. Ibid., p. 29.

30. Ibid.

31. Nicomedes Santa Cruz, "Canto a Angola," *Casa de las Américas* n. 99 (1976): 73.

32. Santa Cruz, *Décimas y poemas, antología*, p. 28.

33. Adriana Tous, *La poesía de Nicolás Guillén* (Madrid: Ediciones Cultura Hispánica, 1971), p. 144.

34. Angel Augier, "The Cuban Poetry of Nicolás Guillén," *Phylon*, 12 (1951): 32.

35. Lowery, "Selected Poems of Nicolás Guillén and Langston Hughes," p. 84.

36. Manuel Navarro Luna, "Un líder de la poesía revolucionaria," in *Recopilación de textos sobre Nicolás Guillén*, Selección y prólogo de Nancy Morejón (La Habana, Cuba: Casa de las Américas, 1974), p. 107.

37. Ibid.

38. Ibid., pp. 107–108.

39. Ibid., p. 108.

40. Nicolás Guillén, *Obra poética*, vol. 1 (La Habana: Editorial de Arte y Literatura, 1974), p. 197.

41. Nicolás Guillén, "Hablando de Miguel Hernández," *Melodía* (La Habana) 2, no. 39 (1937): 11–18. Reprinted in Adriana Tous, *La Poesía de Nicolás Guillén*, p. 144.

42. Guillén, *Obra poética*, vol. 1, pp. 68–69.

43. Ibid., vol. 2, p. 164.

44. Guillén, *Obra poética*, 1, p. 427.

45. Nicolás Guillén, *Tengo*, trans. Richard J. Carr (Detroit: Broadside Press, 1974), p. 7.

46. Ibid.

47. Lowery, "Selected Poems of Nicolás Guillén and Langston Hughes," p. 82.

48. Ibid., p. 251.

49. *Giant Talk: An Anthology of Third World Writings*, ed. Quincy Troupe and Rainer Schulte (New York: Vintage Books, 1975), p. xl.

50. Edouard Glissant, "Free and Forced Poetics," in *Alcheringa: Ethnopoetics*, ed. Michel Benamou and Jerome Rothenberg (Boston: Boston University, 1976), pp. 95–101.

Chapter 15

1. Abel Pacheco, *Más abajo de la piel* (San José: Editorial Costa Rica, 1974), p. 11.

2. Ibid.

3. Leslie B. Rout, Jr., *The African Experience in Spanish America* (Cambridge: Cambridge University Press, 1976), p. 265.

4. Carlos Meléndez and Quince Duncan, *El negro en Costa Rica* (San José: Editorial Costa Rica, 1972), p. 126.

5. In *El negro en Costa Rica*, pp. 161–175.

6. Martha K. Cobb, "Concepts of Blackness in the Poetry of Nicolás Guillén, Jacques Roumain and Langston Hughes," *College Language Association Journal* 18, no. 2 (1974): 262–72.

7. Quince Duncan, *Los cuatro espejos* (San José: Editorial Costa Rica, 1973). All of the quotations from this novel will be taken from this edition. Duncan's other publications include journalistic work, the co-authored volume in note four, two volumes of short stories and an earlier novel, *Hombres curtidos* (1971) that opens with a chapter called "El regreso" where the protagonist leaves the "big city" to return to his home town, to his "pueblo natal" in search of his roots, his "propias raíces," after a fourteen-year absence. Duncan has also edited the anthology, *El negro en la literatura costarricense* (San José: Editorial Costa Rica, 1975).

8. Quince Duncan, "Nuestros blancos, María Cañas y el negro africano primitivo," *La Nación*, 16 September 1972, p. 56.

9. Ibid.

10. Ibid.

11. Emile Snyder, "Aimé Césaire. The Reclaiming of the Land," in *Exile and Tradition*, ed. Rowland Smith (Bristol: Longman and Dalhousie University Press, 1976), p. 39.

12. Isaac Yetiv, "Alienation in the Modern Novel of French North Africa before Independence," in *Exile and Tradition*, p. 86.

13. Ibid., p. 87.

14. Ibid., p. 94.

15. Quoted in Lemuel Johnson, *The Devil, the Gargoyle, and the Buffoon: The Negro as Metaphor in Western Literature* (Port Washington, N.Y.: Kennikat Press, 1971), p. 105.

16. Jean Paul Sartre, "Black Orepheus," trans. John Mac-Combie, *The Massachusetts Review* 6, no. 1 (1964–65): 22.

17. Stephen E. Henderson, "Survival Motion: A Study of the Black Writer and the Black

Revolution in America," in Mercer Cook and Stephen E. Henderson, *The Militant Black Writer in Africa and the United States* (Madison, Wisconsin: The University of Wisconsin Press, 1969), p. 97.

18. Quince Duncan, *Una canción en la madrugada* (San José: Editorial Costa Rica, 1970), p. 83.

19. Henderson, "Survival Motion," p. 117.

20. Ibid.

21. G.D. Killam, "Notions of Religion, Alienation and Archetype in *Arrow of God*," in *Exile and Tradition*, p. 165.

22. Snyder, "Aimé Césaire," p. 34.

23. Malcolm X, in *Black Homeland/Black Diaspora*, ed. Jacob Drachler (Port Washington, N.Y.: Kennikat Press, 1975), p. 139.

24. Ibid.

25. Aimé Césaire, *Return to my Native Land*, trans. John Berger and Anna Bostock (Middlesex, England: Penguin Books, Ltd., 1969), p. 92.

26. Ibid., p. 9.

27. Ibid.

Conclusion

1. St. Clair Drake, "The Black Diaspora in Pan-African Perspective," *The Black Scholar* 7, no. 1 (September 1975): 10.

2. Ibid., p. 12.

3. Ibid., p. 3.

4. Ian Smart, "The Creative Dialogue in the Poetry of Nicolás Guillén: Europe and Africa" (Ph.D. diss. University of California, Los Angeles, 1975), p. 243.

5. Ibid., p. 245. Roberto Fernández Retamar, it should be recalled, has written an important new essay on Latin American culture and he has been accused of resorting in this essay to the term *mestizaje* to characterize the new Latin American reality in Cuba precisely for the "evasive possibilities the term offers", since in a Cuban context, with its black past, to emphasize *mestizaje* is, in a sense, to "veer away from a direct confrontation with Black culture." The point of these accusations—made by Marta E. Sánchez ("Caliban: The New Latin American Protagonist of the Tempest," *Diacritics* 6 (1970): 60)—is that to stress *mestizaje* is to run the risk of highlighting "the absence of the Black" rather than his presence.

6. Arthur P. Davis, "The New Poetry of Black Hate," in *Modern Black Poets*, ed. Donald B. Gibson (Englewood Cliffs, N.J.: Prentice Hall, 1973), p. 153.

7. Nicolás Guillén, *Summa poética*, ed. Luis Iñigo Madrigal (Madrid: Ediciones Cátedra, 1976), p. 36.

8. Miriam (Sugarmon) De Costa, "Social Lyricism and the Caribbean Poet/Rebel," *College Language Association Journal* 15, no. 2 (June 1972): 450.

9. *Giant Talk: An Anthology of Third World Writings*, ed. Quincy Troupe and Rainer Schulte (New York: Vintage Books, Random House, 1975), p. xliii.

10. Amiri Baraka, "Black Nationalism and Socialist Revolution," *Black World*, July 1975: 36.

11. Ibid.

12. *Black Homeland/Black Diaspora: Cross-Currents of the African Relationship*, ed. Jacob Drachler (Port Washington, N.Y.: Kennikat Press, 1975), p. 79.

13. Richard A. Long, "Pan-Africanism: A Re-Evaluation" (Occasional Paper No. 17, Center for African and African-American Studies, Atlanta University, Atlanta, Georgia, p. 4).

14. Ibid.

15. Elizabeth Southerland, *The Youngest Revolution* (New York: The Dial Press, 1970), p. 162.

16. Ibid., p. 167.

17. Ibid.

18. Sylvia Wynter, "Ethno or Socio Poetics," *Alcheringa* (Boston: Boston University, 1976), pp. 78–94.

19. Roberto Fernández Retamar, "Caliban: Notes toward a Discussion of Culture in our America," *Massachusetts Review*, Winter–Spring 1974: 7–72.

20. *Black Homeland/Black Diaspora*, p. 105.

21. In Robert Brent Toplin, "Brazil: Racial Polarization in the Developing Giant," *Black World*, November 1972: 18.

22. Jean Paul Sartre, "Black Orpheus," trans. John Mac-Combie, *The Massachusetts Review* 6, no. 1 (1964–65):52.

23. Francis and Val Gray Ward, "The Black Artist—His Role in the Struggle," *The Black Scholar* 5, no. 2 (January 1971):23.

24. St. Clair Drake, p. 12.

25. Alex Poinsett, "FESTAC '77' Second World Black African Festival of Arts and Culture draws 17,000 participants to Lagos," *Ebony*, May 1977, p. 44.

26. "29 Days that Shook the Black World," *Ebony*, May 1977, p. 48.

27. Ibid.

28. Ibid.

29. Pepe Carril, *Shango de Ima, A Yoruba Mystery Play*. English adaptation by Susan Sherman, Introduction by Jerome Rothenberg and Edward James (Garden City, New York: Doubleday & Co., 1969), p. 27.

30. Ibid., p. 28.

31. Anani Dzidzienyo, "Afro-Brazilians, other Afro-Latin Americans and Africanity: Frozen and Dynamic," (Paper read at the Eighth Annual Meeting of the African Heritage Studies Association, 23 April 1976, in Atlanta, Georgia), p. 4.

32. Ibid.

33. In St. Clair Drake, "The Black Diaspora in Pan-African Perspective," *The Black Scholar* 7, no. 1 (September 1975): 9–10.

34. See Donald B. Gibson, Introduction to *Modern Black Poets* (Englewood Cliffs, New Jersey: Prentice Hall, Inc., 1973), p. 14.

A Bibliographic Guide to Recent Studies on Blacks in Hispanic Literature

In a previous bibliographic guide I outlined some of the recent trends noticeable in research on black themes in Spanish American literature. In that study, "Research on Black Themes in Spanish American Literature: A Bibliographic Guide to Recent Trends," which was published in the *Latin American Research Review* 12, no. 1 (1977), I categorized *trends* in the following subdivisions: Racist Authors and the Heritage of White Racial Consciousness; The Black as Social Symbol; and The Afro-Spanish American Author. In this current *chronological* review, which appeared in a shorter version in *The American Hispanist* 2, no. 15 (February 1977): 2–3, I focus on comprehensive book-length titles (studies and anthologies) that form part of a proliferation in the seventies of works on the black in Hispanic literature.

After a short hiatus following G.R. Coulthard's *Race and Colour in Caribbean Literature* (London: Oxford University Press, 1962), first published in Spanish as *Raza y color en la literatura antillana* (Sevilla: Escuela de Estudios Hispanoamericanos, 1958), Gregory Rabassa's *O negro na ficçao brasileira* (Rio de Janeiro: Edições Tempo Brasileiro, 1965), which has a lengthy introduction that surveys the black in literature, including the Hispanic, and Janheinz Jahn's *A History of Neo-African Literature* (London: Faber and Faber, Ltd., 1968; first published in German in 1966), at least one new title on blacks in Hispanic literature has appeared every year since 1970.

In 1970 Ildefonso Pereda Valdés published *Lo negro y lo mulato en la poesía cubana* (Montevideo: Ediciones Ciudadela), his most recent contribution to the study of the black in Latin America. In this volume Pereda Valdés, the distinguished Uruguayan pioneer in this field, recognizes that there is black poetry and that there is poetry on blacks, and his introduction to what is largely an anthology dwells on this significant distinction. His book is one of the few where black writers are grouped and studied albeit limited to Cuba and to Arozarena, Pedroso, and Guillén. A similar volume on the black writer in his native Uruguay, where there is ample material for such a study or anthology, would be welcome.

Wilfred Cartey's *Black Images* (New York: Teachers College Press, 1970), an updated version of a doctoral dissertation, provides an almost lyrical but thoroughly academic accounting of the literary trajectory of the black image largely in French and Spanish poetry of the Antilles. Moving quickly from the early white poetry about blacks from the Spanish Golden Age through the nineteenth century, Cartey dwells at length on Ballagas and Palés Matos, who miss the essential black man, and on the more aware poetry of Nicolás Guillén, which is not unrelated to the new black image created by the negritude poets writing in French. Cartey's study recognizes the contribution of white writers in making known the black reality in America while pointing up the black's new positive image, largely one of revolt, of his own design.

Rosa E. Valdés-Cruz's *La poesía negroide en América* (New York: Las Americas Publishing Company, 1970) probably was the most widely used anthology, textbook, and commentary in the first half of this decade, coming as it did at a time when interest in black poetry in the Americas was high and earlier anthologies of black poetry by Ballagas, Guirao, Pereda Valdés, Sanz y Díaz, and others were difficult to acquire. Comprehensive in scope, with authors represented in Spanish and in Spanish translation from all over the Americas and from Spain, *La poesía negroide en América* has been a handy tool in the many literature courses that have introduced the black into the Hispanic curriculum. The few objections made to this volume from time to time on academic and technical grounds do not undermine its basic usefulness.

In 1971 Lemuel Johnson published *The Devil, the Gargoyle, and the Buffoon: the Negro as Metaphor in Western Literature* (Port Washington, N.Y.: Kennikat Press). His book, a comparative study, is quite critical of those white writers in English, French, and Spanish who have difficulty accommodating to blackness in human form. Though focusing in part of his book on the black response of Langston Hughes, Nicolás Guillén, and Aimé Césaire to the white world, Johnson's brilliant analysis of the black caricatured as devil, gargoyle, and buffoon in English, French, and Spanish literature underlines the negative, if not racist, nature of these literatures.

In that same year Hilda Perera published *Idapo: el sincretismo en los cuentos negros de Lidia Cabrera* (Miami, Florida: Ediciones Universal, 1971). Her study moved away from the study of black themes in written literature and toward a consideration of black literature in the oral tradition, particularly in Cuba where Lidia Cabrera's many collections of Afro-Cuban folktales have placed her in the forefront of literary and folkloric investigators in this field. This move toward the oral reached its highest expression in November 1976 in Miami, Florida, where an entire "Congreso de Literatura Afro-Americana: Homenaje a Lidia Cabrera," was held at the Florida International University in Lidia Cabrera's honor.

In 1972 Hortensia Ruiz del Vizo published two anthologies of black poetry, one a bilingual anthology, *Black Poetry of the Americas* (Miami, Florida: Ediciones Universal, 1972), with poems in Spanish and others translated into Spanish from French and English, and *Poesía negra del caribe y otras áreas* (Miami, Florida: Ediciones· Universal, 1972), with representation restricted to Spanish-speaking areas in America. These two volumes, unlike the Rosa E. Valdés-Cruz one and others, are unique in that they contain an abundance of poems on black themes written recently by Cuban poets in exile. Her volumes make the singular point that these poets constitute a New School of Black Poetry, and they prove erroneous pronouncements that black poetry as a movement flourished and died largely between the two world wars. Her books give prominence also to black poetry in Colombia though she rejects at the same time (but not convincingly) Colombia's claim that their black native son, Candelario Obeso (1849–84), was a precursor of *poesía negra* as we know it in the twentieth century.

In 1973 Hortensia del Vizo's theory of a New School of Black Poetry received some measure of support from Alberto N. Pamies and Oscar Fernández de la Vega, whose *Iniciación a la poesía afro-americana* (Miami, Florida: Ediciones Universal, 1973) is one of the few volumes up-to-date on this New School in exile. Aside from being a handy collection of hard to get studies of landmark value in the historiography of the black in Hispanic literature, this volume is, at the same time, an intelligent and useful reference book, complete with important dates, extensive (but by no means complete) list of principal authors, and charts that map the development and thematic trajectory of black poetry in Hispanic America.

Mónica Mansour's *La poesía negrista* (México: Ediciones Era, 1973), while covering much the same ground as other similar works, is, nevertheless, unique in that it is more "study" than anthology, more detailed in some areas (colonial and nineteenth century, for example) than other works, though less so in other areas, and more specific in distinguishing between *poesía negrista* and *poesía de la negritud*, though she errs in limiting negritude to African and American literature in French and English only.

Enrique Noble's *Literatura afro-hispanoamericana: poesía y prosa de ficción* (Lexington, Massachusetts: Xerox College Publishing, 1973), is the only volume mentioned in this review designed partly as a reading text for intermediate courses as well as for more advanced courses and seminars in literature. Noble's anthology is also distinguished by its organization which is structured around themes or topics rather than by author or country. This presentation has value in most cases, though the many typographical errors and misspellings detract from the overall quality of the work. Complete with extensive footnotes and vocabulary, this anthology is a useful selection of prose and poetry, even though one could argue with Noble's choices and exclusions in both genres.

The same kind of argument could be put to Stanley Cyrus' *El cuento negrista sudamericano: antología* (Quito: Editorial Casa de la Cultura Ecuatoriana, 1973), although this important collection of *negrista* stories is the only one of its kind. Furthermore, Cyrus' anthology, unlike Noble's volume, includes a substantial number of short stories by Afro-Hispanic authors. Especially useful in this collection are the up-to-date introductions that precede the stories.

In 1974, Rosa E. Valdés-Cruz followed up her *La poesía negroide* with *Lo ancestral africano en la narrativa de Lidia Cabrera* (Barcelona: Editorial Vosgos, S.A.), the second book-length study in three years to analyze the Afro-Cuban folktales of Lidia Cabrera. Her study, like Perera's before her, recognizes the strong white hand of Lidia Cabrera in the transpositions of these black oral tales into written, artistic form.

Also in 1974, Isabelo Zenón Cruz with his *Narciso descubre su trasero: el negro en la cultura puertorriqueña* (Humacaco, Puerto Rico: Editorial Furidi), vol. 1 (followed up in 1975 with vol. 2), startled the Puerto Rican reading public with the first volume of his extensive study and anthology of the black Puerto Rican (a phrase Zenón Cruz prefers to Puerto Rican black) and his literary image. It is an understatement to say that his critical examination or exposé of racism in Puerto Rican literature and society will have as much impact in that country as Francisco Arriví's well-known trilogy *Máscara puertorriqueña*. Also in 1975 Quince Duncan edited *El negro en la literatura costarricense* (San José: Editorial Costa Rica, 1975).

In 1976, six new books in the Afro-Hispanic field appeared, three of them anthologies: *Poesía afroantillana y negrista: Puerto Rico, República Dominicana, Cuba* (Rio Piedras: Editorial Universitaria, Universidad de Puerto Rico, 1976), edited by Jorge Luis Morales; *Antología clave de la poesía afroamericana* (Madrid: Ediciones Alcalá), edited by Armando González Pérez; and *Poesía negra de América* (México: Ediciones Era), edited by José Luis González and Mónica Mansour; Josefina Inclán, *Ayapa y otras Otán Iyebiyé de Lydia Cabrera (notas y comentarios)* (Miami: Ediciones Universal, 1976), the third book in recent years on Lydia Cabrera; my own book, *The Black Image in Latin American Literature* (Albuquerque: University of New Mexico Press, 1976), which explores prose and poetry by black and nonblack writers in the Caribbean and on the Spanish American mainland; and *The African Experience in Spanish America: 1502 to the Present* (Cambridge: Cambridge University Press, 1976), by Leslie B. Rout, Jr. Professor Rout's book, a fine historical overview that deals as well with present and future problems of the Afro-Latino, often provides insightful comments on Afro-Hispanic literary figures.

In 1977 we have *Blacks in Hispanic Literature: Critical Essays*, edited by Mirian de Costa. This book is the first collection ever of critical essays by a group of distinguished Black scholars on Afro-Hispanic liteature, many of them, like De Costa herself, set on structuring a new critical framework for the analysis of this literature.

In 1978 the fourth recent book on Lydia Cabrera appeared, *Homenaje a Lydia Cabrera* (Miami: Ediciones Universal, 1978), a collection of the papers read in her honor at the Congreso de Literatura in November, 1976.

There are many shorter studies (articles) and unpublished works (dissertations, theses, papers) of high quality available, and other book-length studies, collections, and bibliographies underway. I expect to see many of them published before long. Book-length studies on individual black authors are on the increase certainly on Nicolás Guillén (the Tous, Retamar, Ruscalleda, and Morejón volumes, for example, as well as the Augier and Madrigal editions of Guillén's poetry). Even new editions of nineteenth-century works are becoming available, including Ivan Schulman's edition of Manzano's *Autobiografía*, Frederick Stimson's edition of Plácido's poetry, and the recent editions of Martín Morúa Delgado's *Sofía* and *La familia Unzúazu*.

I highlight these studies and many others in a book-length annotated bibliography on Afro-Hispanic authors, literature, and criticism that I am now preparing for Garland Publishers.

Index

73

995139